T0305338

Coopetition

Coopetition
Winning Strategies for the 21st Century

Edited by

Saïd Yami

Associate Professor of Strategic Management at the University of Montpellier and Professor at Euromed Management, Marseille, France

Sandro Castaldo

Chairman, Marketing Department, SDA Bocconi School of Management and Full Professor of Marketing, Bocconi University, Italy

Giovanni Battista Dagnino

Deputy Chair and Professor, Department of Business Economics and Management, University of Catania, Italy

Frédéric Le Roy

Professor of Strategic Management at the University of Montpellier and at GSCM, Montpellier Business School, France

Edward Elgar

Cheltenham, UK • Northampton, MA, USA

Published by
Edward Elgar Publishing Limited
The Lypiatts
15 Lansdown Road
Cheltenham
Glos GL50 2JA
UK

Edward Elgar Publishing, Inc.
William Pratt House
9 Dewey Court
Northampton
Massachusetts 01060
USA

A catalogue record for this book
is available from the British Library

Library of Congress Control Number: 2009940647

Mixed Sources
Product group from well-managed
forests and other controlled sources
www.fsc.org Cert no. SA-COC-1565
© 1996 Forest Stewardship Council

ISBN 978 1 84844 321 1

Printed and bound by MPG Books Group, UK

Contents

Figures

Tables

Contributors

Fabio Ancarani, University of Bologna, Italy

Philippe Baumard, Stanford University (USA) and École Polytechnique, Centre de Recherche en Gestion, France

Maria Bengtsson, Umeå Business School – University of Umeå, Sweden

Sandro Castaldo, Bocconi University, Italy

Michele Costabile, University of Calabria, Italy

Wojciech Czakon, University of Economics in Katowice, Poland

Giovanni Battista Dagnino, University of Catania, Italy

Colette Depeyre, École Polytechnique/University Paris Ouest Nanterre La Défense, France

Hervé Dumez, École Polytechnique – CNRS, France

Jessica Eriksson, Department of Business Administration – University of Umeå, Sweden

Per-Erik Eriksson, Luleå University of Technology, Sweden

Marco Galvagno, University of Catania, Italy

Francesco Garraffo, University of Catania, Italy

Monica Grosso, Bocconi University, Italy

Patrice Guillotreau, University of Nantes, France

Thomas Herzog, Vienna University of Economics and Business Administration, Austria

Frédéric Le Roy, University of Montpellier 1 and GSCM – Montpellier Business School, France

Marcello Mariani, University of Bologna, Italy

Guido Möllering, Max Planck Institute for the Study of Societies, Germany

Ossi Pesämaa, Luleå University of Technology, Sweden

Pierre Roy, University of Montpellier 1, France

Joakim Wincent, Luleå University of Technology – Industrial Economy and Business Administration, Sweden

Saïd Yami, University of Monpellier 1 and Euromed Management, France

Fabrizio Zerbini, Bocconi University, Italy

Introduction – coopetition strategies: towards a new form of inter-organizational dynamics?

Saïd Yami, Sandro Castaldo,
Giovanni Battista Dagnino, Frédéric Le Roy and
Wojciech Czakon

INTRODUCTION

Is coopetition just another fashionable concept or a true revolution in strategic thinking? This question reveals its true meaning when considered respectively from the viewpoints of competition theory (Smith *et al.*, 1992) and cooperation theory (Dyer and Singh, 1998). There is therefore a strong temptation to make it a simple extension of either competition theory or cooperation theory.

With regard to the former, coopetition could become part of the 'competitive paradigm' if cooperation between firms is considered as 'competitive maneuvering' or 'cooperative maneuvering', which can both provide a competitive advantage (Fjeldstad *et al.*, 2004). With regard to the latter approach, coopetition is just another type of cooperation. As such, coopetition research can draw extensively on alliances theory. Concepts such as trust, opportunism and commitment, which are crucial in dyadic cooperative relationships, are likewise applicable to coopetitive relationships.

The aim of this book is to contribute to the discussion and argue that coopetition is neither an extension of competition theory nor an extension of cooperative theory. It is in fact a specific distinctive research object, which calls for dedicated theoretical investigation to develop specific questions for theory, method and managerial practice. This theoretical investigation is still at an early stage, but nonetheless seems promising as a novel approach to intra- and inter-organizational relationship studies.

1

1. COOPETITION: A NEW STRATEGIC
PERSPECTIVE

Since its inception in strategic management, the competitive paradigm has focused on interfirm rivalry (Porter, 1980). The firm's survival requires competitive strengthening, which in turn enables value-creating competitive advantages to be developed (Hill, 1990). Lately, this need has grown considerably in importance. Relatively stable markets have turned 'hypercompetitive' or 'aggressively competitive', or even into 'voracious competition' (Le Roy, 2002). Firms have no other options but to adopt an aggressive or hypercompetitive behavior if they want to strive and survive on the market (D'Aveni, 1994).

At the other extreme, the cooperative paradigm emphasizes the need for firms, divisions and functions to cooperate (Dyer and Singh, 1998). By means of this approach, the firm establishes and strengthens its competitive advantage through strategic alliances, networks or strategic ecosystems (Astley and Fombrum, 1983; Yami and Le Roy, 2007). The ability to form and manage relationships provides access to others' valuable resources, and thus a relational advantage.

Between the competitive paradigm, which suggests rivalry and the shunning of cooperation (D'Aveni, 1994), and the cooperative paradigm, which bases the firm's relational capability on its competitive advantage (Dyer and Singh, 1998), there seems to be clear and unsolved contradiction, though a variety of scholars have suggested that firms should seek the advantages arising from competition as well as those from cooperation (Bengtsson and Kock, 1999; Hamel *et al.*, 1989; Nalebuff and Brandenburger, 1996; Dagnino and Padula, 2002). Competition advantages stimulate the search for new rent-generating combinations of resources, skills and processes. Cooperation advantages allow access to rare and complementary resources. If the firm strives for both types of advantages, it needs to adopt both competitive and cooperative behaviors.

This duality was popularized by Nalebuff and Brandenburger (Brandenburger and Nalebuff, 1995; Nalebuff and Brandenburger, 1996, 1997). From the game theory standpoint, these authors regard coopetition as providing a theoretical background based on the 'value network concept'. Seen from this perspective, coopetition encompassed complementors' interests and goals, which appear when competition and cooperation are simultaneously executed (Figure I.1).

Lado *et al.* (1997) made a second fundamental contribution to the definition of coopetition, even if, paradoxically, they did not use the term. These authors noticed that firms increasingly combined aggressive and cooperative strategies. Using game theory, the resource-based view of the firm and

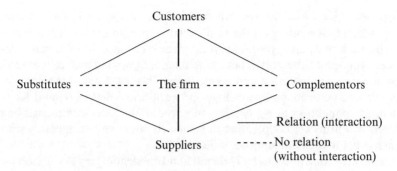

Source: Brandenburger and Nalebuff, 1995

Figure I.1   The value net

Table I.1   Rent-seeking behaviors

		Coopetitive orientation	
		Weak	*Strong*
Cooperative	*Strong*	Cooperative behavior	**Syncretic behavior**
orientation	*Weak*	Monopolistic behavior	Competitive behavior

Source: Lado, Boyd and Hanlon, 1997

social network theory, they argued that cooperation and competition had long been regarded as two extremities of a continuum, which they are not. We need to understand that these are two independent dimensions.

This new approach had a fundamental impact on interorganizational relationship explanations as it introduced four types of 'rent-seeking behaviors' (Table I.1). First, the firm can choose a monopolistic behavior, which is neither aggressive nor cooperative. It implies avoiding any type of competitive or cooperative behavior. Second, choosing cooperative behavior, the firm decides to emphasize cooperation at the expense of competition. Third, choosing competitive behavior, the firm opts for aggressive behavior towards rivals, similar to that in the hypercompetition model (D'Aveni, 1994). Finally, the firm can choose syncretic behavior, thus exhibiting both aggressive and cooperative behaviors. This last option clearly refers to the coopetition concept without actually mentioning it.

Bengtsson and Kock (1999) in their turn made a third valuable contribution to coopetition theory. Their view is essentially grounded in the

network theory and the resource-based view of the firm. The authors
argued that, depending on the firm's relative position in its industry and
on its need for external resources, it can choose between four different relational models (Table I.2). These four relational models are: coexistence,
competition, cooperation and coopetition. This last form combines economic and non-economic exchanges between firms. Bengtsson and Kock
defined coopetition as a 'dyadic and paradoxical relationship emerging
when two firms are cooperating in some activities, while competing with
each other in the remaining activities'.

The three contributions by Nalebuff and Brandenburger (1996), Lado *et
al.* (1997) and Bengtsson and Kock (1999) are regarded as pioneering mile-
stones for coopetition theory as these works are cited in most publications.
Nonetheless, researchers have proposed theoretical extensions that enable
a better understanding of the phenomenon. Dagnino and Padula (2002),
for instance, differentiate four forms of coopetition, which depend on the
number of rival firms and value activities involved in coopetition relationships. They suggest distinguishing dyadic coopetition from network
coopetition and, within them, simple and complex forms of network and
dyadic coopetition (Table I.3).

Since its popularization by Nalebuff and Brandenburger (1996), the

Table I.2   Relationships between firms

		Relative position in the industry	
		Strong	Weak
Need for external	Strong	**Coopetition**	Cooperation
resources	Weak	Competition	Coexistence

Source: Bengtsson and Kock, 1999

Table I.3   Types of coopetition

		Number of Firms	
		Two	More than two
Number of	One	Simple dyadic coopetition	Simple network coopetition
activities in the			
value chain	Multiple	Complex dyadic coopetition	Complex network coopetition

Source: Dagnino and Padula, 2002

coopetition concept has been deemed a new strategic perspective capable of overcoming the limits of the 'old' strategic doctrines: the best performing strategies are coopetition strategies per se. Competitive strategies are inferior, because they only enable the firm to generate competitive advantages. Cooperative strategies too are inferior, as they only generate cooperative advantages. Coopetition strategies enable the firm to reach for both competitive and collaborative advantages. Therefore, coopetition is a beneficial strategy for managers striving for performance improvements. In its normative dimension, the doctrine drives researchers to examine the concept's depth and scope.

2. COOPETITION STRATEGY CONCEPT – THE CHALLENGES

Research on coopetition focuses on a number of questions which remain, however, scantly addressed in depth. The first issue is a purely linguistic one, referring to academia's acceptance of the term 'coopetition'. It is not mentioned in dictionaries, whether English, French or any other language, even if they specialize in economics or management. Only the virtual encyclopedia Wikipedia provides a definition of the term. Are we really allowed to use a term which does not exist in the main vocabularies?

This semantic question raises more fundamental concerns regarding prior research in the field. First, the literature is relatively small, fragmented and sparse. A good part of it does not even use the term 'coopetition'. There are, for example, a number of papers focusing on a combination of competitive and cooperative manoeuvers, which is central to coopetition, without explicitly mentioning it (Teece and Jorde, 1989; Lado *et al.*, 1997). Second, existing literature on coopetition has so far been more oriented towards managers than researchers. With the notable exception of Afuah (2000), most prestigious academic management journals have published relatively little research on this topic.

Another fundamental issue is that the term 'coopetition' is new, but are the underlying phenomena new as well? Could it simply be a traditional phenomenon that is currently observed through a new theoretical lens? Alliance relationships between rivals are, after all, established objects of study. Why should we use new terms to label long-existing phenomena? There are several reasons for this. Firstly, alliances are an increasingly important phenomenon, thus justifying in-depth research, which in turn often produces new concepts. Secondly, contemporary alliances involve many partners and rivals (Dagnino and Padula, 2002; Lecocq and Yami, 2002). New concepts are therefore necessary to capture this growing complexity of alliance relationships between rival firms. Doz and Hamel (1998) suggest the term 'multilateral alliances', while other authors propose 'alliance constellations' (Lazzarini, 2007). A last and – from our viewpoint – most important argument is inherent in the relationships between firms: the coopetition concept is the only one which really captures the core of the problem, which is the paradoxical, simultaneous combination of cooperation and competition.

Observed from this perspective, coopetition can be viewed as a phenomenon that has existed for a long time, but one still on the way to acquiring new and contemporary dimensions and significance. This terminological evolutionary path calls for dedicated research to develop a body of literature specifically focused on coopetition. The idiosyncratic specificity of competition is rooted in both the phenomenon's significance and the nature of the concepts. Coopetition strategies are by nature non-conventional, paradoxical or heterodox. They link two concepts that are contradictory by definition and nature: competition and cooperation. Competitive behavior is defined as a priori excluding cooperation in the long-lived Aristotelian notion of 'non-contradiction'. It essentially refers to seeking goals or aiming at resources, with the success of one rival meaning the failure of all others. Competition excludes – partially or completely – the loser, while the winner takes all by definition. Inversely, cooperative behavior is understood as a priori forestalling competition. It is about sharing resources in a joint effort to achieve a common goal. Benefits are not distributed between the winner and those who lost, but in a negotiated manner to benefit all partners.

Clearly, the concepts of competition and cooperation differ fundamentally and are contradictory. Integrating such concepts necessarily requires a complex approach (the so-called Neo-Platonic *coincidentia oppositorum* or 'the coincidence of the opposites'). This requires a true cognitive change in managerial opinion, which has to date been dominated by the popular Aristotelian dichotomy. Simultaneously thinking cooperation and competition, acting in both a cooperative and competitive way, implies a cognitive revolution in research and in managerial practice. It is much easier to simplify relations with rivals than to define them as 'enemies' in a military metaphor, which excludes cooperation, or to label them as 'colleagues' or 'partners' in a more social metaphor, which instead excludes competition.

Coopetition research development inevitably leads to the questioning of interorganizational relationship norms and definitions, and to new ones. Competitors are no more 'enemies' than they are 'friends', nor any less 'enemies' than 'friends'. This new representation of interorganizational relationships raises true managerial issues at the individual and collective levels. At the individual level, it may be challenging for a firm's employees to understand the new complexity vis-à-vis the more common view that competitors are rivals which are to be fought and defeated. At the collective level, it is necessary to implement managerial solutions enabling the simultaneous development of competitive and cooperative behaviors.

The new coopetitive representation of interfirm relations can be studied on at least three levels of analysis. On the macro level, the issue of inter-country coopetition becomes a major focus in industrial policy. The European Aeronautic Defence and Space (EADS) example shows how France and Germany have successfully managed simultaneous competitive and cooperative relationships. The idea of concurrent cooperation and competition is at the crux of a regional development concept, called 'Competitiveness Poles', implemented in France.

Research has heretofore been the most fruitful on the meso level or at the level of interfirm relationships (see section 1). The micro level has received far less academic attention. The way coopetition is experienced inside the company has rarely been studied, although it remains a major managerial concern when the implementation phase of coopetition strategies becomes imminent (Pellegrin-Boucher, 2006). How should the firm be organized to support both cooperation and competition? How can employees integrate two opposite logics?

This problem is all the more significant in the light of the clear tendency of cooperative relationships to become unstable (Das and Teng, 2000). An adversarial partner firm can at any moment disrupt a coopetition relationship, either due to product line changes, which destroy the scope of the coopetition, or because the rival stops cooperating. Coopetition strategies imply that there can be no long-lasting relationship with an adversarial partner, either in terms of form or content. By its very nature, coopetition is unstable and evolving, but neither the direction nor the pace can be predicted. Coopetition processes can therefore only be conceptualized as dynamic, time-dependent phenomena. This conceptualization drives managers to abandon stability management and instead develop coo-petitive processes, which by definition cannot be completely controlled by purposeful managerial action.

Managerial challenges reveal academic gaps. Coopetitive processes are still a paradoxical logic; in addition, their development trajectory and outcomes are unpredictable. How can we therefore conceptualize a phenomenon that is so far removed from the mainstream linear and causal logic? How can we model relational processes involving competition and cooperation that are, by nature, contradictory? The popularization of the game theory concept produces a strong temptation to draw on it (Nalebuff and Brandenburger, 1996). However, we doubt whether this theoretical approach can be truly applied as soon as we move from abstract economics to an understanding of real-life interfirm relationships. This state of affairs leads to the emergence of a clear necessity to enhance management research in this direction.

3. COOPETITION STRATEGIES – THE RESEARCH OBJECT

The first challenge of a new theoretical approach is usually to define the boundaries of the concept under investigation. Since the seminal work by Nalebuff and Brandenburger (1996), coopetition has been the focus of a growing body of researchers. It had in effect started in Europe, developing from a number of key events. In 2002, there were 13 paper presentations at a European Academy of Management (EURAM) conference track dedicated to coopetition strategy. In 2004, a European Institute for Advanced Studies in Management (EIASM) workshop was held in Catania (34 of the 53 submitted papers were accepted). EIASM presented a second workshop in the series in Milan's SDA Bocconi in 2006 (34 of the 44 presented papers were accepted). In 2007 there was a coopetition track at the EURAM conference (12 of the 24 submitted papers were accepted), followed by a third EIASM workshop in Madrid in 2008. In 2009 a Professional Development Workshop on 'Coopetition strategy: current issues and future research directions' was held at the Academy of Management annual conference in Chicago. An invited workshop on 'Coopetition and Entrepreneurship' has been organized in June 2010 in Montpellier. Finally, in 2010, an EIASM coopetition workshop is scheduled to be held in Montpellier on June 17 and 18, under the broad-spectrum label 'Coopetition and Innovation' and a track named 'Coopetition strategy' will be organized at the IFSAM Conference in Paris.

Special issues of publications also reflect the growing body of literature in the coopetition field. For instance, in *International Studies of Management and Organization* (Vol.37, no.2, 2007), and *Management Research* (Vol.6, no.3), while the *International Journal of Entrepreneurship and Small Business* links coopetition to entrepreneurship (Vol.8, no. 2009). Some books are under way; the first one is for Routledge on *Coopetition Strategy: Theory Experiments and Cases* (Dagnino and Rocco, 2009). This Edward Elgar book is a collection of some of the best contributions extracted from the Paris EURAM track in 2007 and the Milan EIASM workshop on coopetition in 2006.

The emerging coopetition community is founded on the idea that coopetition requires a dedicated theoretical approach. It is noteworthy that different authors, however, capture the concept differently. In its broadest sense, coopetition extends to all actors in the value-creation network (Nalebuff and Brandenburger, 1996). In its most narrow nuance, coopetition addresses key relationships between direct competitors with comparable market offers (Bengtsson and Kock, 1999).

We propose defining coopetition as a system of actors whose interaction is based on partial goal and interest congruence (Dagnino and Padula, 2002). This is the basic concept that clearly differentiates between coopetition, cooperation and competition. Three points of this definition need to be emphasized:

1. Firms' interdependence is both a source of value creation and the location of value appropriation processes.
2. Firms' interdependence is grounded in a positive and variable-sum game that produces benefits which are not necessarily shared equally among the partners.
3. In a positive-sum game, firms' interdependence stems from partially convergent interests.

The idea of a 'coopetitive value creation system' allows reflections on inter-firm relationships in strategic management and, more specifically, allows the resource-based view and emerging network theories to be questioned and enriched. This idea can be extended to different levels of analysis, to include relationships between markets and non-profit organizations, as well as intergovernmental, interest group, trade union, and even state and multi-state relationships.

4. BACKGROUND TO THE BOOK

Fourteen years after its conventional birth in 1996, the coopetition concept has crossed the threshold of adolescence. Accordingly, while coopetition is experiencing a phase of accelerated growth in terms of a publication stream, it simultaneously seems to have accumulated sufficient vigour to confront and intermingle with other relevant management concepts. In our view, this kind of intersection should be very fertile by not only enriching the actual coopetition theorization body but also by supplementing other, more conventional perspectives in strategic management, technology and organization management, marketing and business history.

The novelty of the coopetition concept lies in its introduction of the simultaneity of cooperation and coopetition relations. Conversely, in past research, two independent literatures have always tackled the question of competition (Ferrier, 2001; Smith *et al.*, 1992) and that of cooperation (Dyer and Singh, 1998; Dussauge *et al.*, 2000).

Today's challenge in the coopetition stream is to go beyond the received dichotomy and to include both relations in a unique theoretical background, which is the main goal of this book. Consequently, we believe that this book represents the initiation of the process.

Indeed, as a new framework, coopetition is underutilized in grasping contemporary strategic strategies and, more generally, managerial practices and processes. We feel that we are on the verge of a coopetition era. Accordingly, we believe that this book is one of the first contributions in terms of academic research and managerial practice which truly works towards building and systematizing the coopetition framework in strategy literature.

The aim of this book is twofold. First, since the coopetition concept is a boundary-spanning term concerning different functions in the business organization (marketing, human resources, finance and so on) and a multidimensional construct when observed at the individual, organizational, dyadic and interorganizational levels of analysis, the main question is to theoretically define a unified conceptual framework. Second, discussing coopetition raises the question of its empirical utility and validity in and across multiple contexts and industries.

This book is an opportunity to provide scholars and practitioners with a research contribution that brings together an active academic community mobilizing this new coopetition concept.

5. STRUCTURE OF THE BOOK

The book is divided into three main parts. The first part deals with the emergence and relevance of coopetition strategy. The second presents coopetition strategy in multiple contexts. The third tackles coopetition strategies at the aggregate level.

In the first part of the book, Chapter 1, 'Coopetition: New Ideas for a New Paradigm', by Bengtsson, Eriksson and Wincent aims to contribute to the development of a comprehensive framework based on a review of prior research; this chapter thus supports the development of a coopetitive paradigm for the future. The multidisciplinary nature of research on coopetition has sparked ongoing research on different analytical levels: individual, organizational, dyadic and interorganizational, and network. On each of these levels, the authors scrutinize prior research according to three different themes: the drivers, processes, and outcomes of coopetition. Thereafter, they suggest directions for further research, including the launch of a multidisciplinary agenda to break new grounds, and provide important building blocks for an integrative multi-level model of coopetitive dynamics.

In Chapter 2, 'The Promise of Coopetition as a New Theoretical Perspective in Strategic Management', Marco Galvagno and Francesco Garraffo mainly address the following questions: what does coopetition mean and what are its distinctive elements? How does coopetition shape firms' behavior? Does firms' resource similarity have an effect on coopetitive behaviors? First, the authors review the literature and note important contradictions and ambiguities, suggesting remedies that can direct future studies. Second, they stress that a systematic comparison of the quality and traits of firms' behavior in respect of coopetitive relationships provides new insights into empirical phenomena that have not yet been explained. Third, they advance a set of propositions (largely based on an interfirm relationship approach) regarding the nature of firms' cooperative or competitive behaviors in respect of coopetitors and the relationships between resource similarity and coopetitors' behavior.

In Chapter 3, 'Emerging Coopetition: An Empirical Investigation of Coopetition as Inter-organizational Relationship Instability', Wojiech Czakon highlights that while there is a growing understanding of the deliberate side of coopetition strategies, there are very few studies of this phenomenon as an emerging process. His research aims at filling this gap within a theoretical framework based on interorganizational relationship dynamics. The franchising case study findings suggest that coopetition may emerge within cooperative settings.

The objective of Chapter 4, 'Learning in Coopetitive Environments', by Philippe Baumard is to explore the learning strategies that firms can deploy in coopetitive configurations that offer no other choice than to deploy an 'adverse learning' mechanism to reach their customers, namely through cooperation with their competitors. After exploring the mechanisms of asymmetric learning in the first section, the chapter adopts an ecological perspective (Hawley, 1950) by drawing parallels between animal organization and groups of firms that gain a strategic advantage through asymmetric learning.

In the second part of the book, in Chapter 5, 'Coopetitive Value Creation in Entrepreneurial Contexts: The Case of Almacube', Giovanni Battista Dagnino and Marcello Mariani elaborate on a comprehensive framework in which the emergence of coopetition is linked to the process of configuration of entrepreneurial strategies. In more detail, the chapter focuses on the entrepreneurial firm's strategic role in bridging the gap between the capability space and the opportunity space by characterizing entrepreneurial coopetitive strategies according to the required execution versus innovation objectives. Consequently, the authors show that coopetition can be the appropriate spark that initiates value creation in entrepreneurial contexts. On the basis of a field inquiry performed on 50 business ideas that had been incubated in AlmaCube, the technological incubator of the University of Bologna in Italy, they show that entrepreneurial firms need to select their strategic courses of action by capturing correct and well-timed opportunities, frequently making use of a limited capability baseline.

In Chapter 6, 'The Role of Architectural Players in Coopetition: The Case of the US Defense Industry', Colette Depeyre and Hervé Dumez note that research programs dealing with coopetition focus almost exclusively on firms that compete and cooperate on a horizontal level: the role played by other actors – customers, regulators – has not been investigated. Nevertheless, these latter actors can play an architectural role in respect of coopetitive behaviors and structures. The authors have therefore completed a longitudinal case study within a specific industry in which they analyze three sequences of coopetition and provide a theoretical discussion.

In Chapter 7, 'Exploring How Third-Party Organizations Facilitate Coopetition Management in Buyer–Seller Relationships', Sandro Castaldo, Guido Möllering, Monica Grosso and Fabrizio Zerbini look beyond the coopetitive dyad and explore the managerial option of involving a third party in order to deal with the challenge of developing a dyadic relationship that is both cooperative and competitive. Drawing on evidence from three successful category management projects, they show the general plausibility of using third-party mediation for coopetition management in channel relationships. The authors also shed light on the conditions for successful mediation as well as the mechanisms (such as trust) that mediators use to promote cooperation within distribution channel relationships that are also competitive.

In Chapter 8, 'Coopetition among Nature-Based Tourism Firms: Competition at Local Level and Cooperation at Destination Level', Ossi Pesämaa and Per-Erik Eriksson claim that coopetition is a phenomenon in which firms capitalize on the energy from local competition to outperform other destinations which balance the competition less successfully, through cooperation at a destination level. In this chapter, a game-theoretic simulation is used to investigate cooperating or competing as two different strategies and to discuss their consequences. These consequences are examined by elaboration on different behavior strategies and different perspectives of risk. Specifically, the authors ask what rationale could justify cooperation in nature-based tourism destinations. Do the actors prefer a decision to cooperate in favor of competition based on their perspective of risk?

In the third part of the book, Chapter 9, 'Coopetition within an Oligopoly: Impacts of a Disruptive Strategy', Pierre Roy and Saïd Yami investigate a firm's deviance from a collective fate in an oligopoly and the competitive implications of such a move on the coopetitive relation between dominant firms. In this regard, they study the case of UGC's unlimited access card launched in March 2000 in the French movie theater sector. This project was characterized as a disruptive strategy carried out by just one of the dominant firms and as going against the collective interests of the oligopoly (comprising Gaumont, Pathé and UGC).

In Chapter 10, 'Strategic Management of Coopetitive Relationships in CoPS-Related Industries', Thomas Herzog examines coopetitive constellations from a corporate actor-level perspective. Drawing on the empirical example of the global civil aircraft engine industry as an archetypal CoPS context (Complex Products and Services), this contribution aims to examine why and how strategic action unfolds under coopetitive conditions. Furthermore the author seeks to gain a more profound insight into how companies – which are in many ways linked to global networks that bind them closely to their competitors by means of far-reaching cooperation agreements – cope with coopetitive tension.

In Chapter 11, 'Coopetition Dynamics in Convergent Industries: Designing Scope Connections to Combine Heterogeneous Resources', Fabio Ancarani and Michele Costabile, focusing on scope alliances, argue that the process of widening and combining heterogeneous resources is only successful if the partner companies' combinative capabilities are relatively homogeneous. They claim that within scope alliances, firms should be able to balance a high degree of heterogeneity in technological, commercial and operational resources with a high degree of homogeneity in combinative capabilities. On the basis of three case studies (Symbian, Innéov Fermeté [Nestlé-Oreal], and Kodak), the authors present suggestions regarding the managerial approach that firms should adopt to combine their heterogeneous resources in order to expand their market domain and lead competitive convergence. The authors also highlight directions for future research.

In Chapter 12, 'Successful Strategy for Challengers: Competition or Coopetition with Dominant Firms?', Frédéric Le Roy and Patrice Guillotreau ask the following questions: how can a company challenge the market leader? How can a leading company maintain or lose its leadership? Behavioral norms rule the industry, for example, in terms of production, capacity building and price levels. These collective norms are set by the leading company, which retaliates against any incumbent firm wanting to challenge it. A socio-economic approach is applied to the case of the European tuna industry. The authors show how, in a European context, social exchanges between the different stakeholders led to the coopetitive regulation of economic relations, which allocated a leading position to one of the companies (Saupiquet). They then describe how the entry of new foreign competitors, including Starkist, a US firm belonging to Heinz, challenged Saupiquet's leadership by questioning the industry's coopetitive behavioral norms and led to the rebuilding of both the competitive relationships and market shares for their own benefit.

CONCLUSION

This book provides a handful of theoretical insights and empirical evidence on coopetition. The conclusion is that although some work has been done, the road ahead to improve our knowledge of this intriguing construct is very long. This perspective gives rise to fundamental issues regarding coopetition:

1. The coopetition concept requires broader investigation. What is its real nature? Are there different types of coopetition strategies? What are the most appropriate theoretical grounds for coopetition studies?
2. The context in which coopetition strategies are deployed also needs to be examined. Do some contexts appear to be more appropriate than others? Why and in what form would a coopetition strategy be crafted deliberately? What typical cases illustrate coopetition strategies most significantly?
3. Coopetition processes are as poorly understood as the concept itself. What are the motivations of the actors engaging in a coopetition strategy? What are the antecedents of coopetition strategy emergence? What are the critical issues of coopetition strategy management?
4. The actual performance of coopetition strategy is also under-researched. Do coopetition strategies really provide better results than competition or cooperation individually? What are the performance factors in coopetition strategies? What are the failure factors and drivers of a strategic shift from coopetition to other options?
5. The method of study requires careful choices. Should preference be given to a strictly theoretical approach such as game theory? Should case studies be developed for a better understanding of the nature of coopetition? Can operational measures be developed to facilitate a more quantitative approach?

Further coopetition-oriented research can answer these open questions and contribute to an understanding of the extent of the theoretical potential and the latitude that the coopetition concept can capture and explain. Empirical investigation also appears necessary, even more today, now that coopetition has become a widespread modus operandi in various economic sectors and industries (such automobile, biotech, telecommunications, computers and many others); mainstream strategy research apparently does not appear to be aware of this circumstance. Incorporating empirical phenomena in extant theory could be of the utmost importance to firms in the elaboration and execution of their current and future strategies. It could help managers to better understand the new challenges of interfirm relationships and support them in opting for relational strategies that promise better and deeper value creation.

By looking at coopetition as a distinct research object, we can pave the way for the characterization of a new sub-field of inquiry in strategy. This seems indeed particularly promising for the development of strategic management research and practice. We are therefore at the very beginning of the emerging 'coopetitive investigation path' that tomorrow will possibly become an important part of management studies. We hope many researchers will join us on this emerging and fascinating research path.

REFERENCES

Afuah, A. (2000), 'How much do your co-opetitors' capabilities matter in the face of technological change?', *Strategic Management Journal*, **21**(3), 387–404.
Astley, W.G. and C.J. Fombrun (1983), 'Collective strategy: social ecology of organizational environments', *Academy of Management Review*, **8**(4), 576–587.
Bengtsson, M. and S. Kock (1999), 'Cooperation and competition in relationships between competitors in business networks', *Journal of Business and Industrial Marketing*, **14**(3), 178–190.
Brandenburger, A. and B.J. Nalebuff (1995), 'The right game: use game theory to shape strategy', *Harvard Business Review*, July–August, 57–71.
Dagnino, G.B. and G. Padula (2002), *Coopetition Strategy: A New Kind of Inter-Firm Dynamics for Value Creation*, Stockholm: EURAM.
Dagnino, G.B. and Rocco E. (2009), *Coopetition Strategy: Theory Experiments and Cases*, London: Routledge.
Das, T.K. and B. Teng (2000), 'Instabilities of strategic alliances: an internal tensions perspective', *Organization Science*, **11**(1), 77–101.
D'Aveni, R. (1994), *Hypercompetition*, New York: Free Press.
Doz, Y.L. and G. Hamel (1998), *Alliance Advantage: The Art of Creating Value through Form and Action*, Boston, Massachusetts: Harvard Business School Press, Boston.
Dussauge, P., B. Garrette and W. Mitchell (2000), 'Learning from competing partners: outcome and durations of scale and link alliances in Europe, North America and Asia', *Strategic Management Journal*, **21**(2), 99–126.
Dyer, J.H. and H. Singh (1998), 'The relational view: cooperative strategy and

sources of inter-organizational competitive advantage', *Academy of Management Review*, **23**(4), 660–679.

Ferrier, W. (2001), 'Navigating the competitive landscape: the drivers and conse-quences of competitive aggressiveness', *Academy of Management Journal*, **44**(4), 858–77.

Fjeldstad, Ø., M. Becerra and S. Narayanan (2004), 'Strategic action in network industries: an empirical analysis of the European mobile phone industry', *Scandinavian Journal of Management*, **20**, 173–197.

Hamel, G., Y. Doz and C.K. Prahalad (1989), 'Collaborate with your competitors and win', *Harvard Business Review*, **67**(1), 133–139.

Hawley, A.H. (1950), *Human Ecology: A Theory of Community Structure*, New York: Ronald Press.

Hill, C.W. (1990), 'Cooperation, opportunism, and the invisible hand: implica-tions for transaction', *Academy of Management Review*, **15**(3), 500–514.

Lado, A., N.G. Boyd and S.C. Hanlon (1997), 'Competition, cooperation, and the search for economic rents: a syncretic model', *Academy of Management Review*, **22**(1), 110–141.

Lazzarini, S.G. (2007), 'The impact of membership in competing alliance constel-lations: evidence on the operational performance of global airlines', *Strategic Management Journal*, **28**(4), 345–368.

Le Roy, F. (2002), *La concurrence: entre affrontement et connivence*, Paris: Vuibert.

Lecocq, X. and S. Yami (2002), 'From value chain to value networks: toward a new strategic model', in Sarianna M. Lundan (ed.), *Network Knowledge in International Business*, Cheltenham, UK: Edward Elgar, pp. 9–27.

Luo, Y. (2004), 'A coopetition perspective of MNC–host government relations', *Journal of International Management*, **10**(4), 431–451.

Nalebuff, B. and A. Brandenburger (1996), *La co-opétition, une révolution dans la manière de jouer concurrence et coopération*, Paris: Village Mondial.

Nalebuff, B.J. and A.M. Brandenburger (1997), 'Coopetition: competitive and cooperative business strategies for the digital economy', *Strategy and Leadership*, Nov–Dec, 28–35.

Pellegrin-Boucher, E. (2006), *Stratégies de compétition modalités et implications. Le cas du secteur des ERP et des services*, Thèse de doctorat en sciences de gestion, Université Montpellier 1, Montpellier.

Porter, M. (1980), *Competitive Strategy*, New York: Free Press.

Smith, K.G., C.M. Grimm and M.J. Gannon (1992), *Dynamics of Competitive Strategy*, London: Sage Publications.

Teece, D.J. and T. Jorde (1989), 'Competition and cooperation: striking the right balance', *California Management Review*, **31**(3), 25–38.

Yami, S. and F. Le Roy (2007), *Les stratégies collectives: une nouvelle forme de concurrence*, Caen: EMS.

PART I

The emergence and relevance of coopetition strategy

1. Coopetition: new ideas for a new paradigm

Maria Bengtsson, Jessica Eriksson and Joakim Wincent

INTRODUCTION

Scholars and practitioners have repeatedly observed that the rules of the game in many industries have changed over the past decades. There is increasingly intense competition and a deep inclination towards interorganizational collaboration among firms (Powell, Koput and Smith-Doerr, 1996). A growing number of researchers have also noted that competition and cooperation often coexist and simultaneously influence the strategic operations of firms and other organizations (see for example Gnyawali, He and Madhavan, 2008; Walley, 2007), and the scholarly attention to simultaneous competition and cooperation (that is, to 'coopetition') has increased from the mid-1990s onward. The different lines of inquiry that have developed are many, and several definitions of the concept have resulted. Although the diversity of approaches and perspectives that have been suggested is extensive, Padula and Dagnino (2007) note that the contributions have not gone beyond acknowledging the existence of the phenomenon, naming it, and declaring its importance. There is great potential in outlining new directions and integrating current findings into a comprehensive framework.

In this chapter, we aim to contribute to the development of such a framework based on a review of prior research, and thereby to begin to develop a paradigm of coopetition. In our review of prior research on coopetition, we acknowledge the broader literature on cooperation and competition to push and refine the boundaries of the concept of coopetition and to generate interesting and fruitful ideas for further research. This chapter notes both limitations and challenges that we believe should be addressed to extend current knowledge, and it outlines some intriguing questions that we believe are important for future research.

We begin with the observation that there is limited consensus on what coopetition is and how it manifests in organizations. Our review therefore starts with a discussion of previous conceptualizations and definitions of coopetition, leading up to a discussion of key aspects of a definition that accounts for the various views taken in previous research. Next, we review the current status of the coopetition literature. The multidisciplinary nature of research on coopetition has sparked ongoing research on different analytical levels, and our review mirrors the four different levels of coopetition highlighted in the multidisciplinary approach: individual, organizational, interorganizational, and network. On each level, we scrutinize prior research on the basis of three different themes: (1) the drivers of coopetition, (2) the process of coopetition, and (3) the outcomes of coopetition. We then suggest directions for further research, including the launch of a multidisciplinary agenda to break new ground, and provide important building blocks for an integrative, multilevel model of coopetitive dynamics.

1. CONCEPTUALIZING COOPETITION

The coexistence of cooperation and competition has been recognized in the areas of human resource management, psychology, and strategic management and economics. Although coopetition is often vaguely defined, it centers on an important underlying observation: firms simultaneously engage in two types of interaction with conflicting logics. To highlight some important areas for further progress and to clarify the concept of coopetition, we point out the need to discuss how the cooperative and competitive parts of coopetition are divided between actors in some studies (that is, we compete with some actors and cooperate with others) or between activities in other studies (that is, we compete in this activity but cooperate in other activities). Particularly interesting is that often this is related to the level of analysis (that is, whether the analysis is on an individual, organizational, interorganizational or network level). We shall therefore discuss this question as it relates to the level of analysis.

In Nalebuff and Brandenburger's 1996 book on coopetition, they defined coopetition at a network level as relationships in a value net of customers, suppliers, complementors, and competitors that together add value to the firm. They argued that coopetition in a value net arises, for example, when two computer manufacturers compete with each other but simultaneously complement each other in the value net by cooperating with software producers. Also, two competitors can cooperate to create the value needed to compete with a third firm. Nalebuff and Brandenburger and their followers consequently view coopetition as the sum of many different relationships where the cooperative and competitive part of the relationship is divided between different actors. Such a conceptualization is often used in the literature on coopetition in networks and industrial districts (see for example Dei Ottati, 1994; Lado, Boyd and Hanlon, 1997; Levy, Loebbecke and Powell, 2003; Bonel and Rocco, 2007).

At the interorganizational level, focusing on mutual relationships, Bengtsson and Kock (1999) suggest that coopetition should be defined more narrowly to allow for a better grasp of the tension and complexity that follows when two or more firms simultaneously cooperate and compete. Hence, the authors view cooperation and competition as two interrelated parts of mutual relationships. Bengtsson and Kock also argue that the different parts of the coopetitive relationship are divided between activities; for example, two or more competitors can cooperate in product development or technology upgrades and at the same time compete in taking orders, attracting customers, or attaining market share. A consequence of this view is that coopetition comprises cooperative interaction related to one activity and competitive interaction with the same firm related to another activity (see for example Gnyawali and Madhavan, 2001; Tsai, 2002; M'Chirgui, 2005; Gnyawali, He and Madhavan, 2008; Mariani, 2007; Padula and Dagnino, 2007).

The concept of coopetition has also been used in the literature at the individual level (see for example Lindskold, Betz and Walters, 1986; Tjosvold and Wong, 1994; Tjosvold, Tang and West, 2004; Fisher and Gregoire, 2005; Fang, 2006) and at the organizational or intragroup level (see for example Alper, Tjosvold and Law, 1998; Loch, Galunic and Schneider, 2006; Chen and Tjosvold, 2008). In such studies, coopetition is described as a relationship between two or more persons that occurs on a continuum between full cooperation and full competition, rather than that people may cooperate in certain activities and compete in others. Most of these studies rest on the traditional cooperative paradigm, which emphasizes a win–win structure even if it recognizes that competitive interdependences also arise from diverging interest structures. The cooperative paradigm referred to in such studies reveals that individuals or firms search for collaborative advantages in which the strength and success of a given actor depends on the strength and success of other actors. In this view, the competitive part of coopetition is implicitly a negative thing that needs to be reduced or balanced to make possible the positive outcomes of cooperation. The view of coopetition within firms and between individuals therefore emerges as inherently negative in many studies.

We argue, however, that a coopetitive paradigm is needed on both the individual and the organizational level to acknowledge that both competitive and cooperative interdependencies can influence individuals' actions. Further, it must be acknowledged that combining competitive and cooperative dependencies can be advantageous for interactions and their outcomes. Such reasoning is at the core of coopetition. The dynamic tension inherent in the coopetitive relationship can develop only when actors are involved simultaneously in both parts of an interaction.

We suggest that an important task for the development of a new paradigm on coopetition is to obtain and follow a clearer definition of coopetition. A focus on simultaneous cooperation and competition between actors but divided between activities makes it easier to analytically separate cooperative and competitive interaction in a coopetitive relationship and to understand how the interplay between these activities gives rise to tensions in that relationship. Such an approach acknowledges the dynamic nature of coopetition and its distinctive multilevel range. Therefore, this definition should apply at all levels of analysis. We next elaborate on the current state of coopetition research before suggesting new directions for further research.

2.   THE STATE OF COOPETITION RESEARCH

In a review of the existing research, we found some trends worthy of further elaboration. Prior work has often focused on why coopetition emerges in a specific case; that is, what the drivers of coopetition are, what processes occur during coopetition, and what the outcome of coopetition is. Acknowledging the multidisciplinary approach of prior coopetition research, we believe that such richness is important and should not be neglected in a dialogue on future trends. As already indicated, in different disciplines, scholars tend to focus on different levels of analysis. For example, scholars interested in human resource management or organizational psychology address coopetition among individuals or groups in organizations. Conversely, scholars in strategic management or economics have directed their attention primarily to interorganizational relationships, networks, clusters, or industrial districts. The differences in disciplines guide scholars to focus on distinct drivers, processes, and outcomes of coopetition (Gnyawali, He and Madhavan, 2008) that operate at these levels. Table 1.1 summarizes the main insights from prior work in different management disciplines at different levels of analysis. Next, we discuss the results of Table 1.1, focusing on one level at a time.

Table 1.1 Coopetition levels, drivers, processes and outcomes

Coopetition Level	Drivers (selected examples)	Process ⟶	Outcome (selected examples)
Individual (for example, Fang, 2006; Hatcher and Ross, 1991; Lindskold, Betz and Walters 1986; Loch, Galunic and Schneider, 2006; Tjosvold 1986; and Tjosvold and Sun, 2001)	Cultural traits Individual goals Individual morals and values Personality	In cooperation, individuals strive to get others to be effective and to trust and rely on one another, which leads to shared perspectives and interests. In competition, individuals actively interfere with one another and lack of trust restricts information and resource exchange. A dynamic balance between cooperation and competition is, however, possible.	Creativity Loyalty Productivity Stress
Organization (for example, Alper, Tjosvold and Law, 1998; Chen and Tjosvold, 2008; Loch, Galunic and Schneider, 2006; Tsai, 2002)	Department goals Organizational values Task structures Team procedures	In cooperation, organizational systems communicate that goal attainment helps teams and departments be successful together, and systems are designed for interdependence and resource sharing. Competition facilitates processes aiming to withhold	Market knowledge Organizational coordination Profits/losses Shared knowledge and resources

Table 1.1 (continued)

Coopetition Level	Drivers ——→ (selected examples)	Process ——→	Outcome (selected examples)
Mutual interorganizational (for example, Bengtsson and Kock, 2000; Bonel and Rocco, 2007; Das and Teng, 2000; Khanna, Gulati and Nohria, 1998; Levy, Loebbecke, and Powell, 2003)	Resource sharing and acquisition Reducing the benefits of a competitor (Changes in) structural conditions (for example, cost structure, competitive focus, advantages of scale)	information and ideas between departments and subunits as pursuing own goals and to obstruct the goal progress of others. Organizations must balance incentives to cooperate and to compete in order to ensure both communication and efficiency. Oriented towards cooperation, decision processes are accommodative and aim for mutual problem solving, where dyad members are attentive and responsive to the other's interests. Competition involves less fair, more biased, and less honest behavior, which makes dyadic members strive to fulfil own interests. A fruitful coopetitive	Building channels to foreign markets Knowledge spillover New markets, products and processes Relationship maintenance

Network	Advancing joint interests and pooling resources of common purposes	relationship requires balanced power but may be difficult to sustain over long periods of time.	Coordination
(for example, Carayannis and Alexander, 2004; Dei Ottati, 1994; Gnyawali and Madhavan, 2001; Oshri and Weeber, 2006)	Network structure and positions	When cooperating, dependence is based on trust. When competing, dependence is related to an actor's network strength and position. Conflicts are few in cooperation but arise frequently in competition. There are also clear norms when cooperating. When competing, there are invisible norms and distance between actors. It is difficult to balance coopetition for all parties to reap the benefits, due to vast complexities.	Expand the total market
	Social, cultural, and regulatory changes		Innovation and differentiation
	Technological advances and complexity		Integrated strategies

2.1   Coopetition at the Individual Level – a Paradox?

There are two theories from the social psychology literature that have been
extensively used to account for and explain individual behavior under
various conditions of cooperation and competition (that is, the crude law
of social relations and game theory). As indicated earlier, coopetition at
the individual level is often viewed as a continuum from active cooperation to active competition. Coopetition can exist only if competition and
cooperation are balanced on that continuum, which in itself is a paradox.
For organizations to be able to take part in coopetitive relationships, it is
important that they further understand how cooperation and competition
interact at the individual level. Therefore, we next note some important
aspects of the drivers, processes, and outcomes at the individual level.

As Table 1.1 indicates, there are several possible drivers of the coopetitive process, including morals, personality, and values. Drivers shape the
appearance of the coopetitive process towards either more cooperative
or more competitive qualities. Lindskold, Betz, and Walters (1986) argue
that the atmosphere of a relationship can be more or less cooperative or
competitive and thereby foster certain acts and processes. The degree of
trust and common goals among parties give rise to a certain atmosphere
that determines the shape of the process and the role of the individual in
that process (see Hatcher and Ross, 1991; Tjosvold, 1986; Tjosvold and
Sun, 2001; Fisher and Gregoire, 2005). Fang (2006) notes that, in a business setting, when trust is high, interactions can be fair and gentle, but
when trust is low, individuals are more likely to manipulate one another.
The shape and distinction of the process determines the extent to which
outcomes (for example, innovation, stress, loyalty) occur and can be
fostered.

The focus in the existing literature is on the process of interaction rather
than on the drivers and outcomes of the process, and change is a central
theme of such studies. Lindskold, Betz, and Walters (1986) argue that the
process will change if one party acts in contradiction with the existing
atmosphere of the relationship. For example, the cooperative part of the
relationship can be destroyed if one partly acts deliberately and clearly in
conflict with the existing norms of collaboration. The shifts between cooperation and competition can be rather prominent and swift, and researchers have noted that individuals constantly examine and evaluate the state
of trust and fairness between parties. To this background, the coopetitive
process is often described as 'paradoxical, contradictory, strange, and
inscrutable' (Fang, 2006, p. 55). Loch, Galunic, and Schneider (2006),
however, argue that a balance between taking care of 'me' (that is, competition) and taking care of 'we' (that is, cooperation) is possible if emotions

are accounted for. They explain that positive and negative 'emotional algorithms operate simultaneously, interacting and jointly influencing individuals' behaviour within groups. One of their most striking qualities is the dynamic balance they provide to the dilemma of cooperation versus competition' (Loch, Galunic, and Schneider, 2006, p. 229). Furthermore, they argue that it is disadvantageous, and sometimes destructive, for positive and negative emotions to operate in isolation. Such studies and discussions are promising for the development of a paradigm that acknowledges the dynamic tension and synergies inherent in individual-level coopetitive relationships.

2.2 Coopetition at the Organization Level: Value Creation if Competition can be Managed

At the organization level, coopetition between groups or departments has been studied, and often social network, industrial-organization, game, or emotional appraisal theories have been applied to outline how organizational structures or surroundings incline groups or constellations towards either cooperation or competition. Although this literature partly overlaps with studies of the individual level, there are some clear distinctions. In terms of similarities, though, this literature often describes coopetitive relationships as occurring on a continuum, with competition at one end and cooperation at the other. Another is that cooperation is mainly related to positive outcomes, whereas conflict and competition are matters to be dealt with to gain advantages of cooperation. It also stands clear that while values, structures and goals are often important drivers on both levels, it is the values, structures, and goals of the organizations, not of the individual, that are important when addressing the organizational level.

With respect to the cooperative process, influence and power are essential components in relationships dominated by competitive interaction, but they are considered less important in relationships dominated by cooperative interaction. In the latter, the process is directed more towards generating a common understanding of issues and towards organizational members being responsive to one another to work towards a result that reflects mutual preferences (Tsai, 2002; Loch, Galunic and Schneider, 2006). Therefore, following the research of authors such as Tjosvold, Meredith, and Wong (1998) and Chen and Tjosvold (2008), cooperation occurs when organizational units are positively connected in such a way that each group or department achieves its own goals only if others achieve their goals. In contrast, competition occurs when the goals are negatively tied to one another such that each group or department can reach its own goals only if others do not.

Tsai (2002) notes that cooperation is always present in organizations because an important outcome of the interaction among intraorganizational units is the ability to upgrade knowledge and strive for economies of scope. However, in many ways, these units also simultaneously compete because they are compared on the basis of their success and ability to achieve high returns. Drivers for striking a balance towards either cooperation or competition include the degree of centralized decision making, social interaction, reward systems, and goals assigned. Examples of outcomes include the degree of knowledge spillover, confidence in other teams, and the degree to which resources are pooled or coordinated (Alper, Tjosvold and Law, 1998; Chen and Tjosvold, 2008).

The main argument in the studies reviewed here seems to be that organizations can create value, such as upgraded knowledge, economics of scope, or increased product quality, if they are structured and designed to manage or even reduce competition between groups to allow for the advantages of cooperation to emerge. We, however, question this line of thinking on the basis of our discussion about resolving the 'me' versus 'we' dilemma at the individual level. Loch, Galunic, and Schneider (2006) argued that competitive emotional algorithms, resource striving and status recognition, cooperative emotional algorithms, and reciprocity, friendship, and group identification are needed simultaneously to create a dynamic coopetitive relationship between individuals in groups and between groups. The authors studied groups of individuals in an organizational setting, which they found ideal for studying coopetition, and they found that attempting to foster only competition or cooperation may be destructive. We believe that further studies are needed that focus on the benefits of coopetition at the organizational level, on how to manage coopetition, and on how dynamics of coopetition contribute to value creation.

2.3 Coopetition in Mutual Interorganizational Relationships: Managing a Balancing Act to Sustain Dynamic Tension

Coopetition has often been studied on an interorganizational level with a focus on mutual relationships between two or more organizations, where all organizations are involved simultaneously in cooperation and competition. This literature draws on quite diverse theories, such as those of industrial organization and industrial networks (for example, Bengtsson and Kock, 1999, 2000), the resource-based view, cognitive theory (see Thomas and Pollock, 1999), organizational learning (Khanna, Gulati and Nohria, 1998), and fragments from the broader alliance literature (De Rond and Bouchikhi, 2004). Research on dyad-level coopetition draws on various theories normally used in strategic management research, and depending on the theoretical point of departure, the drivers, process, and outcomes are slightly different. For the sake of simplicity, we use dyadic relationships as the example in this chapter, but we emphasize that coopetition also can develop in triads and relationships with additional partners.

At the relational level, the drivers for coopetition vary but tend to focus on structural conditions and the need to pool resources and competences for innovation, production, or distribution. For example, Bengtsson and Kock (2000) argue that structural conditions in an industry induce competition between firms. At the same time, competition leads to a dependence that may cause some firms to also engage in cooperation. Changes in market conditions are hence frequently cited as drivers of coopetition, following institutional or regulatory change, complementary resource or knowledge profiles (Padula and Dagnino, 2007), or the need for advantages of scale (Mitchell, Dussauge and Garrette, 2002). The drivers all suggest that broader network relationships with embedded dyadic relationships influence why and how coopetition occurs.

Overall, the need to balance coopetitive relationships is highlighted in discussions of the interaction process. Such balance may be necessary to realize a coopetitive dyad, as indicated by Das and Teng (2000), who suggest that simultaneous cooperation and competition may be easier to achieve when partners are reasonably equivalent (for example, in terms of status and size) and have complementary resource bases. Different solutions may be of a structural or motivational nature (for example, improving partners' communication, establishing joint long-term goals) or aimed to handle power issues and alliance dynamics. Throughout the coopetitive process, trust must continuously be re-established, and it may be counterbalanced by the fear of or acts of opportunism and the simultaneous strategic search for flexibility and control (Zeng and Chen, 2003; De Rond and Bouchikhi, 2004). Others suggest that management of knowledge sharing can both alleviate and exploit coopetitive forces or tensions in small and medium-sized enterprises (SMEs), but that few SMEs manage to reap these benefits (Levy, Loebbecke and Powell, 2003).

Alliances and coopetitive interaction may evolve over time: at some points, cooperation may be strong; at others, competition. As a consequence, it can be difficult to sustain coopetition over long periods (Bonel and Rocco, 2007; Padula and Dagnino, 2007). Failure to cope with coopetition and the tensions that arise may 'be responsible for the high failure rate of strategic alliances' (Das and Teng, 2000, p. 86). Coopetitive interaction involves learning processes (Bengtsson and Kock, 1999), and Bonel and Rocco (2007, p. 94) suggest that firms engaging in coopetition may have to adapt their business models 'to exploit emerging new complementarities and to address ensuing interferences due to interactions with coopeting partners'.

The outcomes of coopetition are many according to the literature. Mainly, the advantages suggested include that coopetition results in value creation and facilitates value sharing (Bengtsson and Kock, 2000). Examples include the fact that, through coopetition, companies help or force each other to develop and reach new, creative solutions (Bengtsson and Kock, 1999) and to achieve growth and remain competitive (Thomas and Pollock, 1999). However, there are also potential drawbacks, such as the ending of a coopetitive relationship or the development of a trap or unintended effects (Bonel and Rocco, 2007), and there are potential negative effects and tensions for individual employees (Bengtsson and Kock, 2001).

There has been extensive research on coopetition in various types of mutual alliances. However, even though there is a need to balance competition and cooperation in coopetitive relationships, there is limited knowledge about the tensions that can arise, how the tensions are dealt with, how they develop over time, and what the effects are.

2.4 Coopetition in Networks: The Advantage of Combining Many Different Relations with Different Actors

Studies of coopetition among many actors in a network setting include coopetition within and between industrial districts (Dei Ottati, 1994), industries (Mariani, 2007), research consortia (Carayannis and Alexander, 2004), interest groups (Doucet, 2006), networks of firms, and so on. At the network level, several theoretical approaches have been used, including game theory (Chaudhri and Samson, 2000), structuring approaches (Gnyawali and Madhavan, 2001; Gnyawali, He and Madhavan, 2006), industrial networks (Ims and Jakobsen, 2006), learning and knowledge (for example, Mariani, 2007), resource dependency, and transaction cost theory (M'Chirgui, 2005).

As at the mutual interorganizational level, changes such as deregulation may prompt coopetition strategies (Okura, 2007), and costs and complexity of the technological systems may lead to joint research and development (R&D) (Oshri and Weeber, 2006) and the pooling of resources (Carayannis and Alexander, 2004). Other important drivers of coopetition include; advancing joint interests (Mariani, 2007) or decreasing the benefits of competitors by engaging in collusion (Ims and Jakobsen, 2006; Gnyawali, He and Madhavan, 2006).

Regarding the process of coopetition, tension arises between network partners as a result of simultaneous cooperation and competition.

Gnyawali and Madhavan (2001) illustrate how such tensions may be related to resource asymmetries that arise from the firm's network position and from related aspects such as information and status. Dei Ottati (1994), focusing on industrial districts, suggests that formal, private and public local institutions must monitor opportunistic and protectionist actions and mediate potential disputes in the district. Such coordination is based on local customs and investments in personal reputation, and the mechanisms are relevant to understanding coopetition, even if not all relationships in an industrial district meet our definition of coopetition.

Because of the complexities of coopetition at the network level, the outcome of coopetition may be more beneficial for some actors, and the relationship may constrain other actors. Integrated strategies are a frequent result, as is market expansion. Outcomes can also include reduced costs of claims for insurance firms (Okura, 2007), improved innovation and R&D, maintained coordination, and dynamics in industrial districts (Dei Ottati, 1994). Thus, the potentially beneficial outcomes are similar to those of coopetition at the dyad level. Some of the literature that discusses coopetition at a network level also discusses dyads (for example, Bengtsson and Kock, 1999), and the fact that there are notable similarities and overlaps between the two levels. However, even though explicit comparisons are lacking, it is clear that network-level coopetition is much more complex, and it may be more difficult to balance the coopetitive relationship and ensure that all involved gain benefits of coopetition when more actors are involved. Yet the constellation of firms may be stable, as it can be difficult to break away from the complex interdependences that circumscribe the network-level coopetitive relationship.

Following the view of coopetition as simultaneous cooperation and competition between two or more parties, relationships in industrial districts, clusters, and networks may not always qualify as coopetitive relationships in the sense of simultaneous cooperation and competition among all actors engaged in the relationship. Rather, the sum of the relationships gives rise to competition on the level of the entire network (see Nalebuff and Brandenburger, 1996). In industries and R&D consortia, which we place on this level, it is possible that all parties engaging in the relationship mutually compete and cooperate with all other partners, thus fitting our definition of coopetition. However, such relationships are rarely that symmetrical: some firms have more competitive interactions and others have more cooperative interactions. Instead, coopetition is likely to occur between two networks, industrial districts, or research consortia, even though we found no such examples in our review.

Although more work is needed to clarify coopetition on the network level, we believe that it is important to include the network level in future studies. There are at least two primary issues for further study. First, research should focus on coopetition between different networks, as outlined previously. Second, of particular interest is the study of how cooperative and competitive relationships on the network level influence relationships on the interorganizational level, the tensions that arise, and how such tensions are handled.

3.   DIRECTIONS FOR FURTHER RESEARCH

Several agendas for further research stem from the ideas presented here, which could not only inform more detailed and complex answers to questions presented in prior research but also open up new areas for inquiry. Next, we turn to some of the broader implications that are in need of further elaboration.

3.1   Further Research on Coopetition Levels

Although the conceptualization of coopetition is sometimes vague, the problems in defining coopetition suggest that it captures a complex inter-action process, and that coopetition is evident at the individual, group, interorganizational, and network levels. Currently, most research focuses at disciplines that corroborate the dyad or network level (that is, strategic management), but coopetition can also be studied among individuals and on the group level, such as in the fields of human resource management or organizational and social psychology. Studies of simultaneous cooperation and competition at the individual level were less prone to use the term coopetition, but as we have argued, it is fruitful to apply coopetition at the individual level. We previously stated that coopetition at the individual and organizational levels is considered a dilemma or a paradox, and efforts often aim to reduce competition. Such efforts may, however, decrease dynamics. Loch, Galunic, and Schneider (2006) contribute to a better understanding of these connections by illustrating how emotions play an important part. However, further research needs to explore other potential factors that facilitate fruitful coopetition on the individual and organizational levels. For example, leadership and the structuring of work may have a decisive impact on how to handle coopetition.

Overall, it is evident that we need a clearer picture of the drivers of coopetition, the processes, and the outcomes at each level, as existing research has focused mainly on specific cases and the phenomenon as such. Knowledge about coopetitive processes is restricted and may sometimes be considered a 'black box' phenomenon. Most often the focus is on drivers, processes, or outcomes, or on the relationship between drivers and outcomes of coopetition. We would welcome further studies on the interaction process, as we believe that the interaction process might differ depending on, for example, whether firms' coopetitive interaction is forced (see Bengtsson and Kock, 2001) or whether the firms themselves initiate the contradictory relationship. Future research at the dyad and network levels will benefit from further exploration of the broader coopetition relationship and how it develops over time. Furthermore, the process affects the relationship between the drivers and the outcomes of the process. There is also a need for more studies on the drivers that facilitate cooperation and competition and how they interact, as well as on how coopetition processes over time lean towards competition or cooperation (thus endangering the potential benefits of coopetition), on why dynamics decrease, and on what the outcomes are. In addition, Table 1.1 notes that some drivers and outcomes may be rather similar, which raises the question of how changes in one outcome over time can affect the drivers and the ongoing process of coopetition.

Consequently, we hope to see more longitudinal perspectives in further research, as most published coopetition articles are cross-sectional. Longitudinal studies are especially important for capturing the tensions and conflicts that occur in coopetitive processes on different levels. The study of processes is also incomplete, given the primary interest in outcomes on the interorganizational and network levels, and most studies have tended to analyze the cooperative and competitive processes separately, without exploring the dynamics that presumably are related to coopetition. The attitudes, emotions, and behaviors that characterize and influence coopetition may change over time (Bengtsson and Kock, 2001; Loch, Galunic and Schneider, 2006), and knowledge about how to balance cooperation and competition is far from complete. However, a fruitful path for coopetition research would be to study how to manage the process of coopetition in order to find predictors that facilitate such a balance.

3.2 Multidisciplinary, Multilevel Approaches on Coopetition

Coopetition is not a fixed phenomenon that occurs in isolation, but prior research has often focused on a limited aspect of the phenomenon. Because authors conceptualize coopetition according to the scope of their studies, many individual studies have failed to specify the complexity of the processes involved. Focusing their theorizing on a specific level of analysis, scholars often direct their efforts on the basis of a belief that most meaningful heterogeneity exists at that level and then assume homogeneity on the other levels. For example, when studying organizational-level coopetition, scholars often have assumed that the organization is the most important source of heterogeneity. Detailed explanations then result at one level but not others. Our review and integration of prior work acknowledge that there is heterogeneity at all levels, and an important agenda for further inquiry is the interplay between levels and the interdependencies between those levels. Our interest in integrating the various coopetition levels also leads us to discuss interdependence between levels. Integration of these areas will present challenges, but there is much value in outlining tentative bridges.

Some prior studies have indicated that coopetition exists on different levels, with interactions within and across levels (Bengtsson and Kock, 2001; see also Walley, 2007). Thus, there are dependencies and motivations involved when actors join forces to accomplish certain ends, but there are also numerous sources of conflict and tension that operate side by side. As mentioned previously, coopetition research can greatly benefit from multidisciplinary approaches that take a cross-level perspective. Examples of questions for future research include the following: do drivers of coopetition among lower-level phenomena, such as individuals, travel to macro-level phenomena such as groups? Can coopetition processes at the level of dyads and networks leak to micro-level processes among groups or individuals?

Figure 1.1 shows some examples of possible cross-level interactions, such as how coopetitive drivers, processes, and outcomes on one level can influence drivers, processes, and outcomes on other levels. Theoretically, vertical relationships between all squares in Figure 1.1 are possible. We discuss only a few examples here to highlight the relevance of a multidisciplinary, multilevel analysis of coopetition, and we put forward some propositions to clarify our points. In Figure 1.1, line A illustrates that micro-level coopetition drivers may influence processes at a macro level. For example, individual goals and values may shape the balance of coopetition processes at the organization level by opportunistic behavior that hurts a relationship between two departments. It is equally possible that macro-level drivers shape coopetitive processes at micro-levels. Line B shows one such effect. Thus, organization-level drivers may influence processes at the individual level. For example, when organizations simultaneously cooperate and compete, individuals' circumstances are affected and role conflicts may arise. The possibilities for handling such role conflicts vary, and the individual-level effects have an impact on the organization and on the relationship (and vice versa). Conflicts may lead to creative blocks or hinder advantageous and innovative outcomes, and units may be forced to act inconsistently with internal goals. Such

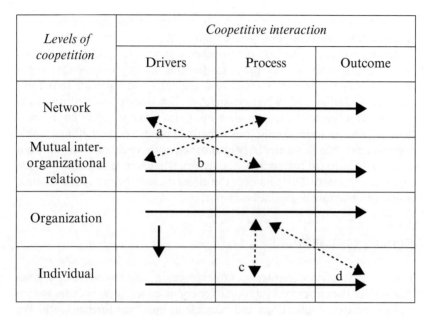

Figure 1.1   Coopetitive interaction across multiple levels

outcomes may have detrimental effects on the relationship between firms.

To complicate matters, we argue that coopetitive processes on different levels are interlinked and can influence each other. Line C illustrates this phenomenon, suggesting that interorganizational-level coopetitive processes influence network-level coopetitive processes. For example, problems balancing the coopetitive relationship and obtaining trust and knowledge sharing in a dyadic coopetitive relationship may lead to similar problems in network-level relationships, and vice versa. Finally, line D illustrates that network-level coopetition outcomes may influence coopetitive processes in interorganizational relationships, and vice versa. Innovative results at the network level can be input in, for example, a dyadic relationship, which may positively improve the interaction but also alter power relationships if one party's position in the network improves at the expense of the dyad partner.

These examples merely illustrate the range of possibilities for further elaboration and are not exhaustive. The main point is that coopetition is well suited for multilevel analyses in order to fully capture the coopetitive dynamics that prior work has not yet focused on. Acknowledging multilevel influences may open the door for more complete theories. Moreover, the possibilities for handling such management problems vary, and any prescriptions will be based on complex analyses.

A wide variety of research approaches and methodologies are useful for studying multilevel coopetition, including traditional survey research and in-depth qualitative studies. Approaches focusing on how macro-levels influence micro-levels may be as challenging as approaches that focus on the inverse. However, to focus on dynamics, we advocate longitudinal survey studies and, when possible, the participation of respondents from several levels of the organization. Qualitative studies may be particularly fruitful in following the coopetitive processes, and ethnographic approaches could be particularly rewarding, as they rely not only on what respondents can tell researchers but also on what people actually do when exposed to coopetition. Whatever the method used, the need for academic cooperation across disciplines is important.

CONCLUSIONS

The objective of this chapter was to explore and discuss some new ideas that rest on the current foundation of coopetition research in order to juxtapose research implications and possible agendas for further work. We explored some new directions for advancing and refining the coopetition paradigm. We also noted some limitations and challenges that should be addressed to extend the current understanding.

In our review and outline for further work, we advocated that multilevel research on coopetition could also benefit from stronger connections across disciplines. Our work, albeit rough and tentative, attempts to contribute to a better understanding of how and when differences occur and to provide some ideas of consequences. We outlined how the multilevel lens and methodology can be a means to integrate existing research on coopetition and to explore new and different sets of questions across levels. We were able to show the existence of coopetitive dynamics across levels. This cross-level approach contributes to the coopetition literature by offering increased theoretical precision for explaining the impact coopetition has on individuals and groups in organizations as well as influences on interorganizational relations and networks. As coopetition increasingly operates under such conditions, the interdependencies across levels add tensions, complexities, and dynamics that would otherwise would have been left unexplained.

Important managerial implications are that coopetition has antecedents and consequences at multiple levels. Managers could try to modify drivers or processes at one level so as to influence those at another. This could inhibit and reduce potential dysfunctional influences of coopetition. For example, managers could avoid fostering disloyal actions by individuals forced to handle the effects of organization-level coopetition. To create effective management tools, managers may need to look beyond traditional management approaches. In the interest of preventing dysfunctional individual influences when the organization simultaneously cooperates with a competitor, managers can model and communicate respectful workplace behavior and skills training of the employees involved.

Our suggestions for research designs that include several coopetition levels and acknowledge a wide range of drivers, processes, and outcomes across levels differ from the traditional designs in this field of research. Our arguments should not be understood as suggesting that further coopetition research should neglect efforts to extend the knowledge of certain levels and pay full attention to multilevel issues. We, also, outlined some specific examples on important issues at each coopetition level. Instead, we mean to acknowledge the complexity involved and the potential for multidisciplinary cooperation to study connections between levels of analysis and how coopetition needs to be better understood from yet new perspectives. As such, we hope that our approach and ideas resonate with scholars who argue for the inclusion of multilevel perspectives to gain valuable insights. Thus, future coopetition research has much to gain from acknowledging the fragmentation, heterogeneity, and interdependence across coopetition levels.

REFERENCES

Alper, S., D. Tjosvold and K.S. Law (1998), 'Interdependence and Controversy in Group Decision Making: Antecedents to Effective Self-Managing Teams', *Organizational Behavior and Human Decision Processes*, **74**(1), 33–52.

Bengtsson, M. and S. Kock (1999), 'Cooperation and competition in relationships between competitors in business networks', *Journal of Business and Industrial Marketing*, **14**(3), 178–194.

Bengtsson, M. and S. Kock (2000), '"Coopetition" in Business Networks – to Cooperate and Compete Simultaneously', *Industrial Marketing Management*, **29**(5), 397–412.

Bengtsson, M. and S. Kock (2001), 'Tension in Coopetition', presented at the 16th Nordic Academy of Management Meeting, Uppsala, Sweden, August 16–18, 2001.

Bonel, E. and E. Rocco (2007), 'Coopeting to Survive; Surviving Coopetition', *International Studies of Management and Organization*, **37**(2), 70–96.

Carayannis, E.G.C. and J. Alexander (2004), 'Strategy, Structure, and Performance Issues of Precompetitive R&D Consortia: Insights and Lessons Learned From SEMATECH', *IEEE Transactions on Engineering Management*, **51**(2), 226–232.

Chaudhri, V. and D. Samson (2000), 'Business-government relations in Australia: Cooperating through task forces', *Academy of Management Executive*, **14**(3), 19–29.

Chen, G. and D. Tjosvold (2008), 'Organizational Values and Procedures as Antecedents for Goal Interdependence and Collaborative Effectiveness', *Asia Pacific Journal Management*, **25**, 93–112.

Das, T.K. and B.S. Teng (2000), 'Instabilities of Strategic Alliances: An Internal Tensions Perspective', *Organization Science*, **11**(1), 77–101.

De Rond, M. and H. Bouchikhi, (2004), 'On the Dialectics of Strategic Alliances', *Organization Science*, **15**(1), 56–69.

Dei Ottati, G.D. (1994), 'Cooperation and competition in the industrial district as an organization model', *European Planning Studies*, **2**(4), 463–483.

Doucet, P. (2006), 'Territorial Cohesion of Tomorrow: A Path to Cooperation or Competition?', *European Planning Studies*, **14**(10), 1473–1485.

Fang, T. (2006), 'Negotiation: the Chinese Style', *Journal of Business and Industrial Marketing*, **21**(1), 50–60.

Fisher, R.J. and Y. Gregoire (2005), 'Competition and Cooperation in Joint Purchase Decisions', *Advances in Consumer Research*, **32**, 311–312.

Gnyawali, D.R. and R. Madhavan, R. (2001), 'Network Structure and Competitive Dynamics: A Structural Embeddedness Perspective', *Academy of Management Review*, **26**(3), 431–445.

Gnyawali, D.R., J. He, and R. Madhavan (2006), 'Impact of Coopetition on Firm Competitive Behavior: An Empirical Examination', *Journal of Management*, **32**(4), 507–530.

Gnyawali, D.R., J. He, and R. Madhavan (2008), 'Coopetition. Promises and Challenges', Chapter 38 in C. Wankel (ed.), *The 21st Century Management: A Reference Handbook*, vol. 1, Thousand Oaks, CA: Sage, pp. 386–398.

Hatcher, L. and T.L. Ross (1991), 'From Individual Incentives to an Organization-Wide Gainsharing Plan: Effects on Teamwork and Product Quality', *Journal of Organizational Behavior*, **12**(3), 169–183.

Ims, K.J. and O.D. Jakobsen (2006), 'Cooperation and Competition in the Context of Organic and Mechanic Worldviews – A Theoretical and Case based Discussion', *Journal of Business Ethics*, **66**, 19–32.

Khanna, T., R. Gulati and N. Nohria (1998), 'The Dynamics of Learning Alliances: Competition, Cooperation, and Relative Scope', *Strategic Management Journal*, **19**(3), 193–210.

Lado, A.A, N.G. Boyd, and S.C. Hanlon (1997), 'Competition and Cooperation, and the Search for Economic Rents: A Syncretic Model', *Academy of Management Review*, **22**(1), 110–141.

Levy, M., C. Loebbecke, and P. Powell (2003), 'SME's, Coopetition and Knowledge sharing: The Role of Information Systems', *European Journal of Information Systems*, **12**, 3–17.

Lindskold, S., B. Betz, and P.S. Walters (1986), 'Transforming Competitive or Cooperative Climates', *The Journal of Conflict Resolution*, **30**(1), 99–114.

Loch, C.H., D.C. Galunic, and S. Schneider (2006), 'Balancing Cooperation and Competition in Human Groups: The Role of Emotional Algorithms and Evolution', *Managerial and Decision Economics*, **27**, 217–233.

Mariani, M.M. (2007), 'Coopetition as an Emergent Strategy: Empirical Evidence from an Italian Consortium of Opera Houses', *International Studies of Management and Organization*, **37**(2), 97–126.

M'Chirgui, Z. (2005), 'The Economics of the Smart Card Industry: Towards Coopetitive Strategies', *Economic Innovation New Technology*, **14**(6), 455–477.

Mitchell, W., P. Dussauge and B. Garrette (2002), 'Alliances with Competitors:

How to Combine and Protect Key Resources?', Paper presented at the Second European Academy of Management Annual Conference, Stockholm, May 9–11.

Nalebuff, B. and A. Brandenburger (1996), *Coopetition*, Gothenburg: ISL.

Okura, M. (2007), 'Coopetitive Strategies of Japanese Insurance Firms. A Game-Theory Approach', *International Studies of Management and Organization*, **37**(2), 53–69.

Oshri, I. and C. Weeber (2006), 'Cooperation and Competition Standards-Setting Activities in the Digitization Era: The Case of Wireless Information Devices', *Technology Analysis and Strategic Management*, **18**(2), 265–283.

Padula, G. and G.B. Dagnino (2007), 'Untangling the Rise of Coopetition: The Intrusion of Competition in a Cooperative Game Structure', *International Studies of Management and Organization*, **37**(2), 32–52.

Powell, W.W., K.W. Koput, and L. Smith-Doerr (1996), 'Interorganizational Collaboration and the Locus of Innovation: Networks of Learning in Biotechnology', *Administrative Science Quarterly*, **41**, 116–145.

Thomas, H. and T. Pollock (1999), 'From I-O Economics' S-C-P Paradigm through Strategic Groups to Competence-Based Competition: Reflections on the Puzzle of Competitive Strategy', *British Journal of Management*, **10**, 127–140.

Tjosvold, D. (1986), 'Organizational Test of Goal Linkage Theory', *Journal of Occupational Behaviour*, **7**(2), 77–88.

Tjosvold, D., L. Meredith and C.L. Wong (1998), 'Coordination to Market Technology: The Contribution of Cooperative Goals and Interaction', *Journal of High Technology Management Research*, **9**(1), 1–15.

Tjosvold, D. and H.F. Sun (2001), 'Effects of Influence Tactics and Social Contexts in Conflict: An Experiment on Relationships in China', *The International Journal of Conflict Management*, **12**(3), 239–258.

Tjosvold, D., M. Tang, and M.A. West (2004), 'Reflexivity for Team Innovation in China: The Contribution of Goal Interdependence', *Group and Organization Management*, **29**, 540–559.

Tjosvold, D. and C. Wong (1994), 'Working with Customers: Cooperation and Competition in Relational Marketing', *Journal of Marketing Management*, **10**, 297–311.

Tsai, W. (2002), 'Social Structure of 'Coopetition' Within a Multiunit Organization: Coordination, Competition, and Intraorganizational Knowledge Sharing', *Organization Science*, **13**(2), 179–190.

Walley, K. (2007), 'Coopetition: An Introduction to the Subject and an Agenda for Research', *International Studies of Management and Organization*, **37**(2), 11–31.

Zeng, M. and X.-P. Chen (2003), 'Achieving Cooperation in Multiparty Alliances: A Social Dilemma Approach to Partnership Management', *Academy of Management Review*, **28**(4), 587–605.

2. The promise of coopetition as a new theoretical perspective in strategic management

Marco Galvagno and Francesco Garraffo

INTRODUCTION

Firms often cooperate with competitors and it is very difficult to carry out this task (Gomes-Casseres, 1994; Harbison and Pekar, 1998; Dussauge, Garrette and Mitchell, 2000). Even if research on interfirm collaboration has begun to explore the issue of relationships among competitors (Lado, Boyd and Hanlon, 1997; Bengtsson and Kock, 2000; Gnyawali and Madhavan, 2001; Gnyawali, He and Madhavan, 2006; Dagnino and Padula, 2007), coopetition is still not a well-defined theoretical perspective in strategic management.

A new theoretical perspective in social science is helpful when it has a conceptual framework that explains and predicts empirical phenomena not explained or predicted by conceptual frameworks already in existence in other streams of research (Shane and Venkataraman, 2000). To date, the phenomenon of coopetition has lacked such a conceptual framework. Rather than explaining a new and different set of empirical phenomena, coopetition has been used, at different levels, in analyzing situations which have been already studied according to the following theoretical perspectives: strategic alliances (Khanna, *et al.*, 1998; Dussauge, *et al.*, 2000; Ancarani and Shankar, 2003), collective strategies (Yami and Roy, 2007), competitive strategies (Lado, *et al.*, 1997; Fosfuri and Giarratana, 2009), co-marketing (Sengupta, 1995), supply chain relations (Cachon and Zipkin, 1999; Kotzab and Teller, 2003), networks (Bengtsson and Kock, 2000; Ritala, Hallikas and Sissonen, 2008; Tidström, 2008), and cooperative R&D projects (Garud, 1994; Miotti and Sachwald, 2003; Belderbos, Carreeb and Lokshin, 2004; Weck and Blomqvist, 2004). As a result, many people could have trouble identifying the distinctive contribution of coopetition research to the broader domain of management, undermining its legitimacy. Researchers in management could ask why coopetition research is necessary if it does not explain or predict empirical phenomena beyond what is known from work in other streams of research. We believe that a good answer lies in an accurate definition of coopetition and in a shared conceptual framework.

This chapter seeks to bring clarity to the notion of coopetition and its relationship to firms' behaviour by addressing the following questions: (a) what does coopetition mean and what are its distinctive elements? (b) how does coopetition shape firms' behaviour? and (c) does firms' resource similarity have an effect on coopetitive behaviours?

This chapter makes three contributions to the literature. First, we review the literature, raising important contradictions and ambiguities in the extant literature and suggesting remedies that can direct future studies. Second, we advance the understanding of firms' behaviour in the presence of coopetition. We believe that a systematic comparison of the quality and traits of firms' behaviour related to coopetitive relationships provides new insights into empirical phenomena not explained yet. Third, we deepen the discussion by advancing a set of propositions (largely based on an inter-firm relationship approach) regarding the nature of the firm's cooperative or competitive behaviours towards coopetitors and the relationships between resource similarity and coopetitors' behaviour.

The chapter is organized as follows. First, we carry out an overview of past research to show how coopetition has been studied in the literature. We then examine ambiguities in the extant literature and how they might be resolved. Next, focusing on the concept of simultaneity, both in terms of market scope and time, we will provide a narrow definition of coopetition, and develop propositions on the relationship between coopetition and competitive and/or cooperative behaviours and resources similarity.

1. PAST RESEARCH ON COOPETITION

The literature refers to coopetition when firms simultaneously cooperate and compete (Lado *et al.*, 1997; Bengtsson and Kock, 2000). The concept of coopetition was introduced in the management literature by two streams of research. One is based on the idea of coopetition as a game, where different players increase the business 'pie' by cooperation and then compete to divide it up (Brandenburger and Nalebuff, 1996). Another one is related to the alliance literature and to the acknowledgment that competitive tensions persist within an alliance (Gomes-Casseres, 1994; Harbison and Pekar, 1998).

The first stream of research has stressed that one of the most important reasons to cooperate is to gain a better position in the market and thus to gain a strategic advantage over competitors (Hamel, Doz and Prahalad, 1989). The second one is based on the idea that cooperation and competition are two opposed forces entangled inside each alliance relationship (Park and Ungson, 2001).

The concept of coopetition has been applied in a number of relevant domains of strategic management studies, including alliances and network relationships as well as channel relationships.

To appreciate the contributions of this literature, it is important to separate studies based on typology of relationship (horizontal versus vertical). The literature suggests (for example, Bengtsson and Kock, 2000) that coopetition can be analysed horizontally (that is, relationships at the same level of value chain or between direct or mutually acknowledged competitors), or vertically (that is, relationships between suppliers and customers). To further gain insights into the contributions of the literature, it is essential to separate studies based on their objective. Some studies have focused on the nature of coopetition; others have explored the various processes and activities needed to develop coopetitive strategies. Still other studies have addressed the antecedents versus outcomes of these strategies. As would be expected, some studies had multiple objects and examined more than one area by covering, for example, the nature of coopetition and the outcome of coopetitive strategies.

Even though our review of the literature is not exhaustive, it serves to show that most research and theory building on coopetition has focused on vertical relationships among firms (that is, channel relationships), ignoring horizontal relationships (that is, direct competitors). We find this gap in the literature to be puzzling given that the concept of coopetition can add something to the management literature only if it is able to go beyond the study of alliances among competitors and the theoretical perspectives already mentioned.

Reviewing the studies in Table 2.1, we note also that prior researchers have predominantly studied coopetition as an interorganizational phenomenon. Few are the studies of coopetition at intrafirm level, among sub-units and/or divisions inside a single firm (for example, Tsai, 2002; Luo, 2005; Luo, Slotegraaf and Pan, 2006). In addition, the literature fails to show unambiguously that firms pursuing coopetitive strategies achieve superior performance (for example, Ritala, Hallikas and Sissonen, 2008). Our review of the literature highlights also the dearth of a common definition of coopetition and the limited number of studies about its antecedents. Lack of agreement about whether the coopetition concept refers to direct competitors or simply to firms operating in the same industry and/ or in the same value chain is perhaps the single largest source of confusion. The literature does not tell us much about coopetition in horizontal

Table 2.1   Overview of past research on coopetition

Typology of relationship	Objective		
	Nature/definition	*Antecedent*	*Outcomes*
Vertical relationship	Lado, Boyd and Hanlon, 1997; Bengtsson and Kock, 2000; Luo, 2007	Gnyawali and Madhavan, 2001; Gnyawali and Park, 2008	Afuah, 2000; Bengtsson and Kock, 2000; Baldwin and Bengtsson, 2004; Oliver, 2004; Quintana-Garcia and Benavides-Velasco, 2004; Gnyawali, He and Madhavan, 2006; Luo, 2007; Luo, Rindfleisch and Tse, 2007; Ritala, Hallikas and Sissonen, 2008
Horizontal relationship			Hamel, Doz and Prahalad, 1989; Quintana-Garcia and Benavides-Velasco, 2004, Bonel and Rocco, 2007, Hokura 2007

relationships. The few studies reported in Table 2.1 tend to be case-study based (for example, Bonel and Rocco, 2007).

Moreover, our review of the literature and the studies summarized in Table 2.1 suggest that prior researchers have not gone much beyond describing and categorizing coopetition as a mix of competitive/cooperative behaviour in an interfirm relationship (see Lado *et al.*, 1997; Bengtsson and Kock, 2000). Although these typologies are useful for studying the phenomenon, unfortunately conceptual issues regarding the content and nature of coopetition remain vague.

According to the literature, coopetition occurs when two or more firms simultaneously pursue competitive and cooperative strategies (Lado *et al.*, 1997). These strategies rely on two diametrically different logics of interaction: conflicting and converging interests (Bengtsson and Kock, 2000, Dagnino and Padula, 2007; Chen, 2008). Lack of agreement about whether the concept of coopetition refers to a cooperation among competitors inside the same market is certainly the largest source of confusion. For example, in their book, Brandenburger and Nalebuff write that 'a player is your competitor if customers value your product less when they have the other player's product than when they have your product alone' (1996: 18). Are they suggesting that a competitor is someone, or anyone, among complementors or other firms that affect a product value?

The confusion increases when time span is incorporated into definitions,

Table 2.2　Key definitions of coopetition

Author	Definiton
Hamel, Doz and Prahalad (1989)	Cooperative relationships among firms having converging strategic goals and diverging competitive goals
Brandenburger and Nalebuff (1996)	A relationship between two firms based on cooperation to develop a new product and create value and then competition to get a share of the market and distribute the returns to the value that has been created
Lado, Boyd and Hanlon (1997)	Syncretic rent-seeking behaviour that describes a firm's strategic orientation to achieve a dynamic balance between competitive and cooperative strategies.
Bengtsson and Kock (2000)	When a firm is simultaneously involved in both cooperative and competitive interactions with the same competitor at the same product area
Gnyawali and Madhavan (2001)	Simultaneous cooperative and competitive behaviour
Dagnino and Padula (2007)	Firms interacting among each other on the basis of a partially convergent interest structure
Luo (2007)	Simultaneous competition and cooperation between global rivals

many of which use the term simultaneously to refer to the activity of cooperating and competing at the same time. Lado *et al.*, in their thoughtful analysis, argue that 'syncretic rent-seeking behaviour describes a firm's strategic orientation to achieve a dynamic balance (or syncretism) between competitive and cooperative strategies' and 'firms that exhibit syncretic rent-seeking behaviour can compete intensely with rivals while they *simultaneously* cooperate like crazy with *other* firms' (1997: 123, emphasis added). Are we to infer that firm A is pursuing a coopetitive strategy when it competes against firm B and at the same time cooperates with firm C?

Table 2.2 presents, in chronological order, a sample of the most well-known definitions that have appeared in the literature to date. As we review prior definitions, we find that they share the idea that coopetition is a sort of balance, inside a single firm, between a cooperative and competitive strategy. This description introduces two elements that may generate different definitions of coopetition: (1) the meaning of simultaneity, and (2) the definition of competitor.

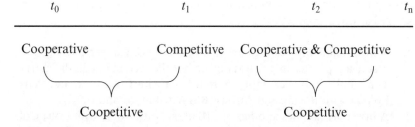

Figure 2.1   The effect of time perspective on the definition of coopetition

1. With regard to the first element, it is widely accepted that coopetition
    occurs when two firms compete and cooperate at the same time. While
    the combination of cooperation and competition is a condition for
    coopetition, what is not clear in the literature is the meaning of simul-
    taneity. Is it used to mean that competitive and cooperative behav-
    iours occur at the same time? And is this time a month, a quarter, a
    year, two or more years? Of course, the simultaneity alone does not
    mean anything; what is important is the time perspective adopted. The
    longer the time perspective, the higher is the likelihood of defining as
    coopetitive a sequence of actions that otherwise would be depicted as
    simply competitive or cooperative. Moving from a shorter to a longer
    time perspective, cooperative or competitive behaviours at t_0 could
    become coopetitive between t_0 and t_n (see Figure 2.1).
2. Regarding the definition of competitor, because coopetition occurs
    between two firms that cooperate while competing in the same market,
    the perspective adopted in delimiting this market defines whether two
    firms can be considered direct competitors or not. Specifically, two
    perspectives can be adopted in defining the competitor: horizontal
    and vertical (Brandenburger and Nalebuff, 1996; Bengtsson and
    Kock, 2000). The horizontal perspective considers a firm to be a
    competitor if it affects another firm's revenues because it operates in
    the same industry, offers similar products and targets similar custom-
    ers (Chen, 1996). The vertical perspective considers a firm to be a
    competitor if it affects another firm's costs because it operates in the
    same value chain or network as supplier, customer or complementor
    (Brandenburger and Nalebuff, 1996; Lado *et al.*, 1997; Dagnino and
    Padula, 2007).

We believe that in any theoretical and/or empirical analysis of coopetition, it is crucial to consider only firms that are direct competitors (that is,
Pepsi and Coca Cola, Boeing and Airbus, GM and Ford), because only

among these firms does competition occur. The following cannot be considered as direct competitors:

1. A firm that competes with another one and not vice versa (that is, the first firm operates in a market niche but the second one in the market as a whole, in our examples Virgin Cola with Coca Cola and Pepsi, Fokker with Boeing and Airbus, BMW with GM and Ford);
2. A firm that supplies another one (that is, NutraSweet with Coca Cola or Pepsi, General Electric with Boeing or Airbus, Brembo with GM or Ford);
3. A firm that does not target the same market segment (that is, IBM and Apple or Ford and BMW).[1]

Our position emphasizes the coopetitor definition from a firm-level perspective, by introducing the idea of market commonality (or overlap), in order to define whether a firm is a proximate competitor or not (Chen, 1996), and by bringing into sharp focus the role of the time perspective, through the concept of simultaneity.

2.   A TWO-STAGE FRAMEWORK OF COOPETITION

We define the concept of coopetition by developing a two-stage framework. In the first stage, we draw on Bergen and Peteraf's model of competitive analysis (2002) and adapt it to our purposes in order to map the coopetitive landscape. In the second stage, we employ the concept of resource similarity (Chen, 1996; Harrison *et al.*, 1991, 2001) to distinguish among firms' coopetitive behaviour, in order to establish how coopetition occurs.

Stage 1: Mapping the Coopetitive Landscape

To build up a hierarchy of competitor/cooperator typology that is central to a precise recognition of a coopetitor, we sort firms based on the degree to which they operate in the same markets (market commonality on a horizontal axis) and on the simultaneity of their interaction, be it cooperative and/or competitive (time on vertical axis) (see Figure 2.2).

According to the grid, firms in the bottom right corner are identified as potential coopetitors in that they have a high market commonality but they are not cooperating. Firms that occupy the upper left corner are also identified as potential coopetitors in that they are cooperating but they

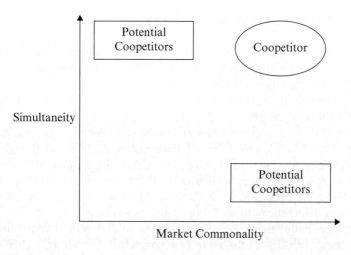

Figure 2.2   Mapping the coopetitive landscape

compete in different markets. Firms that occupy the bottom left corner are entirely outside the coopetitive set at present, although this could change over time as firms change their positions. Finally, firms occupying the upper right corner in the grid are coopetitors.

Therefore, coopetition occurs between direct competitors that perform competitive and cooperative actions at the same time (high simultaneity and high market commonality).

Our definition of coopetition parallels that of Bengtsson and Kock (2000) who characterize the concept as the cooperation among competitors that 'produce and market the same products' (2000: 415).

The distinctions we add are: (1) to make explicit the aspect of the time in which the coopetition has to be considered, and (2) to tie the definition to a specific type of competitor, the direct competitor.

In summary, our definition emphasizes some specific characteristics of the coopetition concept and puts the firm's actions at the centre of the discourse (Gnyawali, He and Madhavan, 2006). Such a choice gives precision, substance, and accuracy to the definition of the coopetitive phenomenon. Consequently, we further exhort researchers to avoid the uncontrolled use of the term 'coopetition' by looking at simultaneity and market commonality to distinguish them from potential coopetitive phenomena (see Figure 2.2: bottom right and upper left corners). Having specified a tighter concept of coopetition, we now build on the literature to develop a set of propositions that further delineate the relationship between coopetition and the firm's behaviour.

Stage 2: Classifying Coopetitors' Behaviour

Since each coopetitor has a unique resource endowment, a definition of
the nature of coopetitors' behaviour should be based on a proper comparison of firms along this dimension.

The concept of resource endowment comes from the literature on
competitor analysis (Abell, 1980; Porter, 1980; Day, 1981; Hatten and
Hatten, 1987) and interfirm rivalry (Karnany and Wernerfelt, 1985; Smith
and Wilson, 1995; Chen, 1996; Gimeno and Woo, 1996). Although this
literature aims to understand and predict the rivalry or interactive market
behaviour between firms in their quest for a competitive position in an
industry (Smith *et al.*, 1991; Zajac and Bazerman, 1991), it can also be
helpful to define the nature of coopetitors' behaviour.

Resource endowment regards the possible similarity of firms in tangible
and intangible assets exploited to gain competitive advantage. Therefore,
we define resource similarity 'as the extent to which a given competitor
possesses strategic endowments comparable, in terms of both type and
amount, to those of another one' (Chen, 1996: 107).

According to this definition, two possible situations may exist between
a pair of coopetitors, as summarized in Figure 2.3. Assuming that coopetition occurs between firms that are direct competitors, because of their
high market commonality, the degree of resource similarity is helpful to
understand the nature of the coopetitive behaviours.

According to our framework, and given that a firm's competitive
position and advantage in the market are defined by its unique resource
endowment (Conner, 1994), a high resource similarity will lead to a competitive coopetition (that is a coopetition with a major degree of competition), while a low resource similarity will lead to a cooperative coopetition
(that is a coopetition with a major degree of cooperation).

In the competitive coopetition, the firms' goal is to invest an amount
of resources sufficient to achieve economies of scale and greater market
power (Dussauge *et al.*, 2000; Harrison, *et al.* 2001). As a result, coopetitors with similar resources are likely to have similar strategic capabilities
as well as competitive actions and strategies, therefore increasing the
degree of competition. In the latter case, different but complementary
resources among competitors (Brandenburger and Nalebuff, 1996) are
useful to achieve knowledge exchange and cross-fertilization through
coopetition and will lead to different competitive actions and strategies,
reducing the intensity of rivalry, and therefore increasing the degree of
cooperation.

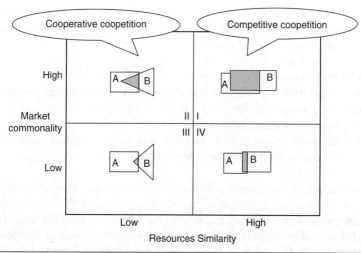

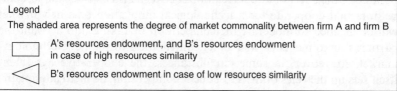

Source: Adapted from Chen (1996)

Figure 2.3   The nature of coopetitive behaviours

3.   PROPOSITIONS

Consistently with the two-stage framework proposed in this chapter, we present some propositions explaining and predicting firms' behaviour when engaged in coopetition. The first two of these propositions follow from the idea that, during coopetition, cooperative and competitive behaviours influence each other.

3.1   How Coopetition Affects Competitive Behaviour

Two firms competing in the same market act and react sequentially and/ or simultaneously in their efforts to gain competitive advantage (Porter, 1985). Literature on competitive dynamics (Lambkin, 1988; Gatignon, *et al.*, 1989; Smith *et al.*, 1989; Golder and Tellis, 1993; D'Aveni, 1994; Gimeno and Woo, 1996; Baum and Korn, 1996; Christensen and Bower,

1996; Lieberman and Montgomery, 1998) identifies several attributes of competition (sequence of actions and responses among first movers, followers, late movers), in terms of:

- timing (Ansoff, 1987; Chen and MacMillan, 1992);
- scope (mono- or multi-point competition) (Karnani and Wernerfelt, 1985; Gimeno and Woo, 1996; Shankar, 1999);
- intensity (number of actions and reactions);
- aggressiveness (mutual aggressiveness or mutual forbearance) (Edwards, 1955; Baum and Korn, 1996).

According to these contributions, the literature on competitive dynamics is a starting point for highlighting the effect of coopetition on attributes of competition. In particular, competitive behaviour towards coopetitors tends to be different in its attributes compared to that towards competitors because of the effect of double relations between firms. For example, competitors that cooperate for a technological innovation or a new market will be inclined to moderate the competition by taking into account the partner's investments as well as its contribution to the new technology/ market. Moreover, in some circumstances, the cooperative agreement itself sets up the rules of the subsequent competition, de facto altering the attributes of competition among partners. As a consequence, when a firm competes with its coopetitor, its behaviour tends to be different from its behaviour towards competitors in terms of timing, scope and intensity as well as aggressiveness. From this it follows that:

Proposition 1: All else being equal, a firm's competitive behaviour towards a coopetitor tends to be different, in terms of timing, market scope, intensity, and aggressiveness, from its competitive behaviour towards a competitor.

The Toyota and PSA agreement for a minicar joint venture in Europe is an example of how coopetition affects competition (Ichijo and Kohlbacher, 2008). Toyota was deeply interested in the minicar segment because of macro-economic factors such as high fuel prices and economic uncertainty. Moreover the minicar was a new segment for Toyota, which did not have a set of loyal customers. For these reasons, Toyota was strongly interested in carrying out a project in developing a new minicar with PSA. The PSA group had two successful models in the minicar segment, the Peugeot 106 and the Citroen Saxo, and it was Europe's second largest car manufacturer. Its capabilities were in good vehicle design, diesel engines, clever advertising and excellent cost position in manufacturing. As a consequence, the agreement in developing a new minicar between Toyota and PSA was a good deal and affected the competition in the minicar market between the two partners. In fact, when the two firms launched the new minicar in the market, they targeted different segments. Toyota focused on young people while PSA targeted women, developing different marketing to avoid strong competition against each other in the same European market.

3.2 How Coopetition Affects Cooperative Behaviour

Similarly, cooperative behaviours towards the coopetitor tend to be different in their attributes from those seen without a simultaneous or previously competitive relationship. The attributes of cooperation (Ring and Van de Ven, 1992) that can be affected by simultaneous competition and cooperation are the market and/or technology scope of the agreement in terms of the market involved compared to the present one, and the technology developed compared to the one already exploited (Khanna, 1998; Ireland, Hitt and Vaidyanath, 2002).

Cooperation is different between coopetitors because competition shapes and affects the scope of the cooperative agreement. If two firms compete in the same market, the cooperative agreement will tend to involve different technologies and/or markets from the existing ones. The reason why competitors will tend to cooperate for new markets and/or technologies is related to the contemporary need to avoid negative effects on current economic results and increase the margins of future performance by sharing investments and increasing the opportunities related to the new market or technology. It follows that:

> **Proposition 2**: All else being equal, a firm's cooperative behaviour towards a coopetitor tends to be different in terms of market and/or technology scope than its cooperative behaviour towards other firms.

The joint venture between Sony and Samsung, called S-LCD, to develop and produce LCD panels for TV screens, the partnership between Microsoft and SAP for developing Duet Software or between LG and Philips for carrying out research and development activities for large TVs are examples of coopetitive agreements focused on new markets and technologies (Gnyawali and Park, 2008). Sony and Samsung or LG and Philips crafted the aim and scope of these coopetitive agreements in relation to the fact that they were direct competitors. By developing new technologies for future markets they did not affect present revenues and profits while contributing to the firms' future economic results.

3.3   How Resource Similarity Affects the Nature of Coopetitors' Behaviour

As already highlighted, coopetitors' resource endowment is helpful in understanding the nature of the coopetitive behaviours. Thus two or more firms with high resource similarities may cooperate and compete with each other, but because of the similarity or dissimilarity of their stock of resources, coopetition will be more on a (1) competitive or (2) cooperative base.

1. Cooperation between direct rivals that have a high degree of resource similarity is justified because of the opportunity to increase the scale of the coopetitive agreement through the same expertise, competences and reputation (Dussauge, *et al.*, 2000). This situation has been defined as a competitive coopetition in that the resource similarity leads to similar competitive actions and strategies, so the degree of competition increases.

    Proposition 3: All else being equal, when resource similarity is high, firms are likely to engage in competitive coopetition.

    The DVD Consortium, established in 1995 by the leading consumer electronics firms in the world (Hitachi Ltd, Matsushita Electric Industrial Co. Ltd, Mitsubishi Electric Corporation, Pioneer Electronic Corporation, Royal Philips Electronics N.V., Sony Corporation, Thomson, Time Warner Inc., Toshiba Corporation, JVC Victor Company of Japan, Ltd), is an agreement among direct competitors with similar resource endowments, established to set up DVD technology as the new standard for the home video market. The partners' resource similarity has been effective in defining the new standard in the home video market, but, at the same time, it has led to similar competitive actions and strategies worldwide, by increasing the degree of competition.

2. Cooperation between direct competitors that have a low degree of resource similarity is justified because of the opportunity to create a linking coopetitive agreement (Dussauge, *et al.*, 2000) through a combination of different and complementary skills and resources that are helpful in creating a new market and/or technology. This situation has been defined as a cooperative coopetition in that the resource dissimilarity or complementarity leads to different competitive actions and strategies, so the degree of cooperation increases. This is consistent with Sarkar *et al.* (2001), as cited by Gnyawali and Park (2008), who highlight how the resource complementarity reduces the risk of opportunism and increases the possibility of organizational learning.

Proposition 4: All else being equal, when resource similarity is low, firms are likely to engage in cooperative coopetition.

The imminent coopetitive agreement between Chrysler and Fiat is an example of cooperative coopetition. Chrysler needs Fiat's small engine technology and expertise in process technologies for small cars, while Fiat needs Chrysler's distribution channel in the US market and reliable equipment in North America, to be used to produce Fiat's new model. Because of their low resource similarity and high resource complementarity, Fiat and Chrysler are likely to base their relationship more on cooperation than competition. Specifically, they will cooperate to learn and exchange knowledge, while competing in different segments.

4. DISCUSSION AND IMPLICATIONS

Coopetition is an important and complex concept that is emerging as a new theoretical perspective in strategic management (Lado *et al.*, 1997; Bengtsson and Kock, 2000; Dagnino and Padula, 2007; Walley, 2007; Chen, 2008; Tidström, 2008). Recognizing this importance and complexity, we have defined it so as to avoid misunderstanding and have developed a framework that proposes a new conceptualization of coopetition by introducing the constructs of market commonality and the simultaneity of firms' interactions. The joint consideration of these two constructs allows us to differentiate among actual and potential coopetitors. Moreover, a third construct, resource similarity, can explain the changing nature of coopetitive behaviour.

Our framework also highlights the importance of a coopetitive relationships for firms' actions and strategic behaviours. And because previous studies have shown that actions and reactions matter to performance (Chen and Hambrick, 1995; Chen, 1996), our ideas are a step forward in the process of linking coopetition to firm performance (for example Luo, *et al.*, 2007; Ritala, *et al.*, 2008). The chapter moves in the direction of Chen (2008), who calls for a formal framework able to explore fully the complexity and richness of competition–cooperation interdependence and interplay (p. 296).

Finally, there is also a practical implication. The two-stage framework can be used to identify actual and future coopetitors, by registering the movement of firms to new positions along the grid. In this way, it is able to offer to executives a more dynamic outlook of how the coopetitive landscape evolves.

Coopetition is a fertile territory for theoretical and empirical investigation. Here, we have focused on developing several propositions intended to advance the understanding of the coopetitive phenomenon and its linkages with firms' behaviour. We hope that other scholars will take up the challenge of further exploring and testing these ideas.

NOTE

1. Cases 2 and 3 are consistent with the vertical perspective of market definition.

REFERENCES

Abell, D.F. (1980), *Defining the business: starting point of strategic planning*, Englewood, N.J.: Prentice Hall.

Afuah, A. (2000), 'How much do your co-opetitors' capabilities matter in the face of technological change?', *Strategic Management Journal*, **21**(3), 397–404.

Ancarani, F. and V. Shankar (2003), 'Symbian: customer interaction through collaboration and competition in a convergent industry', *Journal of Interactive Marketing*, **17**(1), 56–76.

Ansoff, H.I. (1987), 'The emerging paradigm of strategic behaviour', *Strategic Management Journal*, **8**(6), 501–515.

Baldwin, R.G.A and M. Bengtsson (2004), 'The emotional base of interaction among competitors – an evaluation dimension of cognition', *Scandinavian Journal of Management*, **20**(1–2), 75–102.

Baum, J.A.C. and H.J. Korn (1996), 'Competitive dynamics of interfirm rivalry', *Academy of Management Journal*, **39**(2), 255–291.

Belderbos, R., M. Carreeb and B. Lokshin (2004), 'Cooperative R&D and firm performance', *Research Policy*, **33**(10), 1477–1492.

Bengtsson, M. and S. Kock (2000), 'Coopetition in business networks – to cooperate and compete simultaneously', *Industrial Marketing Management*, **29**(5), 411–426.

Bergen, M. and M.A. Peteraf (2002), 'Competitor identification and competitor analysis: a broad-based managerial approach', *Managerial and Decision Economics*, **23**(4/5) 157–169.

Bonel, E. and E. Rocco (2007), 'Coopeting to survive; surviving coopetition', *International Studies of Management and Organization*, **37**(2), 70–96.

Brandenburger, A.M. and B.J. Nalebuff (1996), *Coopetition*, New York, US: Doubleday.

Cachon, G.P. and P.H. Zipkin (1999), 'Competitive and cooperative inventory policies in a two-stage supply chain', *Management Science*, **45**(7), 936–953.

Chen, M.J. (1996), 'Competitor analysis and interfirm rivalry: toward a theoretical integration', *Academy of Management Review*, **17**(3), 197–218.

Chen, M.J. (2008), 'Reconceptualizing the competition – cooperation relationship', *Journal of Management Inquiry*, **17**(4), 288–304.

Chen, M.J. and D.C. Hambrick (1995), 'Speed, stealth, and selective attack:

how small firms differ from large firms in competitive behavior', *Academy of Management Journal*, **38**(2), 453–482.

Chen, M.J. and I.C. MacMillan (1992), 'Nonresponse and delayed response to competitive moves: the roles of competitor dependence and action irreversibility', *Academy of Management Journal*, **35**(3), 539–570.

Christensen, C.M. and J.L. Bower (1996), 'Customer power, strategic investment, and the failure of leading firms', *Strategic Management Journal*, **21**(3), 397–404.

Conner, K. (1994), 'The resource-based challenge to the industry-structure perspective', *Academy of Management Best Papers Proceedings*, 17–21.

Dagnino, G.B. and G. Padula (2007), 'Untangling the rise of coopetition', *International Studies of Management and Organization*, **37**(2), 32–52.

D'Aveni, R. (1994), *Hypercompetition: managing the dynamics of strategic manoeuvring*, New York: Free Press.

Day, G.S. (1981), 'Strategic market analysis and definition: an integrated approach', *Strategic Management Journal*, **2**(3), 281–299.

Dussauge, P., B. Garrette and W. Mitchell (2000), 'Learning from competing partners: outcomes and durations of scale and link alliances in Europe, North America and Asia', *Strategic Management Journal*, **21**(2), 99–126.

Edwards, C.D. (1955), *Conglomerate bigness as a source of power*, in the National Bureau of Economics Research Conference Report, Business Concentration and Price Policy, 331–352, Princeton: Princeton University Press.

Fosfuri, A. and M.S. Giarratana (2009), 'Masters of war: rivals' product innovation and new advertising in mature product markets', *Management Science*, **55**(2), 181–191.

Garud, R. (1994), 'Cooperative and competitive behaviours during the process of creative destruction', *Research Policy*, **23**(4), 385–94.

Gatignon, M., E. Anderson and K. Helsen (1989), 'Competitive reactions to market entry: explaining interfirm differences', *Journal of Marketing Research*, **26**(1), 44–55.

Gimeno, J. and C. Woo (1996), 'Hypercompetition in a multimarket environment: the role of strategic similarity and multimarket contact in competitive de-escalation', *Organization Science*, **7**(3), 322–341.

Gnyawali, R.D., J. He and R. Madhavan (2006), 'Impact of coopetition on firm competitive behavior: an empirical examination', *Journal of Management*, **32**(4), 507–530.

Gnyawali, R.D. and R. Madhavan (2001), 'Cooperative networks and competitive dynamics: a structural embeddedness perspective', *Academy of Management Review*, **26**(3), 431–445.

Gnyawali, R.D. and B.J. Park (2008), 'Drivers of coopetition for technological innovation', Paper Submitted to the EIASM 3rd Workshop *'Coopetition' strategy: stretching the boundaries of 'coopetition'*, Madrid, 7–8 February.

Gomes-Casseres, B. (1994), 'Group versus group: how alliance networks compete', *Harvard Business Review*, **72**(4), 62–74.

Gulati, R. (1998), 'Alliances and networks', *Strategic Management Journal*, **19**, 293–317.

Hamel, G., Y.L. Doz and C.K. Prahalad (1989), 'Collaborate with your competitors and win', *Harvard Business Review*, **63**, Jan–Feb., 133–139.

Harbison, J.R. and P. Pekar Jr (1998), *Smart alliances: a practical guide to repeatable success*, San Francisco, CA: Jossey-Bass.

Harrison, J.S., M.A. Hitt, R.E. Hoskisson and R.D. Ireland (1991), 'Synergies and post-acquisition performance: differences versus similarities in resource allocations', *Journal of Management*, **17**(1), 173–190.

Harrison, J.S., M.A. Hitt, R.E. Hoskisson and R.D. Ireland (2001), 'Resource complementarity in business combinations: extending the logic to organizational alliances', *Journal of Management*, **27**(6), 679–690.

Hatten, K.J. and M.L. Hatten (1987), 'Strategic groups, asymmetrical mobility barriers and contestability', *Strategic Management Journal*, **8**(4), 329–342.

Hokura, M. (2007), 'Coopetitive strategies of Japanese insurance firms', *International Studies of Management and Organization*, **37**(2), 53–69.

Ichijo, K. and F. Kohlbacher (2008), 'Tapping tacit local knowledge in emerging markets: the Toyota way', *Knowledge Management Research and Practice*, **6**(3), 173–186.

Ireland, R.D., M.A. Hitt and D. Vaidyanath (2002), 'Alliance management as a source of competitive advantage', *Journal of Management*, **28**(3), 413–446.

Karnani, A. and B. Wernerfelt (1985), 'Multiple point competition', *Strategic Management Journal*, **6**(1), 87–96.

Khanna, T. (1998), 'The scope of alliances', *Organization Science*, **9**(3), 340–355.

Khanna, T., R. Gulati and N. Nohria (1998), 'The dynamics of learning alliances: competition, cooperation, and relative scope', *Strategic Management Journal*, **19**(3), 203–215.

Kotzab, H. and C. Teller (2003), 'Value-adding partnerships and coopetition models in the grocery industry', *International Journal of Physical Distribution and Logistics Management*, **33**(3), 268–281.

Lado, A.A., N.G. Boyd and S.C. Hanlon (1997), 'Competition, cooperation and the search for economic rents: a syncretic model', *Academy of Management Review*, **22**(1), 110–141.

Lambkin, M. (1988), 'Order of entry and performance in new markets', *Strategic Management Journal*, **9**(3), 127–140.

Lieberman, M.B. and D.B. Montgomery (1998), 'First-mover (dis)advantages: retrospective and link with the resource-based view', *Strategic Management Journal*, **19**(12), 1111–1125.

Luo, X., A. Rindfleisch and D.K. Tse (2007), 'Working with rivals: the impact of competitor alliances in financial performance', *Journal of Marketing Research*, **44**(1), 73–83.

Luo, X., R.J. Slotegraaf and X. Pan (2006), 'Cross-functional "coopetition": the simultaneous role of cooperation and competition within firms', *Journal of Marketing*, **70**(2), 67–80.

Luo, Y. (2005), 'Toward coopetition within a multinational enterprise: a perspective from foreign subsidiaries', *Journal of World Business*, **40**(1), 71–90.

Luo, Y. (2007), 'A coopetition perspective of global competition', *Journal of World Business*, **40**(2), 71–90.

Miotti, L. and F. Sachwald (2003), 'Cooperative R&D: why and with whom? An integrated framework of analysis', *Research Policy*, **32**(8), 1481–1499.

Oliver, A.L. (2004), 'On the duality of competition and collaboration: network-based knowledge relations in the biotechnology industry', *Scandinavian Journal of Management*, **20**, 1–2, 151–171.

Park, S.H. and G.R. Ungson (2001), 'Interfirm rivalry and managerial complexity: a conceptual framework of alliance failure', *Organization Science*, **12**(1), 37–53.

Porter, M.E. (1980), *Competitive strategy*, New York: Free Press.

Porter, M.E. (1985), *Competitive advantage: creating and sustaining superior performance*, New York: Free Press.
Quintana-Garcia, C. and C.A. Benavides-Velasco (2004), 'Cooperation, competition, and innovative capability: a panel data of European dedicated biotechnology firms', *Technovation*, **24**(12), 927–938.
Ring, P.S. and A.H. van de Ven (1992), 'Structuring cooperative relationships between organizations', *Strategic Management Journal*, **13**(7), 483–498.
Ritala, P., J. Hallikas and H. Sissonen (2008), 'The effect of strategic alliances between key competitors on firm performance', *Management Research*, **6**(3), 179–188.
Sarkar, M.B., R. Echambadi, S.T. Cavusgil and P.S. Aulakh (2001), 'The influence of complementarity, compatibility, and relationship capital on alliance performance', *Journal of the Academy of Marketing Science*, **29**(4), 358–373.
Sengupta, S. (1995), 'Some antecedents of exclusivity in bilateral interorganizational relationships', *Marketing Letters*, **6**(1), 33–44.
Shane, S. and S. Venkataraman (2000), 'The promise of entrepreneurship as a field of research', *The Academy of Management Review*, **25**(1), Jan., 217–226.
Shankar, V. (1999), 'New product introduction and incumbent response strategies: their interrelationship and the role of multimarket contact', *Journal of Marketing Research*, **36**(3), 327–344.
Smith, F.L. and R.L. Wilson (1995), 'The predictive validity of the Karnani and Wemerfelt model of multipoint competition', *Strategic Management Journal*, **16**(2), 143–160.
Smith, K.G., C.M. Grimm, and M.J. Gannon (1989), 'Predictors of response time to competitive strategic actions: Preliminary theory and evidence', *Journal of Business Research*, **18**(3), 245–58.
Smith, K.G., C.M. Grimm, M.J. Gannon and M.J. Chen (1991), 'Organizational information processing, competitive responses and performance in the U.S. domestic airline industry', *Academy of Management Journal*, **34**(1), 60–85.
Tidström, A. (2008), 'Perspectives on coopetition on actor and operational levels', *Management Research*, **6**(3), 207–218.
Tsai, W. (2002), 'Social Structure of "Coopetition" within a Multiunit Organization: Coordination, Competition, and Intraorganizational Knowledge Sharing', *Organization Science*, **13**(2), 179–90.
Walley, K. (2007), 'Coopetition: an introduction to the subject and an agenda for research', *International Studies of Management and Organization*, **37**(2), 11–31.
Weck, M. and K. Blomqvist (2004), 'The role of inter-organizational relationships in the development of patents: a knowledge-based approach', *Research Policy*, **37**(8), 1329–1336.
Yami, S. and P. Roy (2007), 'Managing disruption through coopetition', Paper presented at the *7th Annual Conference of EURAM on Current Management Thinking: Drawing from Social Sciences and Humanities to Address Contemporary Challenges*, Paris, 16–19 May.
Zajac, E.J. and M.H. Bazerman (1991), 'Blind spots in industry and competitor analysis: implications of interfirm (mis)perception to strategic decisions', *Academy of Management Review*, **16**(1), 37–46.

3. Emerging coopetition: an empirical investigation of coopetition as inter-organizational relationship instability

Wojciech Czakon

INTRODUCTION

Since the seminal study by H. Mintzberg and J. Waters (1985) we have been aware that any deliberate strategy has its emerging alter ego. Most generally, emergence means 'patterns realized despite of, or in the absence of intentions' (Mintzberg, Waters, 1985), that is, all behaviors, processes and actually implemented strategies which have not been previously planned in a rational or formalized process. Emergence refers to responsiveness, intuition and social embeddedness, and points to the gap between what has been planned versus what is actually being done.

Relationships between firms attract considerable attention from strategic management researchers. For several years academics focused on competitive relationships (Porter, 1980), yet businesses also cooperate with each other, in various ways and forms. Since the early 1980s, we have been able to observe a soaring interest in alliances, joint ventures, collusions, federations, clusters and so on, collectively called interorganizational relationships or IORs (for a review see: Oliver, Ebers, 1998).

The cooperative paradigm revealed itself incomplete in explaining business profitability variance (Dyer, Singh, 1998), just as the competitive paradigm did earlier (Rumelt, 1991). Coopetition is a strategy designed to achieve better performance levels (Brandenburger, Nalebuff, 1996), and ultimately above average profitability, through cooperation with a firm's competitors. When cooperation appears between competitors or, alternatively, competition emerges between cooperating businesses, such phenomena are also called coopetition. Coopetition seems in this context to be a dynamic phenomenon, much more of a process than of a *status rei*.

While our understanding of the deliberate side of coopetition strategies seems to be growing, studies of this phenomenon as emerging processes are very few. My research aims at filling this gap within an IOR dynamics theoretical framework. The franchising case study findings suggest that coopetition may emerge within cooperative settings.

1. THEORETICAL BACKGROUND

Ideally there are four possible relationships between firms (Bengtsson, Kock, 1999): (1) coexistence is a situation where two businesses have no direct relationship with, nor significant influence on each other; (2) competition refers to the pursuit of similar goals, where one player can gain at the expense of the other, a zero-sum game; (3) cooperation is the opposite behavior, consisting of coordinated pursuit of mutual interests and common benefits; (4) coopetition is a deliberate strategy of mixing cooperation and competition at different stages and in different arenas in order to achieve better individual and collective results. Complex, multidimensional, dynamic relationships tie firms to one another (Figure 3.1). Competing units may enter into close cooperation, which they subsequently leave, choosing coopetition, or even abandoning direct relations in favor of operating independently (Peng, Shenkar, 2002).

Cooperative arrangements are voluntarily initiated between firms and involve exchange, sharing or co-development and can include contributions by partners of capital, technology or firm-specific assets (Gulati, Singh, 1998). These interorganizational relationships (Grandori, Soda, 1995) form a significant thread of research. Firms form IORs for various reasons, generally aiming at a cooperative advantage (Kanter, 1994), collaborative advantage (Donada, 2002) or relational rents (Dyer, Singh, 1998). Prior research has provided valuable insights into such motives as: efficiency improvement (Cannon, Homburg, 2001), transaction cost reduction (Jarillo, 1988), access to valuable assets (Dyer, 1996), learning (Hamel, 1991; Powell, Koput, Smith-Doerr, 1996) and uncertainty

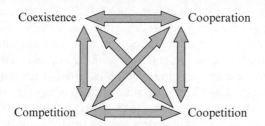

Figure 3.1   Relationships between businesses and their possible dynamics

reduction (Dickson, Weaver, 1997). Viewed from this standpoint, cooperation is an intentional relationship choice aimed at achieving the strategic objectives of the firm.

The operating circumstances of virtually any firm are changing. The speed, direction, continuity and other characteristics of change strongly influence the firm as well as its relationships. Research on dynamics aims at discovering evolution patterns and forces impacting on these change patterns. Many models and theories can be listed in this respect, but all of them fall into one of four categories of ideal type theory (Van de Ven, Poole, 1995): (1) life cycle; (2) teleological; (3) evolutionary; (4) dialectical. Consequently, the current status of IOR dynamics theory is fragmented and incoherent, and calls for theoretical advances (Bell, den Ouden, Ziggers, 2006). Two types of theories appear particularly useful for research on emerging coopetition. Teleological models provide propositions for purposeful action evolution patterns, while dialectical explanations emphasize the factors of instability or opposing forces impacting initial intentions.

The development process framework (Ring, Van de Ven, 1994) and the learning model (Doz, 1996) both rest within the teleological thread of research. The first model suggests that the evolution of any IOR follows a cycle of three stages: negotiations, commitment and execution (NCE). Extant literature suggests that the NCE cycle may begin at any stage: (1) negotiations can be a result of bilateral cooperation seeking (Kanter, 1994); (2) commitment may well be unilaterally aimed at building trust or the reputation of strong reliability (Gulati, Khanna, Nohria, 1994); (3) exchange may develop into a relationship as well (Zaheer, McEvily, Perrone, 1998). The process framework claims that partners evaluate relationships with reference to two criteria: efficiency and equity. Efficiency measures the degree to which a relationship provides more value than it costs. Equity refers to the idea of 'fair dealing', or the feeling of parties about their respective commitment and the sharing of benefits resulting from it. Dissatisfaction results in further cycles or in the disruption of the relationship (Kumar, Nti, 1998). Many cycles allow better achievement of collective and individual benefits (Figure 3.2).

The process framework underscores the role of adaptative processes and the influence of initial conditions on IOR development. The learning model captures these issues (Doz, 1996; Arino, de la Torre, 1998). It emphasizes the role of operating conditions, initial or revised. The central role has been attributed here to learning instead of assessment. The learning model also brings adaptation – the willingness and capability to adjust – to our attention. Yet both models narrow the focus on to two possible outcomes: development or dissolution.

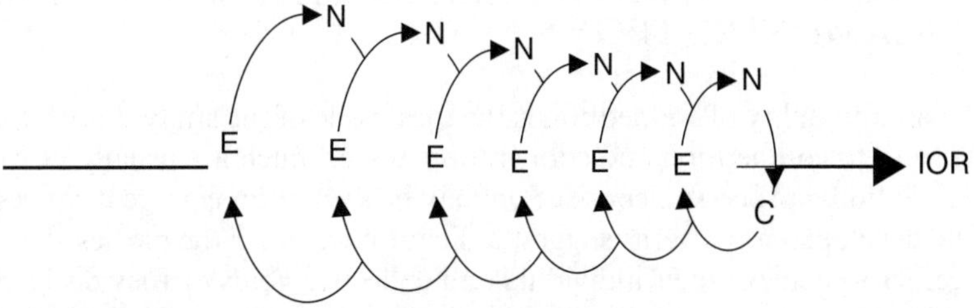

Figure 3.2   Sequence of development cycles

Yet the initial conditions which justified or induced (Ahuja, 2000) the relationship formation are rarely durable. Over time, complex dynamics occur and impact on the structure and processes of cooperation. Deliberate change occurs as the result of a negotiation process – it is called a development process (Ring, Van de Ven, 1994). If partners don't come to an agreement in the face of changes during cooperation, then unilateral decisions may emerge within the cooperative context. A major change or dissolution which has not been planned from the perspective of one or more partners is called instability (Inkpen, Beamish, 1997). Instabilities are one of the major issues in the strategic cooperation field, as about 50 per cent of all alliances or joint ventures become unstable (Das, Teng, 2000). When parties are driven by the pursuit of a mutually beneficial goal or individual benefits, their cooperation requires a pattern of intentional evolution. Dialectics come to be complementary to the teleological theories to the extent that changes can be initiated either by an intentional assessment and learning process, or by a major cooperative imbalance. If conflicting forces fall below similar levels, imbalance appears (Das, Teng, 2000), triggering change to the initially planned pattern (Zeitz, 1980).

Very little empirical research has so far been undertaken in this respect, focusing instead on the balance concept – the relationship develops as long as conflicting forces stay in balance. So far, researchers have considered balance in terms of opposite pairs: (1) design – emergence (Gulati, 1995); (2) control – autonomy (Ahuja, 2000); (3) vigilance – trust (Das, Teng, 1998); (4) conflict – compromise (De Rond, Bouchikhi, 2004); (5) competition – cooperation (Jorde, Teece, 1989); (6) individualism – collectivism (Astley, Fombrun, 1983); (7) contraction – expansion (Parkhe, 1993); (8) replication – innovation (Tracey, Clark, 2003). Prior research suggests that they form a space of choices, whether in the form of gradable continua or bipolar alternatives (Clarke-Hill, Li, Davies, 2003).

2.   IS COOPETITION A DELIBERATE POSITIVE-SUM GAME STRATEGY?

The intentionality of coopetition is the focal issue of the study. I posit that contrary to competition and cooperation alone, which are usually viewed as intentional processes, coopetition may be seen as an emergent process. IOR development patterns suggest a dichotomy: either the parties still go together to achieve their individual and collective goals or they decide to pursue their goals separately. Both ways, the teleological models would be viable as long as this alternative choice reflects all decision options. Yet coopetition can be seen as the third available option, which leads to the first research question:

> **Research question 1**: Is emerging coopetition a distinct path in interorganizational relationship evolution, aside from a collective decision to further develop the relationship or to dissolve it?

If a party seeks goals with guile (Jap, Ganesan, 2000) regardless of the interests of his or her partner, such behavior is called opportunism. This leads to the second research question:

> **Research question 2**: Is instability driving interorganizational relationship partners to coopete in the form of opportunism in cooperative settings?

Competition between partners may appear and jeopardize their cooperative relationship. The study contributes to our understanding of the emergent process and its correlates.

3.   RESEARCH DESIGN

There are three major reasons for using case studies to build a theory: the early development stage of knowledge in the study field; examination of a contemporary phenomenon in its real-life context; and when the boundaries between the phenomenon and the context are not clearly evident (Yin, 1981). All seem to be valid for the investigation of emerging coopetition.

3.1   Focal Case

A particularly appropriate setting in which to study emerging coopetition is a bank's franchising network. This setting is appropriate for several reasons. First, franchising is a typical contract offered to entrepreneurs willing to do business along standard lines, under a common logo and management, but also under separate ownership. Relationships between the franchisor and its partners are standardized. The diversity of typical networks can thus be reduced to multiple observations of behaviors in highly similar circumstances in a centralized network. Secondly, banking is a sector renowned for rigid and highly formalized procedures. Documentary analysis offers the opportunity to access codified knowledge and allows for triangulation with other data sources. Thirdly, a deliberately built franchising network is asymmetrical in terms of the partner's power and benefit sharing. This is expected to induce emerging strategies from franchisees.

The object of study, a retail bank in Poland, is one of the top five retail banking institutions in the country's market. With about 450 of its own branches, it covers the territory of southern and central Poland well, but is relatively weak in the rest of the country. One of the major strategic objectives is to expand territorially.

3.2 Data Collection and Analysis

Four sources of evidence were selected: retrospective individual interviews, documentary information, direct observation and internet forum observation. First, retrospective individual interviews were conducted with the bank's managers. Three semi-structured interviews with the bank's top executive responsible for the indirect sales department were performed: two in November 2005 and another in March 2006. A set of 30 questions was usually prepared and communicated to the respondent by email. During the interview a discussion developed the originally crafted data input. One non-structured interview was conducted with the sales manager of a local branch of the bank in order to gather evidence on phenomena observable in direct cooperation with franchisees.

Secondly, documentary information was collected from the franchisor. In total, there were 590MB in 257 computer files such as: procedures, decisions, rules of cooperation, standard agreement forms, check lists, project description, business plan, master plan of the franchising project, manual of the franchisee, manual of the supervising branch director and operating procedures. Thirdly, direct observation of a single franchising point of sale was performed between June 2005 and July 2006. A typical location was chosen – a small city of 20000 people, and a typical size for the franchising point of sale – two desk clerks. Fourthly, an internet forum was set up, animated by the franchisees themselves, with the first data posted in March 2005 and the last data gathered in June 2006. These posts were copied to a 31 000 word text file and covered several topics, mostly the problems which franchisees encountered in their franchise operations, many of them relating to the bank's procedures or the franchising system itself. The extensive dataset gathered was triangulated and analyzed using complexity reduction techniques such as data stratification with regard to data source, problems addressed and process focus. The findings were further reviewed in the light of extant literature (Eisenhardt, 1989) relative to the instability of interorganizational relationships, providing extensions and advances for coopetition theory.

4. RESULTS

4.1 The Initial Framework

The bank's strategy focused on rapid market expansion at reasonably low costs. Among other projects, the franchising network appeared in 2003. Opening a bank's own branch is an investment about thirty times more expensive than setting up a franchisee's point of sale, which is financed additionally by the franchisee. Franchising network project profitability has been estimated by the franchisor at an Internal Rate of Return (IRR) of at least 70 per cent for a five-year period. As for the franchisees, the payback time was estimated at six months on average and the suggested monthly income achievable was 10 000 euro.

Franchising network formation followed at a rapid pace. Instead of a highly formal recruitment procedure, the bank chose to use social capital (Lin, 2001) by offering partnership to entrepreneurs indicated by local branch directors. Negotiations were restricted to technical topics such as location, cash limits and employee qualifications. The commitment of partners took the form of the acceptance of mutual terms and signature of a contract, and was executed very quickly. The network size topped 460 franchisees within two years of project launch.

4.2 The Tensions

The structural settings of the franchising contract are rigid, formal and asymmetric. While it became clear that the franchising model was a largely successful strategic move, several tensions with franchisees appeared. Very soon after cooperation started, the franchisees assessed cooperation against efficiency and equity criteria, which led many of them to renegotiation attempts. Franchisees claimed that 'I dream of having a small part of the interest from the credits I sold' or that '[the franchisees] should negotiate commissions on credits and accounts, because otherwise I do not see any future in that business'. Yet the bank manager acknowledged with satisfaction that 'no such negotiation has been successful so far'. It is evidence of a lack of adaptability on the part of the bank, hampering relationship development.

First, asymmetries relative to income flow sharing were claimed on the forum to be 'for every 1000 of ours [the franchisee's], they [the bank] are getting 3000 on average'. For a typical mortgage loan, the sharing of income was calculated as 3.6 per cent for the franchisee versus 96.4 percent for the bank. Generally the pie sharing by the franchisees was considered to be 'miserable'. Second, power asymmetries were noticed relative to the product range limited by the contract or to the cooperation process. The loan decision couldn't be discussed, which drove a franchisee to state 'The worst of our problems are branches, more specifically branch's directors'. This hampered sales, as one franchisee stated 'I just lost another loan customer because they couldn't check the documents for two days'. Also, the remuneration for the franchisee was paid by the bank in bulk, based on transactions records, at the end of the month. This made negotiations very delicate. Third, the flexibility of sale conditions was restricted, even compared to credit brokers, who could provide a considerably better offer to the customer: 'I have sent 15 loan applications last week; they were all turned down, while all these applications have passed through a credit broker'. Fourth, the bargaining position towards the bank was very weak because 'we are treated as separate vendors', as one franchisee reported on her phone conversation with the bank's manager. Despite the fact that the franchising network generates 15 per cent of total bank turnover, having no single representative to negotiate cooperation terms allowed the bank to state: 'as soon as you get a comparable sales volume as brokers your commissions will be comparable also'.

4.3 The Reactions

Under such circumstances, some franchisees chose to dissolve the contract and sell their franchise, justifying it in emails, forum posts or even auction portals: 'because of the rapid development of my other activities' or 'because of moving abroad' or else ' because of family reasons'. Others chose to keep their contract but to seek additional profits unilaterally. Several such actions were announced, proposed to other franchisees and discussed on internet forums. Most notable were: (1) setting up an association to represent franchisees of the bank; (2) intentional infringement of the exclusivity clause; and (3) selling customer databases to competitors.

The franchising association initiative appeared in emails sent by some franchisees to each other by the end of 2005, because of disclosed cases of direct competition of credit brokers and the bank's branches with the franchisees. The franchisees were told that the credit brokers got better conditions because they sold more, yet the franchising network as a whole represented some 15 per cent of mortgage loan income. In bulk, the franchising network was the most valuable partner of the bank, but had no single representation: 'we need to have a single representation if we are to expect any improvements'. Therefore an association was initiated to increase franchisees' bargaining power and improve their share of the cooperation benefits.

Intentional exclusivity clause infringement by the franchisees was a reaction to a low approved loans ratio. It ranged from brokering bank products to offering only other banks' products. Thus franchisees became agents of competitors within the bank sales structure. When competitors are able to approve a loan faster, then they get the customer. Some franchisees also opened another credit agency just next door to their franchise in order to maximize revenue from the customer. As one franchisee said: 'it is easy – the franchise is formally yours, while the credit bureau next door is in the name of another member of your family. It allows income to be increased by some 20%'. Several offers of cooperation were also sent to franchisees by competitors through email or by invitation via the internet.

Customer data selling to the most aggressive competitors, such as credit card issuers' was a different issue. The price of one piece of customer data seemed to be fixed on the market, suggesting a routine procedure. It might be an interesting source of income for the franchisee. Quantitative data about the extent of this process are not easily accessible, because the respondents knew that such behavior was not legal, infringing the franchising contract.

The discrepancies revealed by the relationship assessment drove franchisees to engage in negotiation cycles. No adaptability was shown by the bank, inducing in a propensity for competition to emerge within cooperative settings.

5.   DISCUSSION

Viewed from the strategic intent standpoint, coopetition is revealed here to be an emerging phenomenon, consistent with features of both the emerging strategy and types of strategies within the continuum planned–emergent (Mintzberg, Waters, 1985). Coopetition here is the franchisee's strategy realized despite initial partners' intentions. There is evidence that it is: (1) entrepreneurial, because of its adaptability; (2) unconnected, as it originates in enclaves and spreads on the network; and (3) imposed, as it originates in the environment.

From the relationship development stance, cooperation is usually designed from goals, scope, governance structure and expected parties' commitment specification. The path followed by partners in the relationship formation phase is consistent with the NCE cycle (Ring, Van de Ven, 1994). During cooperation, assessment may show unsatisfactory results or processes. Another cycle should then be engaged in for mutual adjustment – developing cooperation or, alternatively, dissolving it. Prior literature views this choice as dichotomous. My study provides evidence of a third option – to continue cooperation and seek profits unilaterally within and beyond the IOR. The coopetition process typically has two stages: value creation and value appropriation. Partners cooperate to 'expand the pie', but then compete for a share of it. The franchising case provides evidence that competition between partners appears at the 'pie sharing' stage, without being previously planned by at least one partner. This third option of relationship development – to keep cooperation and add competition to it, seems therefore consistent with the nature of IOR instability (Inkpen, Beamish, 1997).

Proposition 1: Emerging coopetition is an alternative to interorganizational relationship dissolution, a choice to keep profits from cooperation and simultaneous unilateral rent seeking.

This finding is consistent with the view that there are two levels of coopetition: network and dyadic (Dagnino, Padula, 2007). The network-level coopetition in the franchising case creates positive-sum game effects, and has an anticipated value appropriation regime. Dyadic-level coopetition follows the negotiated value creation and appropriation regime, but additional competitive actions emerge. Franchisees strive for a more equitable share and process modifications, while the franchisor sticks to the initial agreement. Consequently, three types of franchisees' reactions have been found: acceptance of the initial conditions, contract dissolution and unilateral rent seeking within and beyond the IOR. Unilateral rent seeking can be harmful to the franchisor. Franchisees' association formation, credit brokering and customer data selling exemplify such actions and propensities, which are clearly opportunistic.

Proposition 2: Emerging coopetition is a form of opportunistic behavior, where one partner seeks the fulfilment of his own goals within a cooperative setting, regardless of the common goals and the interests of his partner.

Yet emerging coopetition is a reaction to several tensions between partners – relationship assessments revealed discrepancies and initiated attempts to engage in negotiations. The franchisor's lack of flexibility and relationship asymmetries induced competition within cooperative settings. Prior research points to intentional network density increase, that is, relationship formation between partners of the focal agent, in order to foster interorganizational learning and cooperative advantage (Dyer, Nobeoka, 2002). My study findings suggest that network density also increases through action orchestrated by actors other than the central agent. There is evidence that network density increased through relationship formation between franchisees, focused on learning: problem articulation, practice sharing and joint action initiatives.

Proposition 3: Relationship formation between franchisees fosters network learning and the spread of emerging strategies.

Interorganizational learning brings about coopetition, yet its antecedents are to be seen in relationship setting and franchisor behaviour. Furthermore, new relationships have been formed outside the boundaries of the franchising network, notably with the bank's competitors. This is evidence of a boundary spanning propensity, regardless of franchising contract terms, clearly prohibiting such action. This propensity is also a reaction to the franchisor's lack of flexibility, communication gaps and relationship asymmetries. The franchising network study suggests a relationship between structural relationship features and the propensity to coopete. The structural lack of flexibility of the franchising contract unleashes competition where it was not expected, and is harmful to the franchisor. It arises from the lack of communication between partners and lack of will on both sides. This suggests a possible impact of the structural features of a network – flexibility and asymmetry – on the propensity to coopete.

The process framework model of relationship dynamics needs to be extended (Figure 3.3) by no-development options, such as dissolution or opportunism. Also, the model should involve adaptability as an assessment criterion. Emerging coopetition would thus be modelled as a modification of the NCE cycle. The franchising case suggests that there is no direct, deterministic link from one stage of the cycle to the other. Rather, partners choose from available options. Specifically, when: (1) negotiations fail, the outcome may be dissolution of the contract or commitment; (2) if commitment is assessed as unequal or inefficient it may lead to execution of the contract or to opportunism; (3) if execution is estimated to be unequal or inefficient it may lead to further negotiations or to emerging coopetition.

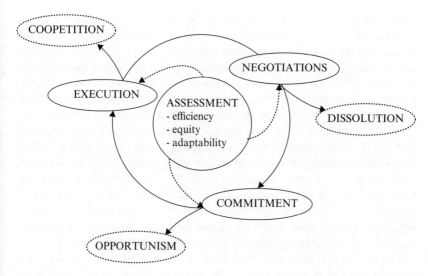

Figure 3.3   Emerging coopetition in the IOR development process

CONCLUSIONS AND LIMITATIONS

Coopetition strategy has been defined so far as a deliberate use of coop-eration and competition in order to achieve a positive-sum game and better performance for partners. By deliberate, we understand usually that at least one partner has planned coopetition, and other partners have agreed to jointly follow this strategy. Yet strategy is 'walking on two legs' (Mintzberg, Waters, 1985) and emergent patterns are realized as well. From this standpoint, coopetition may emerge as either competition within cooperative relationships or cooperation within competitive set-tings. My study reveals emerging coopetition as unplanned competition in cooperative settings.

The study findings contribute to coopetition theory development four-fold. First, it provides evidence that a view of coopetition as a deliberate, negotiated strategy is oversimplified. Coopetitive strategies may emerge within cooperative settings as a unilateral and potentially opportunistic choice. It may take the form of unilateral rent seeking within a cooperative relationship by partners. Despite low satisfaction from cooperation, they choose to keep cooperative advantages. Second, the nature of coopetition needs to be revised. The term 'simultaneous cooperation and competition' refers to a brief period, whereas coopetition strategies are implemented over long periods. Indeed, coopetition implies that the balance between cooperative and competitive behaviors changes, but both are observable. Third, coopetition and interorganizational dynamics theory are strongly linked. Clearly the phenomenon is dynamic: partner, relationship, network and environment driven. Also, the study addresses the academic gap in interorganizational relationship dynamics by extending existing models with additional options. Coopetition appears as the third option of relationship development, beyond mutual adaptation or dissolution alone. Fourth, the study suggests links between endogenous relationship factors to coopetition emergence. Coopetition seems to be induced in the cooperative arrangement by both structural variables – flexibility and asymmetry, and a process variable – network learning. Whether it is leveraging of common resources for the outside activities of a single partner or bargaining for a higher share in jointly generated value, emerging coopetition goes beyond the initial agreement and does so because it did not evolve.

The managerial implications of the study suggest the need to adapt and learn from coopetitors. Otherwise, the scope of intentional action remains rigid, while partner activities may appear to be harmful. Imbalances, while rather typical of business networks, may fall beyond the level of partners' tolerance. A close monitoring seems to be justified and needed.

The research agenda calls for empirical investigation of coopetition strategy path dependence. In other words teleological theories appear to be better suited for the study of coopetition than lifecycle-like paths. This implies the need to incorporate such concepts as interorganizational learning and relational capabilities into the theoretical framework of coopetition strategy. Also, the impact of structural factors on coopetition needs to be further investigated.

The limitations of this research come mostly from the method of study. A single case usually shows a business reality well, but generalization requires going beyond one's data. Although it seems empirically grounded, further research is needed with reference to the structural correlates of emergent coopetition. Nevertheless coopetition dynamics seem to be a promising direction of research, contributing to a better understanding of the phenomenon.

REFERENCES

Ahuja, G. (2000), 'The Duality of Collaboration: Inducements and Opportunities in the Formation of Interfirm Linkages', *Strategic Management Journal*, **21**(3), 317–343.
Arino, A. and J. de la Torre (1998), 'Learning from Failure: Towards an

Evolutionary Model of Collaborative Ventures', *Organization Science*, **9**(3), 306–325.

Astley, W.G. and C.J. Fombrun (1983), 'Collective Strategy: Social Ecology of Organizational Environments', *The Academy of Management Review*, **8**(4), 576–587

Bell, J., B. den Ouden and G.W. Ziggers (2006) 'Dynamics of Cooperation: On the Brink of Irrelevance', *Journal of Management Studies*, **43**(7), 1607–1619.

Bengtsson, M. and S. Kock (1999) 'Cooperation and Competition in Relationships between Competitors in Business Networks', *The Journal of Business and Industrial Marketing*, **14**(3), 178–189.

Brandenburger, A. and B. Nalebuff (1996) *Coopetition*, New York: Doubleday.

Cannon, J.P. and C. Homburg (2001), 'Buyer–Supplier Relationships and Customer Firm Costs', *Journal of Marketing*, **65**(1), 29–43.

Clarke-Hill, C., H. Li and B. Davies (2003), 'The Paradox of Co-operation and Competition in Strategic Alliances: Towards a Multi-Paradigm Approach', *Management Research News*, **26**(1), 1–20.

Dagnino, G. and G. Padula (2007), 'Untangling the Rise of Coopetition: the Intrusion of Competition in a Cooperative Game Structure', *International Studies of Management and Organization*, **37**(2), 32–52.

Das, T.K. and B.S. Teng (1998), 'Between Trust and Control: Developing Confidence in Partner Cooperation in Alliances', *The Academy of Management Review*, **23**(3), 491–512.

Das, T.K. and B.S. Teng (2000), 'Instabilities of Strategic Alliances: An Internal Tensions Perspective', *Organization Science*, **11**(1), 77–101.

De Rond, M. and H. Bouchikhi (2004), 'On The Dialectics of Strategic Alliances', *Organization Science*, **15**(1), 56–69.

Dickson, P.H. and K.M. Weaver (1997), 'Environmental Determinants and Individual Level Moderators of Alliance Use', *Academy of Management Journal*, **40**(2), 404–425.

Donada, C. (2002), 'Generating Cooperative Gain in a Vertical Partnership: a Supplier's Perspective', *Canadian Journal of Administrative Sciences*, **19**(2), 173–183.

Doz, Y. (1996), 'The Evolution of Cooperation in Strategic Alliances: Initial Conditions or Learning Process', *Strategic Management Journal*, **17**(Special Issue), 55–83.

Dyer, J. (1996), 'Specialized Supplier Networks as a Source of Competitive Advantage: Evidence from the Auto Industry', *Strategic Management Journal*, **17**(4), 271–291.

Dyer J. and K. Nobeoka (2000), 'Creating and Managing a High Performance Knowledge-Sharing Network: The Toyota Case', *Strategic Management Journal*, **21**(Special Issue), 345–367.

Dyer, J. and H. Singh (1998), 'The Relational View: Cooperative Strategy and Sources of Interorganizational Competitive Advantage', *The Academy of Management Review*, **24**(4), 660–679.

Eisenhardt, K.M. (1989), 'Building Theory from Case Study Research', *The Academy of Management Review*, **14**(4), 532–550.

Grandori, A. and G. Soda (1995), 'Inter-firm Networks: Antecedents, Mechanisms and Forms', *Organization Studies*, **16**(2), 183–214.

Gulati, R. (1995), 'Social Structure and Alliance Formation Patterns: A Longitudinal Analysis', *Administrative Science Quarterly*, **40**(4), 619–652.

Gulati, R., T. Khanna and N. Nohria (1994), 'Unilateral Commitment and the Importance of Process in Alliances', *Sloan Management Review*, **35**(3), 61–69.

Gulati R. and H. Singh (1998), The Architecture of Cooperation: Managing Coordination Costs and Appropriation Concerns in Strategic Alliances, *Administrative Science Quarterly*, **43**(4), 781–814.

Hamel, G. (1991), 'Competition for Competence and Interpartner Learning within International Strategic Alliances', *Strategic Management Journal*, **12**(Special Issue), 83–103.

Inkpen, A.C. and P.W. Beamish (1997), 'Knowledge Bargaining Power, and Instability of International Joint Ventures', *The Academy of Management Review*, **22**(1), 177–202.

Jap, S. and S. Ganesan (2000), 'Control Mechanisms and the Relationship Life Cycle: Implications for Safeguarding Specific Investments and Developing Commitment', *Journal of Marketing Research*, **37**(2), 227–245.

Jarillo, J.C. (1988), 'On Strategic Networks', *Strategic Management Journal*, **9**(1), 31–41

Jorde, T. and D. Teece (1989), 'Competition and Cooperation: Striking the Right Balance', *California Management Review*, **31**(3), 25–37.

Kale, P., H. Singh and H. Perlmutter (2000), 'Learning and Protection of Proprietary Assets in Strategic Alliances: Building Relational Capital', *Strategic Management Journal*, **21**(3), 217–237.

Kanter, R.M. (1994), 'Collaborative Advantage: The Art of Alliances', *Harvard Business Review*, **72**(4), 97–102.

Kumar, R. and K. Nti (1998) 'Differential Learning and Interaction in Alliances Dynamics: A Process and Outcome Discrepancy Model', *Organization Science*, **9**(3) 356–367.

Lin, N. (2001), *Social Capital: A Theory of Social Structure and Action*, Cambridge: Cambridge University Press.

Mintzberg, H. and J. Waters (1985), 'Of Strategies, Deliberate and Emergent', *Strategic Management Journal*, **6**(3), 257–272.

Oliver, A.L. and M. Ebers (1998), 'Networking Network Studies: An Analysis of Conceptual Configurations in the Study of Inter-Organizational Relationships', *Organization Studies*, **19**(4), 549–583.

Parkhe, A. (1993), 'Strategic Alliance Structuring: A Game Theoretic and Transaction Cost Examination of Interfirm Cooperation', *Academy of Management Journal*, **36**(4), 794–829.

Peng, M. and O. Shenkar (2002), 'Joint Venture Dissolution as Corporate Divorce', *Academy of Management Journal*, **16**(2), 92–105.

Porter, M.E. (1980), *Competitive Strategy*, New York: The Free Press.

Powell, W., K.W. Koput and L. Smith-Doerr (1996), 'Interorganizational Collaboration and the Locus of Innovation: Networks of Learning in Biotechnology', *Administrative Science Quarterly*, **41**(1), 116–145.

Ring, P.S. and H. Van de Ven (1994), 'Developmental Process of Cooperative Interorganizational Relationships', *Academy of Management Review*, **19**(1), 90–118.

Rumelt, R.P. (1991), 'How Much Does Industry Matter?', *Strategic Management Journal*, **12**(3), 167–185.

Tracey, P. and G.L. Clark (2003), 'Alliance, Networks and Competitive Strategy: Rethinking Clusters of Innovation', *Growth and Change*, **34**(1), 1–16.

Van de Ven, A.H. and M.S. Poole (1995), 'Explaining Development and Change in Organizations', *The Academy of Management Review*, **20**(3), 510–540.
Yin, R.K. (1981), 'The Case Study Crisis: Some Answers', *Administrative Science Quarterly*, **26**(1), 58–65.
Zaheer, A., B. McEvily and V. Perrone (1998), 'The Strategic Value of Buyer–Supplier Relationships', *Strategic Management Journal*, **34**(3), 20–26.
Zeitz, G. (1980), 'Interorganizational Dialectics', *Administrative Science Quarterly*, **25**(1), 72–88.

4. Learning in coopetitive environments

Philippe Baumard

INTRODUCTION

Coopetitive environments (Brandenburger and Nalebuff, 1996) are characterized by situations where firms simultaneously compete and cooperate with competitors. Such situations impede the generation of proprietary and discretionary learning, by forcing competitors to selectively share critical knowledge about their assets (Baumard, 2008). Coopetition can arise from partial or incomplete interest in a rival's domain, where it does not require a full entry or deployment into it. Dagnino and Padula (2009) hence note that coopetition is not restricted to situations of simultaneous cooperation and competition, but rather extends to every form of strategic interdependency, where partially congruent and divergent interests need to be managed simultaneously. How do they differ from more traditional 'collective strategies' (Hawley, 1950; Astley and Fombrun, 1983)?

Whilst collective strategies are temporary arrangements that increase the chance of success of previously or geographically competitive firms, coopetition translates into a more durable form of inescapable coexistence. In order to distinguish between the forms of dependency that link firms in such a fate, Astley and Fombrun (1983) have borrowed from Hawley's (1950) work on the coexistence between species in a biotope to describe the forms of durable arrangements that maintain the flow of interactions between firms. They suggest that the dependence upon a shared resource (commensalism), the mutual and symmetric dependence on core assets (symbiotic relations), or the dependence of a smaller player upon an architecture generated by a large incumbent (parasitism) trigger different environmental configurations, such as federations or conglomerates.

While mixed motives (Axelrod, 1984; Schelling, 1960) and knowledge exchange within inter-firm networks (Grandori and Neri, 1999) have been studied extensively, little attention has been given to strategies of learning that firms must deploy in order to be successful in a setting where they have to learn from, or learn with, a competitor. While coopetitive arrangements are not conditionally antagonistic, the learning that occurs in the midst of an agreement, where copyright laws, industrial secrecy and non-disclosure agreements are the sole barriers to protect the firm's discretion, is often felt to be an adverse experience (Baumard, 2008). 'Adverse learning' is a term used in education sciences to describe learning that triggers anxiety, emotional blockage, phobias and poor responses (Menec *et al.*, 1995). Studies focus on providing alternative learning strategies that would help students in adverse learning situations to overcome such obstacles. Two streams of research, one coming from the works of Burrhus Frederic Skinner (1968) on associative learning, and one coming from the works of Piaget (1972) on participative learning have focused on human antagonistic learning. Skinner observed that subsequent responses of a learner are much influenced by what follows the initial learning. In his experiments, Skinner also showed that rats resist complete conditioning, and invent a behavior that does not respond mechanically to the stimulus. They adapt to adversity by creating a routine that bypasses the trick that has been designed to create an aversion (usually an electric shock), and still allows access to their food. Whereas Skinner's theory of behavioral chain received harsh criticism, noticeably by Chomsky, Piaget's theory of reciprocity in learning brought an in-depth understanding of adverse learning in childhood. Piaget did not focus on a stimulus–response scheme, but rather in understanding the forms and logic the child uses when faced with a lack of response, trying to assimilate and accommodate contradictory or adverse inputs. For Piaget, the journey into learning the mechanisms of learning, from birth to childhood, is one of slow and gradual asymmetric gains. The child learns simultaneously to define who he or she is, constructing an ontology of being, while inventing and discovering the epistemology of his or her interactions.

Economists and etiologists have also studied antagonistic learning. We shall see in this chapter how unexpectedly parallel these studies were. Akerlof (1970), in his market for lemons, developed a seminal example of adverse learning in an economic trade-off situation. He showed that buyers can engage in adverse selection when facing antagonistic and uncertain learning settings (in his example, when buying an untrustworthy second-hand car). Lorenz (1966), in his study of animal and human aggression, disclosed similar examples of reluctant and adverse learning, noticeably when animals must accommodate a non-cooperative partner in order to achieve a vital learning mechanism for food and reproduction. Hence, 'unbalanced' or 'adverse' learning is inherent in most human and animal activities, but has not received adequate attention by management and strategy scholars.

Nevertheless, unbalanced learning in coopetitive dealing has gained a worldwide momentum with the rise of compensation mechanisms, involving for instance the return of know-how or R&D capabilities to gain access to emerging markets. The objective of this chapter is to explore the learning strategies that can be deployed by firms in coopetitive configurations with no other choice than deploying an 'adverse learning' mechanism to reach their customers through cooperation with their competitors. After exploring the mechanisms of asymmetric learning in the first section, the chapter adopts an ecological perspective (Hawley, 1950) in drawing parallels between animal organization and groups of firms in gaining a strategic advantage through asymmetric learning.

1. STRATEGIC LEARNING THROUGH ASYMMETRIC LEARNING

1.1 Asymmetric Learning

Coopetitive situations are similar to settings described by Akerlof (1970) in his 'market for lemons': two parties are seeking to get the most out of their interaction, seeking cooperation to reduce information asymmetries, while engaging in competition to get the most out of the deal. In Akerlof's seminal example, the market for used cars would diminish, even to the point of collapsing, if the fear created in the buyer by the information asymmetry reaches the point of preferring to pay more for a new car and less uncertainty. In such a double-bind context, the buyer of the 'lemon' will try everything he or she can to reduce the information asymmetry, by means of trust enabling, seduction and eventual intelligence gathering from fellow buyers who visited the same shop. Unfortunately, as he or she soon discovers, buying a used car is a situation where the moral hazard is inescapable, for the asymmetry ultimately plays in favor of the seller.

Adequate learning strategies can reduce the information asymmetries between the two parties. As Stigler suggested (1961: 224), partners in such an adverse selection scheme often rely on the reputation of the other party to compensate for the fact that they cannot afford or access the search for complete information on the correct price. As Stigler puts it: 'Ignorance is like subzero weather: by a sufficient expenditure its effects upon people can be kept within tolerable or even comfortable bounds, but it would be wholly uneconomic entirely to eliminate all its effects' (*op. cit.,* p. 224). The problem with coopetitive situations is that both parties mirror each other, being simultaneously reciprocal buyers and sellers. They need to unveil a minimum level of information to engage in cooperation, while keeping from sight a sufficient level of information to preserve their competitive stance. In other words, both parties need to 'sell' part of their information to the other party, while at the same time 'buying' themselves some discretionary and competitive knowledge on their partner in order to be able to eventually compete, sooner or later. They are symmetrically ignorant of the other's actual performance, not knowing if they are in a situation of 'lemon for lemon' or 'gold for gold'.

This situation is similar to an employer meeting a prospective employee: the applicant does not know if the firm is a lemon or a paradise; the employer does not know if the applicant is a lemon or a world-class. Spence (1973) proposed a specific learning strategy for such two partially ignorant parties cooperating in a competitive situation. He named it 'signaling'. Previous experience has taught employers that higher education in their employees returns higher profits, while applicants know that firms that can afford better trained professionals usually pay them more and provide better workplaces. Of course, the intrinsic value of the higher education, and likewise, the intrinsic value of the workplace, do not stop the model from working. In other words, escaping information asymmetry can be achieved through games of convention (Lewis, 1969). The applicant's education does not possess a known price, even if it had a cost. Its appreciation is a social convention, and usually labelled as such, for example, 'Ivy League'. The firm's reputation also does not come with a price, but much evidence can be found in 'precedents', a term used by Lewis to denote the existence of common knowledge shared by the parties on the state of the social convention.

A convention is a highly ambiguous approximation of a price. In the market for lemons, Akerlof (1970) puts a buyer in the position of choosing between prices for a car (which may be a lemon), or walking away, and eventually buying a new car. In most coopetitive situations, the choice to stay or go does not come with a price. If there are prices, they are so dispersed in the intertwined implications of their collateral effects on future cooperation and competition, that even Stigler's concept of 'dispersion' would not capture the dilemma facing the coopetitive partners. As a consequence, partners in coopetition trade 'conventions' that are crafted for the purpose of trying to stay in the game, while not chasing away the partner from its cooperative predisposition. An adequate etiological myth to illustrate such coopetitive strategies might be found in Hesiod's *Theogony*. Hesiod relates how the Greeks tricked Zeus when faced with choosing between self-starvation and satisfying the God's demand. Prometheus assembled a pack of bones and fat made of the sacrificial animal, keeping the meat aside, hence cooperating with the Gods, while not totally betraying them.

1.2   An Ecological Perspective

The factor that prevents Prometheus from informing Zeus that his people are lacking food is not malignity, but fear. As Mariani (2007) showed in his analysis of an Italian opera house consortium, coopetition is rarely a deliberate situation desired by partners. It is more likely to be emergent and somewhat undesired. When thrown into coopetition, firms face a change in their ecological arrangements with other firms that can be compared to a change of biological equilibrium in a living organism, or in nature. Several authors have borrowed from biology and ecology to describe organizational phenomena. McKelvey (1982), in *Organizational Systematics*, borrows the principles of natural selection to try to apply them to populations of organizations. Nelson and Winter (1982) draw an analogy between organizational routines and genetic characteristics. For the latter, routines that match environmental conditions allow firms to survive, while firms failing to adopt adequate routines disappear. In the same perspective, Astley and Fombrun (1983) borrowed Hawley's (1950) characterization of living organisms' interactions within an ecosystem to describe interactions between firms, building extensively on concepts such as commensalism, antagonism, symbiosis, parasitism and so on. Hence, by seeking to explain how firms survive by drawing analogies with ecology, these authors have laid the primary stones of the study of strategic learning (Starbuck, Barnett and Baumard, 2008). However, staying loyal to a functionalist tradition, strategic management literature that has borrowed from ecology and biology has performed a discretionary selection, stopping the analogy at a mere description of interactions, and putting aside what in fact motivates the adoption of an antagonistic behavior rather than a cooperative one.

Studies of cooperation and competition, by and large, have put too much emphasis on intent and the deliberate nature of competitive configurations. Even the work of Astley and Fombrun (1983), which borrows intensively from Amos Hawley's (1950) study of biotic communities, fails to underline the instinctive and 'natural' organization of those interactions. In fact, the authors state that their analysis 'highlights the importance of collective, as opposed to individual, forms of organizational adaptation' (p. 578), to suggest the importance of 'collective strategy: the joint mobilization of resources and formulation of action within collectivities of organization' (ibid.). It is unfortunate that organizational theory only borrowed the surface and salient aspects of ethology and biology, for much of the most interesting part of this body of science lies at the very low level of animal behavior in the face of uncertainty and ambiguity (Burkhardt, 2005).

In particular, Lorenz (1966) introduced four different dimensions in an attempt to explain animal behavior: the immediate response to a stimulus, which could be compared to a competitive reaction such as a retaliation; the inherent and programmed behavior (ontogenetic), which can be compared to the works of population ecology; the mimetic and homothetic behaviors (Lorenz, 1966; 1970), which are rooted both in genetic inheritance and imitation, and can be compared to institutionalism; and finally, functional adaptation, which is learned from experience of other species and the natural environment, and which seems to have attracted most attention from the management literature (Astley and Fombrun, 1983).

Lorenz defended the idea that these four dimensions of behavior continuously interact while an animal is experiencing a wide variety of events and learning challenges. Although his theory of instinctive behavior was partially invalidated by early critics (Lehrman, 1953), he was the first to underline that the failure of human strategic learning does not lie in the lack of learning abilities, but on the contrary, and contrary to animals, in the excess of learning functions that humans are using. Finally, animals live in coopetitive settings. Cooperation, either symbiotic, parasitic or commensalist is a necessity, not a choice. Likewise, competition, which happens simultaneously and eventually among the same species, is also a vital component for feeding and social organization (Mesterton-Gibbons and Adams, 1998). Therefore, animals need to adapt, whether the context is one of cooperation or competition. Bence (1986) notes that some species have developed skills in 'antagonistic learning', that is, adopting a behavior that precludes feeding efficiently on more than one type of prey at a time. He observes that mosquito fishes decrease their feeding rate as they increase their attack specialization on profitable prey. Krane and Wagner (1975), however, showed that a modification of such a behavior can be 'imprinted' on animals, to use Lorenz's term, by associating an electric shock with a specialized food (in that case, saccharin with rats). Yet Charles River's rats defy theorization by being able to cooperate with the experimenters, hence accessing their food, even with the burden of an adverse and antagonistic learning. Faced with contradictory choices, animals do engage in learning behaviors that are adverse to their objectives, and manage cooperation and competition simultaneously. The question raised by such an observation is: why do theorizations of coopetition not assume that human beings can do just the same?

1.3 Cooperating and Competing at the Same Time

Like Spence's (1973) applicants for a job, animals have an intensive use of 'signaling' to reduce informational asymmetries, discourage aggression, or engage in courtship. This signalling activity is highly conventional, ceremonial and codified (Lorenz, 1966). In the event of courtship, which Lorenz describes as a simultaneous activity of aggression, animals also use what Stiglitz (1975) has labelled 'screening'. This is a technique used by an economic agent trying to reduce an informational asymmetry to extract discretionary information from another. Within a group of similar job applicants, an employer has a keen interest in finding out who are the most qualified, without letting them know that he is after this information. In a situation of coopetition, a firm is in a similar situation. It has a strategic interest in 'screening' partners, among which it competes and cooperates, without letting them know that such a screening is taking place. Animals have a very similar problem when they try to mate, and this is largely due to social conventions and perceptions of hierarchy (Lorenz, 1966).

Lorenz observed that animals resort to 'redirected activity' when provoked and when they are unable to retaliate on the animal originating the aggression. Hence, they start a very aggressive move towards the provocateur, drop it at the last minute, and redirect their aggression towards the closest neighbor. This redirection of aggression has two functions: first, it informs the provocateur that its offense has been acknowledged, and second, it provides a simultaneous 'screening' by reasserting the hierarchy of the dominant male in the social structure. Similar behaviors have been observed in human competitive signalling among populations of salesmen (DePaulo, 1988) and in product announcements from firms trying to 'bluff' the competition (Robertson *et al.*, 1995). In both instances, the bluff signalling has two purposes: first, to deceive the receiver into believing in the sender's superiority (maintaining or enacting an information asymmetry), and simultaneously, to inform the receiver that the firm may engage in an irreversible move if the current equilibrium becomes threatened (screening).

What the animal is also doing when redirecting its aggression to its closest neighbor is to take a 'hint' at the status of both its cooperative and competitive perceptions within its social group (Lorenz, 1966). In doing so, a much larger risk is involved in trying to solve both problems at the same time. If the provocateur, most likely a female during the mating season, stands in the way, this unwanted aggression, on both sides, even if initiated by one of the parties, will terminate any prospects of future relations. If the aggression is redirected, but unsuccessful, the dominant male loses its status within the group, and consequently, both prospects of cooperation (in this case, mating) and competition (in this case group dominance) are lost. This is a high level of risk for just taking a 'hint', and as Schelling noted:

Taking a hint is fundamentally different from deciphering a formal communication or solving a mathematical problem; it involves discovering a message that has been planted within a context by someone who thinks he shares with the recipient certain impressions or associations. One cannot, without empirical evidence, deduce what understandings can be perceived in a nonzero-sum game of maneuver any more than one can prove, by purely formal deduction, that a particular joke is bound to be funny (Schelling, 1960: 163–164).

The gorillas of Lorenz or Parker *et al.* (1999) are in a very similar situation: a provocation has been deliberately thrown to call for the gorilla's attention, but the signal carries simultaneously several meanings and several intents. It is directed as much towards the gorilla's attention, as towards the attention of the social group. Taking a 'hint' either cooperatively or competitively are not available options. The 'hint' must be obtained while managing simultaneously a competitive relation (with the social group, and with the provocateur to assert his/her legitimacy) and coopetitive relation (with the provocateur to maintain the boundary, and with the social group to assert membership of the pack).

1.4 Attention Sharing and the Dilemma of Coopetitive Stance

Managing cooperation and competition simultaneously increases the problems of attention and sense making in managing competitive dynamics. Ocasio (1997) defended the idea that firm behavior is mostly the result of how firms channel and distribute their attention. Although Ocasio is more interested in revisiting Simon's behavioral theory (Simon, 1947, 1955) of the firm by proposing another limitation to human bounded rationality, he justly points out that managerial attention is situated, structurally distributed between tasks and limited in span and depth (see the model in Figure 4.1).

Ocasio (1995, 1997) presents two opposing perspectives on the effect of economic adversity. On the one hand, he cites Kiesler and Sproull (1982), who advocated that failures of economic performance induce corrective actions, and on the other, he presents the theory of threat-rigidity effects (Staw *et al.*, 1981), which argues that adversity leads to more control and more rigidity. The author then suggests that both phenomena are simultaneous. Mimetic isomorphism brings repertoires of responses that can rigidify the firm's response to environmental adversity, while the same adversity triggers at the same time a higher amount of 'paralleled' problemistic search. In other words, there is a trade-off between the attention given to maintaining group acceptance and conformity (mimetic isomorphism) and trying to get an advantage (problemistic search). Indeed, Ocasio teaches that executives have problems which are in nature very

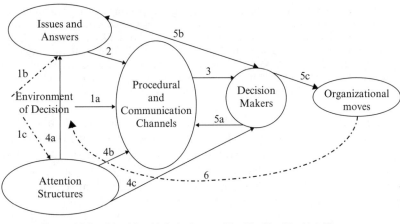

Temporal Sequence is indicated, from left to right, by the placement of the origin of the solid and dotted lines

Source: Ocasio (1997) p. 192

Figure 4.1   Ocasio's (1997) model of situated attention and firm behavior

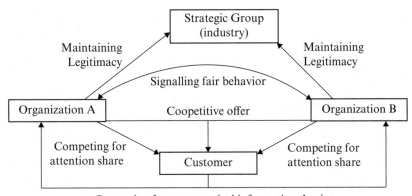

Figure 4.2   Signalling and learning behavior in coopetition

similar to gorillas. One interesting twist of Ocasio's theory would be to analyze such double-bind effects by mirroring the situation of organization A with hypothetical organization B. Figure 4.2 demonstrates this; however, it should be borne in mind that more than two firms can be intertwined in the very same configurations. Both organizations are thus trying to maintain legitimacy to their respective strategic groups. Meanwhile, because of their coopetitive stance, they must reciprocally signal (Spence,

1973; Stiglitz, 1975) a fair behavior to their competitor-partner. A missing element in Ocasio's model, however, is the role of the customer, who is likely to be ignorant of the coopetitive nature of the goods he or she consumes (see Figure 4.2).

Although the customer is buying a 'bundled' or 'integrated' offer, there is still an intense rivalry between the organizations involved over grabbing their share of attention. Hence, both organizations are likely to compete for asymmetrical informational gains gathered in the privileged space they maintain with the customer, despite the running coopetition. Customers find themselves in a situation quite similar to a buyer of a 'lemon' (Akerlof, 1970): while they purchase the overall offer on the basis of the aggregator's reputation, their selection of the respective components is an adverse selection, as they purchase the coopetitive offer not knowing the intrinsic performance of its various components.

In Akerlof's seminal example, both buyer and seller can eventually rely on their own examination of the car. Although engine performance varies greatly in make and year, even with the same brand of car, the general state of the car, and the general aspect of the pipes, carburettors, and so on, can be thoroughly inspected. General knowledge is also available from word-of-mouth and specialist registries. Knowing that buyers could access external knowledge, classic car sellers may try to 'obfuscate' evident liabilities in their cars. A well-known practice is to wax, blacken and shine engine components in order to conceal the fact that they are very worn. The rise of electronic and software components, however, has rendered obfuscation more possible and less detectable, to a point that can both challenge Akerlof's theory and explain the sustainability of paradoxical configurations such as coopetitive agreements.

Obfuscation is the concealment of meaning in communication by the application of placebic and neutrally functional capabilities to a techno-logical set or chunk of knowledge. Obfuscation is not necessarily driven by malevolent intents. Faced with incompleteness, indeterminacy, irrelevance and incommensurability, managers often rely on industry recipes that temporarily obfuscate their lack of responses (Spender, 1989). For instance, a doctor can use such obfuscation in order to conceal the meaning of a diffi-cult operation to an overly worrying patient. Linsley and Lawrence (2007) found large firms' annual reports to display a very low readability level when it came to communicating risks to the public. Similarly, Bournois and Point (2006) found that commentary letters from CEOs in annual reports themselves contain a high level of obfuscation regarding imminent losses, future profits and confidence. Rutherford (2003) produced similar findings when he studied extensively the textual complexity of Operating and Financial Reviews (OFR). Kono (2006) saw in obfuscation a core mechanism of modern democracies. In his study of trade policies of 75 countries, Kono found that democracy promotes 'optimal obfuscation' by forcing policy makers to a more acute management of transparency, which mostly relies on sophisticated obfuscation of communications to trade partners.

The use of obfuscation in strategic alliances rose steadily with the generalization of 'obfuscated codes' in software development. Coping with a weak legal intellectual protection for software, many large software firms started to obfuscate their source codes before integrating them into commercial products, or when leading co-developments with partners that could be, or become, competitors. Obfuscation allows the maintenance of a paradoxical alliance by preventing opportunistic behavior in shared learning (Larsson *et al.*, 1998). Obfuscated codes allow software to run with the exact same performance as the non-obfuscated version. 'Optimal obfuscation' in international trade negotiations does not prevent commerce relations from growing in volume and profitability. They allow, however, the sharing of critical know-how with a competitor, such as an algorithm to fly a plane at a very low altitude, allowing this competitor to gain learning on low-altitude flights for improvement in other domains, such as aerodynamics, without compromising the balance between cooperation and competition.

Advances in learning require the concentration of knowledge of specific assets, so as to develop rents or cumulate enough experience to take a market lead. Such learning curves consume large shares of companies' R&D investments. Obfuscated sharing allows continuing development and the acquisition of knowledge rents. Advantageously, the use of obfuscating strategies does not imply that the sharing firm needs to impose causal ambiguity on itself. Causal ambiguity has been defined by Lippman and Rumelt (1982) as a coincidental or deliberate retention of knowledge 'concerning the nature of the causal connections between actions and results', which can include uncertainty 'as to what factors are responsible for superior (or inferior) performance' (Lippman and Rumelt, 1982: 420). While causality cannot be established in an obfuscated code, its transformation is simply based on the addition of artificial and placebo complexity that performs its application at the same level of performance, and does not prevent the buyer from using the code, nor from eventually inspecting the obfuscated code.

Obfuscation techniques were not developed with collaboration in mind. The technique has a long history that began with the birth of ancient societies. Detienne and Vernant (1991) have described how duplicity of meaning and deed constitutes the architecture of *mêtis*, know-how or cunning that allowed Greek heroes to defeat their enemies by design, not brute force.

More recently, Lin Foxhall (2007: 107) described how olive tree growers in Ancient Greece used obfuscation in order to deter imitation or conceal the real usage of their land from the jurors of their jurisdiction when in dispute with their neighbors. Hence, narrative obfuscation was frequently used in Ancient Greece, playing with a language that allows puns, word play and versatility of sense making. While obfuscation has a long history, it never achieved the perfection that software technologies have brought to this technique, that is to say to achieve a perfect duality, a perfect dissociation between intelligibility and functional authenticity.

2. EXAMPLES FROM THE TELECOMMUNICATION AND MEDIA INDUSTRY

In the previous paragraphs, we saw that signalling is essential to coopetitive collaboration as it reduces the mutual temptation for opportunistic behavior between the involved partners. Borrowing from ecology and ethology, we induced that excessive learning impedes the performance of coopetitive arrangements, because it increases tensions and antagonistic learning. Observing ape behavior, we inclined towards a proposition that 'redirected activity' may play a central mechanism in avoiding direct confrontation between two firms in a coopetitive dyad. Following Schelling (1960), we inferred that weathering out a problematic relation in a coopetitive dyad involves 'taking hints' on the competition, a deed impractical and hardly realizable with discretion. Investigating the need for discretion and distracting attention further, we learned from Ocasio (1997) that firms constantly arbitrate in a trade-off between conformity with the dyadic partner (mimetic isomorphism) and individualistic search. The problem was then to find a solution to 'sharing without sharing', 'cooperating without cooperating', and 'competing without competing'. We finally discovered that modern obfuscation techniques were used in Ancient Greece for this exact purpose between olive tree growers, forced to cooperate with other farmers, but protecting their farming techniques by obfuscating their disclosure using the versatility of the Greek language (Foxhall, 2007). In other words, obfuscation allows the mediation of destructive signalling by drowning antagonistic learning within a placebic set of sharable information.

Telecommunication is a coopetitive industry. The rise of digital technologies in its infrastructures and service production led the industry towards complex arrangements, with multi-level competition and cooperation at different layers of the service delivery. For example, Apple Inc. delivers digital music through its online digital stores iTunes. The revenue model of the online store is mimetic and symbiotic with the historical economic model of the music publishing industry. Apple Inc. ensured a proper signalling policy towards the Recording Industry Association of America (RIAA) by adopting a pricing structure that respects digital rights management and the historical economic model of this industry. Although this precaution sent the right signal to the recording industry, Apple Inc. rapidly collected 'asymmetrical informational gains' (see Figure 4.2) by capturing most of the attention share of the customer, and developing an in-depth understanding of consumer behavior that the Cupertino firm did not share with its 'coopetitors' in the recording industry.

Although the delivery system used by Apple seems transparent to its coopetitors, it is highly obfuscated. Algorithms used for the display of customer preferences and recommendation engines are proprietary to Apple Inc., and not shared with the recording industry. Even if the whole economic model was readable and understandable by the recording industry, the meaning of the change introduced by the system was inherently concealed to the recording industry, which in good faith pursued this deadly cooperation with the Cupertino firm. While the recording industry was steadily losing market shares in 2003–2008, Apple Inc. gained exceptional growth. Obfuscation created a long-term strategic advantage for the firm that grasped most of the attention share of the customers.

Not all winning strategies imply the establishment of a symbiotic agreement with the 'coopetitors'. New entrants can also adopt parasitism by stealing the attention share from the main incumbent and developing the same strategy that we described in relation to Apple Inc. The 'LastFM' venture is an exemplar of such a strategy. LastFM is an Internet radio. Because it uses the right to broadcast without recording digital music, the firm has obfuscated one major legal backdrop in order to enter this coopetitive market. Pursuing a parasitic strategy, LastFM is both a website platform and a software component that self-instals within the iTunes platform. When installed, the software 'listens' to music played by the user and records its consumption of digital music on any media: on the computer itself, on the digital music player iPod, and on multiple others.

Users have already nicknamed this 'scrobbling'. Scrobbling is the act of constantly recording one's preferences in order to re-use the accumulated learning in another functional environment. For instance, users can go hiking for many hours, listening to their portable music, and when returning home, connect their portable music player, such as an iPod, and upload the chronology of the listening, both to the iTunes software, and directly to the LastFM database. The LastFM software will then upload the entire library and its evolution to its own central databases. Of course, once this library is present on LastFM server, the company can provide a 'radio' that plays authors and composers present in the iTunes platform. But it can also do more. Because many customers are 'scrobbling' and sending their accumulated learning to the LastFM platform, the firm accumulates their learning and can use sophisticated collaborative technologies to create a new learning available for each customer: a powerful recommendation engine that can help customers extend their primary musical tastes to new authors and composers. LastFM's strategy is an exemplar of the use of obfuscation to gain an asymmetric advantage in a coopetitive arrangement. Similarly to the trick played by Apple Inc. on the recording industry, LastFM is implementing an obfuscated routine within the platform of its 'coopetitor': it delivers transparently a legal function (listing in a database what the customer listens to), but beyond this placebo 'façade', pursues the creation of valuable meaning, which in turn becomes the core of its economic model. After its significant success in grabbing attention share, LastFM was acquired by the CBS Corporation. Hence, it has become a core instrument of coopetition between the CBS group, owning and publishing content, and the Apple platform, distributing that content.

Obfuscation is also a core mechanism in another firm at the center of a coopetitive ecosystem: Google from Mountain View, CA. By listening to customer behavior at multiple points (search engine, electronic mail, electronic geographic software), the firm has developed a convergent and obfuscated learning infrastructure which allows it to operate an antagonistic learning, usually not tolerated by users when visible, and to bring back the fruit of this learning directly in its economic model. When the customer has the means to identify the obfuscation, the technology is indeed rejected. Although its performance was superior to most built-in search engines, the Google Desktop solution never succeeded in gaining a commensurate market share. The problem was that this application 'calls home' frequently, that is, it repatriates its obfuscated learning to the main servers of the firm for further exploitation. Although customers do not see and do not understand what learning is taking place, they can still detect that an unauthorized outgoing communication is happening, usually blocked by specialized software such as a firewall.

'Obfuscated learning' and 'obfuscated components' are not provided in disguise. They do not constitute a violation of the law. However, the sophistication of modern obfuscation techniques make it very improbable for a partner in a coopetitive arrangement to be certain that the announced and visible functionalities are truly the ones performed. Hence, like the gorilla which cannot decided if the invitation is an aggression or a collaboration, firms are forced to 'take a hint', either by redirecting aggression as a means of signalling, or by blurring, or bluffing, the obfuscated learning that accompanies the collaboration. Such a case occurred when the 'inhabitants' of Second Life, a large persistent virtual world where users develop replicas or phantasmagoric versions of reality, discovered that the owner of the company, Philip Rosedale, known as Philip Linden in the virtual world, was also a main component in the virtual world's regulation. Second Life is a coopetitive environment, whose organization and development is shared between its inhabitants (and customers of Linden Labs) and Linden Labs itself, which owns the architecture and provides the services.

Originally, the virtual world started as an experiment, and little thought was put into its democratic processes, for Second Life was nothing more than an entertainment platform. As the world grew, it absorbed most of the deviant behaviors of the real world, so the owner of the platform, which is legally liable in the real world, started to impose regulation on behaviors. However, inhabitants compete as much as they cooperate in such a world. They compete for attractive parts of the land, such as isolated islands, as in the real world. They cooperate, as the 'life' of the virtual world depends on a minimal cooperation and game play. Linden Labs, no doubt with the intent of 'doing good', started to apply discretionary and obfuscated sanctions to deviant inhabitants who might have decided that laws 'from the outside' could not be applied in a virtual and phantasmagoric world. As long as the various interventions were obfuscated, the virtual world continued to grow, with little disturbance of its precarious coopetitive equilibrium. But mistakes were made. And harmony was gone: 'redirected aggression' took place in many forms: inhabitants started to own and run 'independent press', both in the virtual world and in the real world. Democratic rules were requested. A supplier of electronic voting systems from the real world was suggested in good faith by the Labs, but the inhabitants redirected most of their aggression on the supplier, and then on the founder of the virtual world. Excessive discretion and lack of discretion both contributed to an unbalanced ecosystem, riddled with conflicts.

In the three above examples, obfuscated learning serves the purpose of mitigating coopetition. In the LastFM case study, the obfuscated learning allowed the firm to benefit from the iTunes platform without infringing copyright laws, while obtaining its own learning grounded in another learning ecosystem. Interestingly, on LastFM's own platform, the songs of the 'discovered' new music artists can be purchased through other vendors, in direct competition with iTunes, but cannot be purchased on the iTunes platform. Apple Inc. introduced its own recommendation engine in September 2008 but this has an intrinsically poorer performance as it sources its learning in its own closed ecosystem.

The Second Life case study is different. Obfuscated learning was made explicit as Linden Labs was struggling with a rapid growth of petty criminality in its virtual environment. Explicit and direct discretion was exerted, not without humor by, for instance, building a virtual jail inspired by the final chapter of Philip K. Dick's *Substance Death,* that is, a never-ending field where inhabitants are forced to drive a virtual tractor until completion of their sanction. Here we discover that tolerance of obfuscated learning strategies by customers plays a central role in maintaining a coopetitive environment perceived as well balanced and fair by users. Google Inc. experienced similar difficulties when customers groups claimed than a ten-year archive of their learning was an exaggerated measure, and was not justified by the delivery of services. The firm from Mountain View agreed to revise its recording process, and subsequently moved its obfuscated learning strategies into other domains such as geo-location and the creation of its own web browser, where it can operate freely a range of various obfuscated learning devices.

3. TOWARDS A THEORY OF OBFUSCATED COOPERATION

Coopetition is an emerging paradigm. The combination of globalization and commoditization forces firms to integrate more and more generic components from competitors into the assembly of their offers to customers. The quest for larger market coverage also induces firms to share a coopetitive space facing a single customer, such as the iTunes platform. In our investigation, we compared coopetitive dyadic situations, such as a reciprocal adverse selection inspired by the works of Akerlof (1970), Spence (1973) and Stiglitz (1975). We first concluded that such a configuration would lead the coopetitive dyadic partners to deploy parallel learning mechanisms in order to obtain asymmetric learning gains 'bypassing' their fair collaboration agreement with their coopetitors (Figure 4.2). Inspired by the practices of Ancient Greek olive tree growers (Foxhall, 2007), we then suggested that competing and cooperating within the same learning system was possible if both learning devices were mutually obfuscated. In doing so, the coopetitive firm is still signalling a 'fair behavior', or at least a legal behavior, to other members of the coopetitive platform, but can at the same time build its own discretionary learning (see Figure 4.3).

Several authors have proposed typologies of coopetitive strategies; notably, Dagnino and Padula (2009) suggested distinguishing simple dyadic coopetition from complex network coopetition by differentiating the level of interfirm relations (macro, meso, micro) and respective

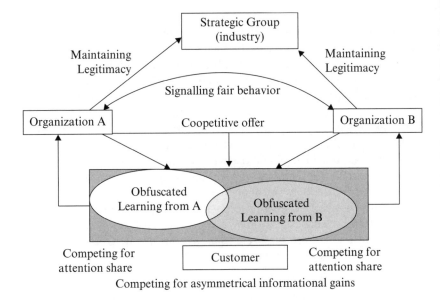

Figure 4.3   Obfuscated learning in coopetitive spaces

gains in terms of knowledge and economic value. Likewise, we would like to propose several categories of learning strategies within a coopetitive framework. These categories do not represent a finding, but rather probable alleys of empirical research that may contribute to a more structured study of coopetitive management of growth and innovation.

3.1   Mixed Motive Cooperation, Benevolence and Contrition (RSTL)

The first generic learning strategy we propose is situated within the classic context of perfect competition, perfect information and mutual transparency behavior. Such contexts are traditional to laboratory experiments of game theorists. We call this strategy 'reciprocal symmetric transparent learning' (RSTL, see Table 4.1). In such a context, the market regulates competition (Clifton, 1977), and 'players' accommodate their behavior in order to win over the cooperative dynamics. The learning strategy is hence transparent, and it aims to obtain from the partner, by the symmetric games of dissuasion, persuasion and conviction, an expected behavior.

When information circulates freely amongst partners, corrective actions are taken on the behavioral determinants of the interaction. Partners use signalling intensively (Spence, 1973; Robertson *et al.*, 1995), but signals easily get jammed and misunderstood. Coopetition hence depends heavily

Table 4.1   A proposed typology of learning strategies

Generic Strategies	Competition	Cooperation	Coopetition
RSTL Reciprocal Symmetric Transparent Learning (Both parties learn, shared outputs)	Perfect competition and perfect information market competition (Clifton, 1977).	Mutual benevolence and early signalling create cooperative learning gains (Axelrod, 1984).	Tit-for-tat strategies (Axelrod, 1984) and commensalism (Astley and Fombrun, 1983).
AOAL Asymmetric Open Adverse Learning (Both parties need to openly learn in a mutually adverse situation)	Individual adaptation to maintain learning despite adversity (Skinner, 1968; Bence, 1986; Menec *et al.* 1995). Burden of antagonistic learning is borne by subject.	Use of signalling to reduce uncertainty in adverse selection (Stigler, 1961; Akerlof, 1970; Spence, 1973) while balancing discretionary attention and conformity (Ocasio, 1997)	Contingent altruism when cooperation is expensive (Hammond and Axelrod, 2006) and Lorenz's (1966) redirected activity, for example, 'taking a hint' (Schelling, 1960).
NAOL Non-Adverse Obfuscated Learning (One party is learning without disclosure with a non-aggressive purpose)	Use of industry jargon to preserve discretion (Spender, 1989) and obfuscation for selective filtering of audiences (Linsley and Lawrence, 2007).	Cooperation without direct or readable reciprocity (Riolo *et al.* 2001). Obfuscation is used to prevent opportunistic behavior (Larsson *et al.*, 1998).	Obfuscation is used to maintain causal ambiguity (Lippman and Rumelt, 1982) in sharing sensitive components of a cooperative system (for example, olive tree growing: Foxhall, 2007).
COAL Competitive Obfuscated Adverse Learning (One party engages in parasitic adverse non-disclosed learning)	Obfuscated learning has a purpose of cunning (Detienne and Vernant, 1991) or 'parasitism' (Astley and Fombrun, 1983).	Search for an 'optimal obfuscation' (Kono, 2006) allowing cooperation without compromising strategic independence.	Obfuscation is used to disguise antagonistic behavior within a cooperative ecosystem. Limit is tolerance to obfuscation.

upon complex 'tit-for-tat' strategies (Axelrod, 1984). When messages are misunderstood, partners correct them by adding generosity, for example by compensating a losing party once the deal has been won. Vice versa, a partner that has betrayed the fragile gentleman's agreement of coopetition can still engage in cooperation after being punished for his selfish behavior (Wu and Axelrod, 1995). Natural biotopes (Hawley, 1950) and animal packs (Lorenz, 1966) display similar learning strategies. They are, as Axelrod and Dion (1988) noted, used similarly by nations, bats, birds and monkeys.

3.2   Asymmetric Open Adverse Learning (AOAL) Strategies

In a context of free information and a perfect market, one can always walk away from an adverse situation. The expectation, or the inescapable constraint, of an ongoing relationship can dramatically change the perspective. In the various examples we found in the literature, Charles' River rats modify their aversion to shocks in order to continue feeding, and Mosquito fishes over-specialize their hunting strategy, despite individual risks, to protect their feeding regime. Organizations engage in similar antagonistic learning when they face an abrupt change in environmental trends, and decide to develop an adverse learning strategy within their core to accommodate the change. Intel pursued RISC architectures, despite its path dependency on previous architectures. Microsoft developed an Internet browser, despite its path dependency on static operating systems. Apple engaged in DRM-free distribution of digital music, despite its symbiotic economic model based on the defense of digital rights with the RIAA.

These learning strategies are developed openly. Signalling is here used to reduce uncertainty in an adverse selection scheme (Stigler, 1961; Akerlof, 1970). When direct cooperation becomes too expensive, traditional 'tit-for-tat' strategies become inefficient. Hence, firms engage in 'contingent altruism', that is, trying to 'discover ever more minimal conditions for the evolution of altruism' by selecting with parsimony the recipients of temporary favoritism (Hammond and Axelrod, 2006: 333). In reviewing the literature, we found similar behaviors within gorilla packs, when dominant males need to protect their competitive status in the pack, while simultaneously displaying a cooperative stance for mating purposes (Parker *et al.*, 1999). Firms, like gorillas, 'take a hint' (Schelling, 1960), and eventually use redirected aggression as both a signalling and intelligence gathering tactic. We named such strategies: 'asymmetric open adverse learning' (AOAL). There is no concealment. Gorillas are quite explicit about their intents. They are conducted openly. In fact, visibility is key, for all players must clearly see their meaning in terms of direct and indirect reciprocity. They are swift and dynamic. Timing is key, for the gain in asymmetry will only be temporary, as the overall strategy is still pursuing the goal of maintaining ongoing and future relationships. The successful development of the iTunes platform and business model could well be the archetype of such a strategy.

3.3 Obfuscated Learning Strategies: Adverse and Non-Adverse

Our observation of the co-existence of partially cooperative and partially antagonistic partners around the ITunes platform suggests that obfuscation may actually play a major role in handling causal ambiguity and friction in long-lasting coopetition. Non-Adverse Obfuscated Learning (NAOL) has a long history in coopetitive settings. We found examples of obfuscated technical secrets of production in Ancient Greece (Foxhall, 2007), when olive tree growers needed to partially share access to their domains without sharing the specific asset of their regional trade. Spender (1989) gave similar examples of the use of industry jargon which allowed industry peers to cooperate, even when working for competitors. More recently, several works have studied the role of obfuscation in creating 'selective perceptual filtering' in company documents or official communications (Linsley and Lawrence, 2007).

In a cooperative agreement, 'non-adverse' obfuscation is used to prevent opportunistic behavior (Larsson and *et al.*, 1998). As the cooperation has no direct or readable reciprocity, for example in a fast evolving population of temporary partners such as open source communities, partners may try to trigger 'indirect reciprocity . . . when benevolence to one agent increases the chance of receiving help from others' (Riolo *et al.*, 2001: 441). NAOL strategies are indeed quite frequent. Algorithms for low altitude flying, which are essential to the growth of the airline construction industry, are shared between constructors under obfuscation. Obfuscation is not used with an aggressive purpose, but solely to allow the growth of new applications and exploration of new domains, while maintaining causal ambiguity (Lippman and Rumelt, 1982). Technology allows for coopetition where 'no memory of past encounters is required' (Riolo *et al.*, 2001: 441). Hence, instead of adopting a 'sociological' perspective on coopetition, here the technology makes simultaneous cooperation and competition possible between partners who do not need to physically meet and who do not need to question their respective strategic intent; this, finally, defies the resource-based view of coopetitive agreements (see Table 4.1).

The fourth proposed generic learning strategy in a coopetitive environment is 'competitive obfuscated adverse learning' (COAL). The purpose of obfuscation here is still to allow cooperation with a competitor without disclosing discretionary information and trade secrets. But concealment also plays a more competitive role. We observed such a strategy when we analyzed the growth of LastFM within the iTunes platform ecosystem. LastFM achieved a better learning and better recommendations according to users, than the embedded learning engine within its host's platform. Contrary to other Internet radios based on collaborative filtering, such as Pandora, LastFM directly installs an obfuscated routine within the user's ITunes platform, and hence, learns directly from his or her listening habits. This kind of articulation is not per se a parasitic behavior, as LastFM ends up extending the primary demand for digital music by achieving improved discovery and returning demands to the iTunes commercial platform. On the contrary, LastFM performs an 'optimal obfuscation' (Kono, 2006), allowing cooperation without compromising strategic independence (of both partners). The learning strategy that LastFM has to deploy is nevertheless adverse, as it is legally allowed to 'borrow' consumer's preferences with their agreement, but is not allowed any recording or storage on its own platform. As in both Ancient Greek olive tree growing, and examples from Detienne and Vernant (1991), the limit of deployment of such a learning strategy lies in the social tolerance of obfuscation (see Table 4.1).

CONCLUSION

The objective of this chapter was to explore different 'learning strategies' that can make coopetition possible and profitable for partners. Our inquiry started by examining the corrective behaviors (generosity, contrition, signaling of good faith, signalling of conventions and so on) that are deployed by coopetitive partners to weather the ambiguities and tensions of paradoxical simultaneous cooperation and competition. We learned from game theory (Axelrod, 1984) that appropriate signalling can induce partners to maintain a paradoxical agreement, and eventually for one of those partners to triumph over it. In a second step, we examined the role of knowledge within the coopetitive interaction. Looking at classic works of biology (Hawley, 1950), etiology (Lorenz, 1966) and economics (Akerlof, 1970), we hypothesized that discretion and transparency could be achieved simultaneously, thus diminishing the need for corrective signalling. We found various examples of 'obfuscated processes' in the telecommunications and media industry, that is, cooperative processes where meaning is concealed but authenticity and functionality preserved. We then synthesized these discoveries into four proposed 'generic' learning strategies that may be used to sustain, or triumph over a coopetition.

These propositions trigger many questions. First, the apparent paradox of competing and collaborating at the same time can be set aside, as obfuscated learning does not threaten the balance of coopetitive agreements. Second, the use of obfuscated learning strategies can displace and distort situations that can be read, at first glance, as pure coopetitive archetypes. The case study of LastFM is exemplar: the firm is sourcing its customer base within the platform of its competitor, but then creates a totally different ecosystem based on the discovery of 'unknown unknowns' (artists that the user did not know about), yielding its profits from the discovery function. While the presence of LastFM within the iTunes platform seems symbiotic in its façade, it is indeed a rather antagonistic learning and strategy. Third, studies of coopetition generally assume that knowledge and learning possess the same ontology for both partners in a coopetitive agreement. This assumption over-emphasizes the paradox of the arrangement, overlooking the fact that coopetitive ecosystems can indeed develop a harmonious growth without hurting partners. Fourth, most studies of coopetition focus on the managerial skills that allow for a better management of the tension between competition and cooperation, while obfuscated learning strategies underline the role of economic and technological design in the sustainability of coopetitive economics.

REFERENCES

Akerlof, G.A. (1970), 'The Market for "Lemons": Quality Uncertainty and the Market Mechanism', *Quarterly Journal of Economics*, **84**(3), 488–500.

Astley W.G. and C.J. Fombrun (1983), 'Collective Strategy: Social Ecology of Organizational Environments', *Academy of Management Review*, **8**(4), 576–587.

Axelrod, R. (1984), *The Evolution of Cooperation*, New York: Basic Books.

Axelrod, R. and D. Dion (1988), 'The Further Evolution of Cooperation', *Science*, **242**(9) 1385–1390.

Baumard, P. (2008), 'An Asymmetric Perspective on Coopetitive Strategies', *International Journal of Entrepreneurship and Small Business*, **8**(1), 6–22.

Bence, J.R. (1986), 'Feeding Rate and Attack Specialization: The Roles of Predator Experience and Energetic Tradeoffs', *Environmental Biology of Fishes*, **16**(1–3), 113–121.

Bournois, F. and S.P. Point (2006), 'A Letter from the President: Seduction, Charm and Obfuscation in French CEO Letters', *Journal of Business Strategy*, **27**(6), 46–55.

Brandenburger, A.M. and B.J. Nalebuff (1996), *Coopetition*, New York: Doubleday.

Burkhardt R. (2005), *Patterns of Behavior: Konrad Lorenz, Niko Tinbergen, and the Founding of Ethology*, Chicago: University of Chicago Press.

Clifton, J.A. (1977), 'Competition and the Evolution of the Capitalist Mode of Production', *Cambridge Journal of Economics*, **1**(2), 137–151.

Dagnino, G.B. and G. Padula (2009), 'Coopetition Strategy: A New Kind of Interfirm Dynamics for Value Creation', in G.B. Dagnino and E. Rocco (Eds), *Coopetition Strategy: Theory Experiments and Cases*, London: Routledge.

DePaulo, B.J. (1988), 'Research on Deception in Marketing Communications: Its Relevance to the Study of Nonverbal Behavior', *Journal of Nonverbal Behavior*, **12**(4), 253–273.

Detienne, Marcel and Jean-Pierre Vernant (1991), *Cunning Intelligence in Greek Culture and Society*, Trans. Janet Lloyd, Chicago: University of Chicago Press.

Foxhall, L. (2007), *Olive Cultivation in Ancient Greece: Seeking the Ancient Economy*, Oxford: Oxford University Press.

Grandori, A. and M. Neri (1999), 'The Fairness Properties of Interfirm Networks', in A. Grandori (Ed.), *Inter-Firm Networks*, London: Routledge.

Hammond R.A. and R. Axelrod (2006) 'Evolution of Contingent Altruism when Cooperation is Expensive', *Theoretical Population Biology*, **69**, 333–338.

Hawley, A.H. (1950). *Human Ecology: A Theory of Community Structure*, New York: The Ronald Press Company.

Kiesler, S. and L. Sproull (1982) 'Managerial Responses to Changing Environments: Perspectives on Problem Sensing from Social Cognition', *Administrative Science Quarterly*, **27**, 548–570.

Kono, D. (2006), 'Optimal Obfuscation: Democracy and Trade Policy Transparency', *American Political Science Review*, **100**(3), 369–384.

Krane, R.V. and A.R. Wagner (1975), 'Taste Aversion Learning with a Delayed Shock: Implications for the Generality of the Laws of Learning', *Journal of Comparative and Physiological Psychology*, **88**(2), pp. 882–889.

Larsson, R., L. Bengtsson, K. Henriksson and J. Sparks (1998) 'The Interorganizational Learning Dilemma: Collective Knowledge Development in Strategic Alliances', *Organization Science*, **9**(3), 285–305.

Lehrman, D.S. (1953) 'A Critique of Konrad Lorenz' Theory of Instinctive Behavior', *Quarterly Review of Biology*, **298**, 337–363.

Lewis, D. (1969), *Convention: A Philosophical Study*, Cambridge, MA: Harvard University Press.

Linsley, P.M. and M. Lawrence (2007), 'Risk Reporting by the Largest UK Companies: Readability and Lack of Obfuscation', *Accounting, Auditing and Accountability Journal*, **20**(4), 620–627.

Lippman, S.A. and D.P. Rumelt (1982), 'Uncertain Imitability: An Analysis of Interfirm Differences in Efficiency Under Competition', *The Bell Journal of Economics*, **13**(2), 418–438.

Lorenz, K. (1966), *On Aggression* (Das Sogenannte Böse zur Naturgeschichte der Aggression), San Diego: Harcourt, Brace & Co.

Lorenz, K. (1970), *Studies in Animal and Human Behavior*, Vols I and II, Cambridge, MA: Harvard University Press.

Mariani, M.M. (2007), 'Coopetition as an Emergent Strategy: Empirical Evidence from an Italian Consortium of Opera Houses', *International Studies of Management and Organization*, **37**(2), 97–126.

McKelvey, B. (1982), *Organizational Systematics: Taxonomy, Evolution, Classification*, Berkeley: University of California Press.

Menec, V.H., R.P. Perry and C.W. Struthers (1995), 'The Effect of Adverse

Learning Conditions on Action-Oriented and State-Oriented College Students', *Journal of Experimental Education*, **63**, 281–299.

Mesterton-Gibbons, M. and E.S. Adams (1998), 'Animal Contests as Evolutionary Games', *American Scientist*, **86**, 334–341.

Nelson, R.R. and S.G. Winter (1982), *An Evolutionary Theory of Economic Change*, Cambridge, MA: Harvard University Press.

Ocasio, W. (1995), 'The Enactment of Economic Adversity: A Reconciliation of Theories of Failure-Induced Change and Threat-Rigidity', *Research in Organizational Behavior*, **17**, 287–331.

Ocasio W. (1997), 'Towards an Attention-Based View of the Firm', *Strategic Management Journal*, **18**, 187–206.

Parker, S.T., R.W. Mitchell and H.L. Miles (Eds) (1999) *The Mentalities of Gorillas and Orangutans in Comparative Perspective*, Cambridge: Cambridge University Press.

Piaget, J. (1972). *To Understand Is To Invent*, New York: The Viking Press, Inc.

Riolo, R., M.D. Cohen and R. Axelrod (2001), 'Evolution of Cooperation without Reciprocity', *Nature*, **414**(22), 441–443.

Robertson T.S., J. Eliashberg and Talia Rymon (1995), 'New Product Announcement Signals and Incumbent Reactions', *Journal of Marketing*, **59**(July), 1–15.

Rutherford, B. (2003), 'Obfuscation, Textual Complexity and the Role of Regulated Narrative Accounting Disclosure in Corporate Governance', *Journal of Management and Governance*, **7**(2), 187–210.

Schelling, Thomas C. (1960), *The Strategy of Conflict*. Cambridge, MA: Harvard University Press.

Simon, H. (1947), *Administrative Behavior*, New York: Macmillan.

Simon, H. (1995), 'A Behavioral Model of Rational Choice', *Quarterly Journal of Economics*, **69**, 99–118.

Skinner, B.F. (1968), *The Technology of Teaching*, New York: Appleton-Century-Crofts.

Spence, A.M. (1973), 'Job Market Signaling', *Quarterly Journal of Economics*, **87**(3), 355–374.

Spender, J.C. (1989), *Industry Recipes: An Enquiry into the Nature and Sources of Managerial Judgment*, Oxford: Basil Blackwell.

Starbuck, W.H., M.L Barnett, and P. Baumard (2008), 'Payoffs and Pitfalls of Strategic Learning', *Journal of Economic Behavior and Organization*, **66**(1), 7–21

Staw, B.M., L.E. Sandelands and J.E. Dutton (1981), 'Threat-Rigidity Effects in Organizational Behavior: A Multilevel Analysis', *Administrative Science Quarterly*, **26**, 501–524.

Stigler, George J. (1961), 'The Economics of Information', *Journal of Political Economy*, **69**(3), 213–225.

Stiglitz, J.E. (1975), 'The Theory of Screening, Education and the Distribution of Income', *American Economic Review*, **65**(3), 283–300.

Wu, J. and R. Axelrod (1995) 'How to Cope with Noise in the Iterated Prisoner's Dilemma', *Journal of Conflict Resolution*, **39**, 183–189.

PART II

Coopetition strategy in multiple contexts

5. Coopetitive value creation in entrepreneurial contexts: the case of AlmaCube

**Giovanni Battista Dagnino and
Marcello Mariani**

INTRODUCTION

In the burgeoning coopetition strategy literature, scant attention has been paid so far to the role of the coopetitive system of value creation in entrepreneurial contexts. With the aim of epitomizing such a system, we draw attention to the fact that coopetition does not simply emerge from coupling competition and cooperation issues, but rather, it implies that cooperation and competition merge together to form a new kind of strategic interdependence between firms. Accordingly, coopetition strategy concerns interfirm strategy that allows the firms involved to manage a partially convergent interest and goal structure and to create value by means of coopetitive advantage.

Drawing on a parsimonious set of theoretical antecedents (Dagnino and Padula, 2002; Dagnino and Mariani, 2007; Padula and Dagnino, 2007), this paper elaborates a comprehensive framework in which the emergence of coopetition is linked to the configuration process of entrepreneurial strategies. In more detail, the paper focuses on the strategic role of the entrepreneurial firm in bridging the gap between the capability space and the opportunity space, by characterizing entrepreneurial coopetitive strategies according to the required objectives of execution versus innovation. Consequently, we show how coopetition can be the appropriate spark to initiate value creation in early stage entrepreneurial contexts, where entrepreneurial initiatives have to select their strategic courses of action by capturing the right well-timed opportunities, frequently making use of a limited capability base. A few business mini-cases extracted from the initiatives incubated and developed within AlmaCube illustrate how coopetitive analysis can be supportive of entrepreneurial strategies under the budding regime of coopetition. AlmaCube is a technological incubator established and run by the University of Bologna in Italy, where coopetition (competition in financial and marketing means and cooperation in infrastructure and common knowledge base) emerges in early entrepreneurial contexts. Finally, the notion of entrepreneurial coopetitive strategy, where the entrepreneurial actors involved interact coopetitively, is introduced and depicted as an appealing concept effective in recognizing the potential for creating and sustaining coopetitive value creation in young entrepreneurial contexts.

In order to exemplify the role of coopetitive value creation in entrepreneurial contexts, this chapter is structured into four sections. In section one, the three main theoretical antecedents of this work are illustrated (that is, the definition of strategy as a dynamic process of gap bridging between the capability space and the opportunity space, the concept of a coopetitive system of value creation, and the importance of cooperation in entrepreneurial and uncertain contexts); the research questions are also introduced. In section two, a specific nuance of the strategic process of gap bridging between capabilities and business opportunities is formalized with reference to coopetitive strategies. Accordingly, the concept of coopetitive gap bridging is introduced, illustrated and discussed with specific reference to entrepreneurial-driven strategies. Section three provides a description of coopetitive gap bridging in early stage entrepreneurial contexts by means of empirical examples drawn from Italian university-based business ventures that were later spun off. The final section proposes a few theoretical implications and suggests new itineraries for further research on coopetitive strategy in young entrepreneurial contexts.

1. THEORETICAL BACKGROUND

How can coopetitive strategies emerge and be leveraged in entrepreneurial contexts? What are their major features? In order to tackle these questions, it is fundamental to recall several theoretical concepts that may serve as foundation stones upon which our analysis will be developed.

First, it is relevant to call to mind the crucial role firm capabilities play in seizing strategic opportunities. As clarified in extant strategy literature (Dagnino, 2003; Dagnino and Mariani, 2007), firm strategy can be seen as a fundamentally dynamic process directed towards bridging the strategy gap between the capability space (CS) and the opportunity space (OS) over time. More specifically, firm capabilities (Langlois, 1995; Teece *et al.*, 1997; Capron and Mitchell, 1998; Eisenhardt and Martin, 2000; Zollo and Winter, 2002) – be they operational or dynamic (Helfat and Peteraf,

2003) – are undertaken and deployed to seize the strategic opportunities (Kirzner, 1997; Winter, Fang and Denrell, 2003) that the firm is able to perceive (Penrose, 1959; Miller, 2003) in the opportunity space.

Both spaces are coevolutionary in nature (Lewin and Volberda, 1999; Murmann, 2003) and display the property of feedforward (Levinthal and Myatt, 1994; Dagnino, 2003). Moreover, firm capabilities display their own individual lifecycle (Helfat and Peteraf, 2003), which in turn influences the modal capability lifecycle of the firm (Mariani and Dagnino, 2007), thus determining different degrees of effectiveness of strategic gap closure and, in the end, in the overall process of formulation and implementation of strategy.

The process of strategic gap bridging is influenced by (1) the introduction of an entrepreneurial innovation; and (2) the reduction of the degree of environmental uncertainty. In particular, innovations may initiate new capabilities able to seize opportunities present in the opportunity space and may influence the probability of an actual reduction of the strategy gap to zero, thus inducing either an expansion or a contraction of the realized gap set (RGS). Entrepreneurial innovations can be introduced by universities and leading research centers which create new businesses (Roberts and Peters, 1981; Sobocinski, 1999). While neglected until the mid-1980s, in the last two decades, the role of universities in incubating and supporting newly founded companies has received increasing attention (Cooper, 1985; George *et al.*, 2000). More specifically, this burgeoning number of entrepreneurship centers and incubators established by universities helps entrepreneurs to develop business plans, provides space for their operations and offers guidance on effective technology commercialization (Zahra and Hayton, 2004).

Extant literature has paid careful attention to:

- inter-organizational relationships such as: strategic alliances; cooperative research arrangements such as R&D consortia; industry–university collaborative arrangements; strategic alliances that include marketing or product development partnerships; equity joint ventures; and technology licensing arrangements (Hitt *et al.*, 2000; Das and Teng, 2001; Oliver, 2001; Zahra and George, 2002);
- R&D consortia that are a specialized form of alliance and, more specifically, non-equity agreements among two or more firms where all partners share the costs and results of R&D (Doz *et al.*, 2000; Barnett *et al.*, 2000);
- industry–university collaborative arrangements leading to university spin-offs (Nicolau and Birley, 2003), licensing arrangements (Shane, 2002) and cooperative industry–university alliances.

Our analysis seeks to focus on the strategic gap bridging in such entrepreneurial contexts as the ones cultivated by universities. More specifically, Doz *et al.* (2000) demonstrated the formation process of R&D consortia: they may either emerge naturally or, instead, result from the intervention of some triggering entity. The emergent forms are a consequence of the identification by members of common interests and shared external threats such as the emergence of new technologies, new competitors from abroad, or new governmental interventions. These consortia are likely to be composed of firms from the same or similar industries. In contrast, triggered or engineered forms of consortia are shaped in response to some organizational catalyst, such as a trade association or governmental agency (for example, the National Science Foundation). These consortia will frequently be composed of members from diverse industries actually lacking a common strategic agenda. A second feature of consortia emphasizes the purpose for which they are actually formed (Barnett, Mischke and Ocasio, 2000). While some consortia take shape for quite highly specific purposes, such as the development of technology standards, others conversely exist essentially to explore basic pre-competitive research.

In fact, not all strategies in entrepreneurial contexts and, as a consequence, strategic gap bridging processes, are equal. In many cases, strategic interdependence among firms plays a crucial role (Contractor and Lorange, 1988). More specifically, we can distinguish three relevant situations:

1. a situation where strategic interdependence takes place among firms with a divergent interest and goal structure (that is, the competitive frame of reference);
2. a situation where strategic interdependence takes place among firms with a convergent interest and goal structure (that is, the cooperative frame of reference);
3. a situation where strategic interdependence takes place among firms with a partially convergent interest and goal structure (that is, the coopetitive frame of reference).

The three situations portrayed above are able to engender three comparatively different systems of value creation that are respectively: (a) the competitive system of value creation, (b) the cooperative system of value creation and (c) the coopetitive system of value creation (Dagnino and Padula, 2002).

Building on the premises above, in the next section we shall discuss the concept of the coopetitive system of value creation, originally linking it to the idea of a dynamic gap bridging process.

2. COOPETITIVE STRATEGY AND COOPETITIVE GAP BRIDGING

If we accept the view that firm strategy can be seen as a fundamentally dynamic process directed towards bridging the strategy gap between the capability space and the opportunity space over time (Dagnino, 2003; Dagnino and Mariani, 2007), it is important to characterize competition, cooperation and coopetition on the basis of the gap bridging process between the capability space and the opportunity space.

More specifically, competitive gap bridging takes place when two or more firms (business organizations) with divergent interests and goal structures bridge the CS/OS gap by leveraging their respective capabilities to seize the identical opportunity individually. Cooperative gap bridging takes place when two or more firms (business organizations) with a (totally) convergent interest and goal structure bridge the CS/OS gap by leveraging complementary (or matching) capabilities to seize the same opportunity conjointly. Coopetitive gap bridging takes place when two or more firms (business organizations) with a partially convergent interest and goal structure bridge the CS/OS gap by leveraging complementary capabilities to seize one or more opportunities conjointly while seizing other additional opportunities separately.

Indeed, within coopetitive arrangements, two or more firms (organizations) with a partially convergent interest and goal structure which are conjointly seizing one or more opportunities may also seize additional opportunities independently from each other. An illustration of this idea of coopetitive gap bridging is shown in Figure 5.1. As may be observed from this figure, Firm A and Firm B deploy different capabilities in order to seize the available opportunities: more specifically, Firm A deploys capabilities $C1_A$, $C2_A$, $C3_A$, whereas Firm B deploys capabilities $C1_B$, $C2_B$, $C3_B$, $C4_B$.

In particular, Firms A and B (displaying partially convergent interests and goal structures) coopetitively bridge the CS/OS gap by respectively leveraging the complementary capabilities $C1_A$, $C3_A$ and $C2_B$, $C3_B$, $C4_B$ to seize conjointly opportunity O4, while separately seizing opportunity O10 by means of capabilities $C2_A$ and $C4_B$. A cooperative use of firm capabilities is illustrated by means of a dashed line, whereas a competitive deployment of firm capabilities is exemplified by a dotted-and-dashed line.

In our perspective, a rather disparate collection of eight firm strategy types fall along this continuum. Consistent with Mintzberg and Waters (1985: 270), in Table 5.1 we identify the following strategies: planned, entrepreneurial, ideological, umbrella, process, unconnected, consensus, and imposed.

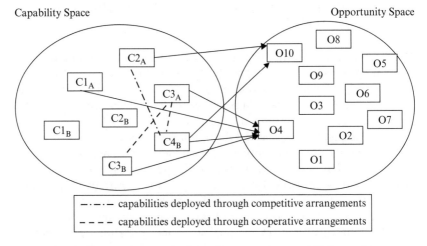

*Figure 5.1   Coopetitive gap bridging between the capabilities and
opportunities of firms A and B at time t*

Drawing on the established typological distinction indicated above, we
can dig more deeply into the concepts of realized gap bridging and realized
gap set as follows:

1. planned gap bridging (PlanGB), which concerns the set of strategy
    gaps that are bridged through planned strategies, can be defined as the
    Planned Gap Set (PlanGS);
2. the entrepreneurial gap bridging (EntrGB) process refers to the strat-
    egy set undertaken by an individual in personal control of an organi-
    zation and successful in imposing his or her specific vision on it. This
    set of strategies (EntrGS) implies the existence of intentions deriving
    from one individual who, nonetheless, in principle does not need to
    formally articulate or elaborate them (because he or she is the 'one
    and only' to run the firm and therefore is not subject to any kind of
    external interference);
3. ideological gap bridging (IdeolGB). At the very basis of this process,
    we can identify the ideological gap set (IdeolGS), including all the
    strategies deployed intentionally, these intentions being organiza-
    tional and not individual as in the case of PlanGS and EntrGS;
4. umbrella gap bridging (UmbrGB). The set of strategies these processes
    are based upon can be defined as the Umbrella Gap Set (UmbrGS);
5. process gap bridging (ProcGB). We can identify a process gap set
    (ProcGS) as the set of strategies designed by the central leadership,
    allowing other actors the flexibility to evolve strategy patterns within it;

6. unconnected gap bridging (UnconGB). The set of strategies on which this bridging process rests can be depicted as an unconnected gap set (UnconGS);
7. consensus gap bridging (ConsGB). The set of strategies that is undertaken in this case is defined as the consensus gap set (ConsGS);
8. imposed gap bridging (ImpGB). This process of gap bridging takes place on the basis of a gap set identifiable as ImpGS.

At the level of the realized gap set (RGS), our decision is to focus especially on the key concept of EntrGS. Our analytical choice reflects our perception of this gap set as the most essential and critical for framing the firms' evolutionary paths and most significant with regard to the coevolutionary matching of capability space and opportunity space in entrepreneurial contexts (Dagnino and Mariani, 2007). In more detail, we emphasize the essential function and the key role of the individual entrepreneur, who has direct control of his/her firm, effectively imposing his/her specific vision. Accordingly, entrepreneurial gap bridging strategies imply the existence of individual intentions, which will in essence drive the firm's evolution and guide it to thrive (or fail), bridging the capability space and the opportunity space in changing environments. It may be that these entrepreneurial-driven strategies are time and path dependent: for a time, they may be successful in capability–opportunity matching and then become less successful or unsuccessful because of the single entrepreneur's inability to pre-empt or adapt to evolving contextual features. And they are more successful in as much as they follow a predefined path that has in fact epitomized the firm's success previously.

What is important to stress is that, in our case in point, entrepreneurial gap bridging may fundamentally become coopetitive if the gap bridging process occurs when two or more entrepreneurs with partially convergent interest and goal structures bridge the CS/OS gap by leveraging matching capabilities in order to seize jointly one or more opportunities while separately grabbing others. This may potentially and incrementally demonstrate intriguing and distinctive characteristics in the context of nascent entrepreneurial ventures, as we shall empirically exhibit in detail in the next section.

3. COOPETITIVE GAP BRIDGING IN EARLY STAGE ENTREPRENEURIAL CONTEXTS

In this section we provide an explanation of coopetitive gap bridging in young entrepreneurial contexts by using a set of real business examples

Table 5.1   A comprehensive description of strategy types

STRATEGY	MAJOR FEATURES
Planned	Strategies originate in formal plans: precise intentions exist, formulated and articulated by central leadership, backed up by formal controls to ensure surprise-free implementation in a benign, controllable or predictable environment; strategy is mostly deliberate
Entrepreneurial	Strategies originate in a central vision: intentions exist as the personal, unarticulated vision of single leaders, and thus are adaptable to new opportunities; organizations are under the personal control of the leaders and located in protected niche environments; strategy is relatively deliberate but can be emergent
Ideological	Strategies originate in shared beliefs: intentions exist as collective vision of all actors in inspirational form, and are relatively immutable, controlled normatively through indoctrination and/ or socialization; organizations are often proactive vis-à-vis the environment; strategy is quite deliberate
Umbrella	Strategies originate under constraints: the leadership is in partial control of organizational actions, and defines strategic boundaries or targets within which the other actors respond to their own forces or to complex and perhaps also unpredictable environments; strategy is partly deliberate, partly emergent and partly deliberately emergent
Process	Strategies originate in process: the leadership controls the process aspects of strategy (hiring, structure and so on), leaving the content aspects to the other actors; strategy is partly deliberate, partly emergent (and, again, partly deliberately emergent)
Unconnected	Strategies originate in enclaves: the actor(s) are loosely coupled to the rest of the organization, and produce(s) patterns of their own actions in the absence of, or in direct contradiction to the central or common intentions; strategy is organizationally emergent whether or not deliberate for actor(s)
Consensus	Strategies originate in consensus: by means of mutual adjustment, actors converge on patterns that become pervasive in the absence of central or common intentions; strategy is quite emergent
Imposed	Strategies originate in the environment: the environment dictates the patterns of actions, either through direct imposition, or through implicitly pre-empting or bounding organizational choices; strategy is mostly emergent, although it may be internalized by organizations and rendered deliberate

Source: Mintzberg and Waters (1985: 270); Dagnino and Mariani (2007: 326)

drawn from Italian university-based business ventures. First we present the underpinnings of the data collection process, then we proceed to the scrutiny of the Start-Cup case, which is based on 50 business venture ideas that were incubated inside AlmaCube, the academic incubator of the University of Bologna in the years 2000–2008.

3.1 Data Collection

An in-depth qualitative approach has been adopted in the present study because it is quite consistent with our exploratory and descriptive aim (Glaser and Strauss 1967; Miles and Huberman 1984; Strauss 1987; Eisenhardt 1989).

The research methodology deployed consists of a few cases with a longitudinal perspective (Pettigrew 1988) and observation. The study of cases is preferable to other research methodologies (such as experiments and questionnaires) (a) when little is known about a phenomenon and current perspectives seem inadequate since they have little empirical substantiation (Eisenhardt 1989) and (b) when we intend to answer questions related to the 'why' and the 'how' of certain aspects or phenomena (Yin 1981, 1984).

The central notion in using cases is to try to develop theory inductively. The theory is emergent in that it is situated in and developed by recognizing patterns of relationships among constructs within and across cases and their underlying logical arguments (Eisenhardt and Graebner, 2007)

The study focuses on coopetitive dynamics in an entrepreneurial context, namely 50 business venture ideas that have been incubated and developed within AlmaCube, the technological incubator established and run by the University of Bologna in Northern Italy. Cofounded jointly with Foundation Cassa di Risparmio in Bologna and Foundation Alma Mater, University of Bologna, to promote and sustain entrepreneurship in the local university system, AlmaCube is closely connected to the Start-Cup business plan competition that takes place each year. AlmaCube offers space and logistic services to young initiatives and start-ups (for example, Internet connections, data communication infrastructures, general services) as well as relational capital through direct links to local economic and political institutions and individual actors. AlmaCube does not participate financially in the hosted business initiatives, but nonetheless actively promotes and facilitates funding contacts and processes with professional investors. AlmaCube regularly hosts the initial phases of the start-up process, but cannot shelter production-related activities or, more generally, the expansion phase of the business. The presence of a start-up in the incubator is initially limited to one year, with possible extension for an additional year. The decision is subject to the discretionary judgment of the AlmaCube Steering Committee.

The fact that we used the entire population of business ideas (50 mini-cases) developed in a specific high-velocity entrepreneurial context, such as the incubator of the University of Bologna, is closely connected to the advantage of studying multiple cases and therefore helps reinforce the consistency and validity of the analysis.

Two main data sources were used in the course of this investigation: (1) semi-structured interviews and (2) archival documents and press accounts.

3.1.1   Semi-structured interviews

Nine interviews were conducted (from June 2007 to March 2008), with the following individuals: three of the founders of the business ideas that were incubated by AlmaCube, one major representative of AlmaCube and two major representatives of Start-Cup (the business plan competition launched by the University of Bologna in 2000).

Because of their position and tenure, these individuals were 'knowledge-able about the issues being researched and able and willing to communicate about them' (Kumar *et al.* 1993) and were, therefore, included in this study. Interviews averaged from 1 to 1.5 hours. They concerned topics such as the processes through which the business ideas were selected for financing and later incubated, and the kind of relationships and linkages that were established between the individuals who had formulated the business ideas during the incubation period. Two researchers conducted all the interviews. Notes were compared after each interview to ensure accuracy and to improve the consistency of the study (Eisenhardt 1989). Moreover, several repeat interviews were conducted (Glaser and Strauss 1967; Gersick 1988). The results of the research were finally tested with the interviewees in order to increase the external validity of the research constructs (Kirk and Miller 1986; Maxwell, 1996).

3.1.2   Archival sources

Published information about the business ideas incubated in AlmaCube was thoroughly reviewed, including press releases, leaflets, pamphlets, Internet matter and materials generated by AlmaCube and the individuals whose businesses were incubated. Detailed information about the business ideas incubated and their main features was found in a handful of AlmaCube's confidential internal reports.

On the whole, multiple sources have allowed the collection of both qualitative and quantitative data (Jick 1979; Miles 1979; Miles and Huberman 1984; Yin 1984), which were analyzed and subjected to a proper triangulation (Kirk and Miller 1986; Eisenhardt 1989). Interestingly, soft data (such as those deriving from semi-structured interviews) have been used to explain and interpret hard data (Mintzberg 1979).

3.2 The Start-Cup Case

The analysis of 50 business venture ideas that were incubated in Almacube, between 2000 and 2008, indicates how many of them (which later became independent start-ups), did actually coopete or compete and cooperate at the same time. We shall examine the cooperation and the coopetition sides of the coin in the paragraphs that follow. However, we first need to underscore that coopetition between and among nascent entrepreneurs is customarily a requisite resource-driven strategy leading to opportunity seizing. This is because early stage entrepreneurs – while generally having detected or created an opportunity – inevitably possess a limited capability base.

On the one hand, they competed over the financial resources that were provided annually to the winners of the Start-Cup competition, the business plan competition initially launched by the University of Bologna in 2001[1] (see, for example, the cases of Ars Srl, Silicon Biosystmes S.p.A and Termocontrol in the year 2000). In some cases, they also competed in the marketplace (especially in marketing activity): see, for example, the cases of Optit Srl and Xelia SNC, two businesses which operate in the ICT industry.

In more detail, it is interesting to note in Table 5.2 that 25 out of 50 business ventures had been winners of the Start-Cup competition. Twenty of them won the Start-Cup award by being placed first, second or third in the competition, while five of them won an intermediate phase of the same competition. In terms of cash awarded, five of the start-ups received less than 5000 euros, while 15 of them received between 5000 and 10000 euros. Three start-ups succeeded in getting more than 10000 euros. Therefore, at least in part, according to the different years in which the contest took place, they actually competed for financial resources.

On the other hand, during the incubation period, and sometimes also when they became start-ups and were later spun off from the university incubator, the entrepreneurs that had submitted their business ideas shared the very same material infrastructure of the incubator (AlmaCube) and also a specific common base of knowledge (knowledge infrastructure).[2] As regards material infrastructure, they shared the office space made available in the same building and the supporting secretarial and IT services offered by AlmaCube as well as the people who were available to support them in their strategic and day-to-day operational decisions.

Table 5.2   AlmaCube monitoring table

NAME	ACTIVITY[1]	Business idea was born inside		
		University or public research center	Private research center/other firm	Other
Silicon Biosystems S.p.A	Biomedical	University of Bologna		
Pro-Gamma Srl	ICT			X
GARWER Srl	Environment and territory	ENEA[3]		
IMAVIS Srl	ICT	University of Bologna – School of Mathematics		
Opere Srl	ICT			X
Termocontrol Srl	Devices, sensors and diagnostics		Private research center	
3WPS Srl	ICT			X
Vortika Srl	ICT			X
Porcari Srl	Meccanica e Automazione			X
WineSquare	ICT			X
Wirelessfuture Srl	ICT		Marconi Foundation	
ComCube Srl	ICT			X
Bioidea Srl	Cosmetics			X
RETINAE Srl	Mechanics and Automation			X, spin-off from a firm

Start Cup		Host incubator	Foundation year	Year 2007		
Winner of the Start Cup competition	Value of award achieved (in Euros)			Turnover (in Euros)	People employed[2]	Number of patents registered
Winner Start cup 2000 – I place	51 000	no	1999	10 000 (production to start in 2008, so far performed research and developed prototypes)	35	
		AlmaCube	1999	500 000	5	
		AlmaCube	2000	100 000	2	
		AlmaCube	2000	230 000	9	
		AlmaCube	2000	150 000	1	
Start Cup 2000 – winner intermediate phase	15 000	no	2000	70 000.00	3	2
		AlmaCube	2001	260 000	3	0
Start Cup 2002–winner intermediate phase	2500	AlmaCube	2001	250 000	4	
Winner Start Cup 2002 – I place	50 000	no	2001	non-active	non-active	non-active
Winner Start Cup 2001 – I place		AlmaCube	2001	non-active	non-active	non-active
		AlmaCube	2001	320 000	6	
Start Cup 2001 – winner intermediate phase	6000	no	2001	120 000	2	
Start Cup 2002–winner intermediate phase	10 000	no	2001	15 000	1	
		AlmaCube	2002	300 000	4	

Table 5.2   (continued)

NAME	ACTIVITY[1]	Business idea was born inside		
		University or public research center	Private research center/other firm	Other
Ergo Consulting Srl	Agribusiness	University of Bologna – School of Engineering		
Nextend Srl	ICT			X
Ars Srl	Chemical and Biochemical	University of Bologna		
Ssyntegrator Srl	ICT			
ENVIS Srl	Environment and territory	ENEA – Section Management of idric resources		
U-SERIES Srl	Environment and territory	ENEA		
CARPE CIBUM SOC. COOP	Agribusiness	University of Bologna – School of Engineering		
Biodec Srl	Biomedical			X
BitBang Srl	ICT			X
Koinema Srl	ICT			X
Sherpa Srl	ICT			X
Neopress Srl	Electronics	University of Bologna		
SCRIBA NANO-TECNOLOGIE Srl	Nanotech	National Research Council		
MAVIGEX Srl	ICT	ARCES – School of Engineering – University of Bologna		
WayMedia Srl	ICT			X
ArcadiaLab Srl	Biomedical	University of Bologna		
Polycrystalline Srl	Chemical and Biochemical	University of Bologna		

Start Cup		Host incubator	Foun-dation year	Year 2007		
Winner of the Start Cup competition	Value of award achieved (in Euros)			Turnover (in Euros)	People employed[2]	Number of patents registered
		AlmaCube	2002	130 000	5	
		AlmaCube	2002	190 000	4	
Winner Start Cup 2000 – II place		no	2002	non-active	non-active	non-active
		AlmaCube	2002	liquidation	liquidation	liquidation
		AlmaCube	2003	200 000	6	
		AlmaCube	2003	340 000	7	
Winner Start Cup 2003 – III place	Zero	AlmaCube	2003	90 000	5	
Start Cup 2001 – winner intermediate phase	2000	AlmaCube	2003	100 000	6	
		AlmaCube	2003	1 000 000	8	
		AlmaCube	2004	220 000	5	
Winner Start Cup 2003 – II place	5000	AlmaCube	2004	liquidation	liquidation	liquidation
Winner Start Cup 2003 – I place	10 000	no	2004	non-active	non-active	non-active
Winner Start Cup 2004 – II place	5000	AlmaCube	2005	450 000	10	15
		AlmaCube	2005	70 000	3	
		AlmaCube	2005	291 300	5	
		AlmaCube	2005	50 000	3	1
Winner Start Cup 2005 – II place	4000	no	2005	350 000	4	

Table 5.2   (continued)

NAME	ACTIVITY[1]	Business idea was born inside		
		University or public research center	Private research center/other firm	Other
Bronteion Srl	ICT	University of Bologna		
Gyro GPS	Electronics	University of Bologna		
PHENBIOX Srl	Pharmaceuticals	Department of Industrial Chemistry and Materials of the University of Bologna		
ANUFA Srl	Environment and territory	University of Bologna		X
WIA Srl	ICT	University – School of Engineering of Cesena		
Econoetica Srl	ICT			X
NAIS Srl	Mechanics and Automation	University of Bologna		
OPTIT Srl	ICT	University of Bologna – School of Engineering		
XELIA SNC	ICT			X
ALBA PROGETTI SOC. COOP.	Environment and territory			X
Mexage Srl	ICT			X
Openliven Srl	ICT			X
Simavian Srl	Electronics			
Protek-consulting	ICT	University of Bologna		

Start Cup		Host incubator	Foundation year	Year 2007		
Winner of the Start Cup competition	Value of award achieved (in Euros)			Turnover (in Euros)	People employed[2]	Number of patents registered
Winner Start Cup 2005 – I place		no	2005	non-active	non-active	non-active
Winner Start Cup 2004 – I place	10000	no	2005	non-active	non-active	non-active
Winner Start Cup 2006 – I place	5000	Almacube	2006	23000	2	
Winner Start Cup 2005 Imola section – I place	8000	Incubator of Imola	2006	30000		
Winner Start Cup 2005 Imola section – II place	4000	Incubator of Imola	2006	20000	5	
		AlmaCube	2006	240000	6	
		AlmaCube	2007	18000	2	
Winner Start Cup 2006 Imola section – I place	5000	Incubator of Imola	2007	30000	3	
Winner Start Cup 2006 Imola section – II place	5000	Incubator of Imola	2007	7000	2	
Winner Start Cup 2006 – Imola section – III place	5000	Incubator of Imola	2007	–	4	
		AlmaCube	2007	0	4	
		AlmaCube	2007	40000	2	
Winner Start Cup 2006 – II place	5000	AlmaCube	2007	0	2	
		AlmaCube	2007	30000	2	

Table 5.2   (continued)

NAME	ACTIVITY[1]	Business idea was born inside		
		University or public research center	Private research center/other firm	Other
ITALIANA SOFTWARE	ICT	University of Bologna – School of Engineering		
WINDESIGN	Environment and territory			X

Notes:
1. Aerospatial; Agri-food; Environment and territory; Devices, sensoring and diagnostic; Architecture and cultural goods; Biomedical; Biotech; Chemical and biochemical; Electronics; Pharmaceutical; ICT; Materials and acoustics; Mechanics and automation; other.
2. Number of people that, with typical and/or atypical contracts, have been in paid employment with the company.
3. ENEA stands for Ente Nazionale per L'Energia Atomica (National Agency for Atomic Energy).

As concerns knowledge infrastructure, two types of social knowledge practices (Polanyi, 1962; Weick and Roberts, 1993; Spender, 1996) were shared: (a) social explicit knowledge or objectified knowledge (Spender, 1996), encompassing shared databases, process manuals and information systems that help to distribute knowledge among incubated businesses (Youndt and Snell, 2004); and (b) social tacit knowledge or collective knowledge (Spender, 1996), including social practices and routines (Nelson and Winter, 1982), such as methods that help employees develop new ideas and innovative approaches that give rise to extra-rational learning processes and contribute to aligning employees and organizational goals (Schiemann, 2006).

4.   FINDINGS

The analysis shows that Bologna's case well exemplifies the dynamics of an entrepreneurial coopetitive game. More specifically it showed entrepreneurs' fierce competition over financial resources in the Start-Cup contest and, concurrently, their deep cooperation in material and knowledge

Start Cup		Host incubator	Foun-dation year	Year 2007		
Winner of the Start Cup competition	Value of award achieved (in Euros)			Turnover (in Euros)	People employed[2]	Number of patents registered
Winner Start Cup 2007 – Imola section – II place	5000	no	2008	–	2	
Winner Start Cup 2007 – Imola section – I place	5000	no	2008	–	3	

infrastructures inside the incubator once they managed to get incubated. As previously stated, the case of AlmaCube is a notable instance of what we term 'entrepreneurial coopetitive gap bridging', which occurs when two (or more) entrepreneurs with partially convergent interests and goal structures match the gap between the capability space and the opportunity space by leveraging the ability to seize one (or more) opportunities jointly, while grabbing other opportunities individually.

On the basis of what we have reported and discussed so far, we introduce the notion of entrepreneurial coopetitive strategy, where the entrepreneurial actors involved interact coopetitively. As we shall argue in the next and final section, in our understanding, this is an engaging concept effective for recognizing the potential for creating and sustaining coopetitive value creation, particularly in young and nascent entrepreneurial contexts.

CONCLUSIONS AND RESEARCH AGENDA

In this chapter we have carefully accounted for and discussed the coopetitive entrepreneurial interaction that occurred inside AlmaCube, the academic incubator of the University of Bologna, between the years 2000 and 2008. A study of 50 business ventures incubated and developed within Almacube, where coopetition (competition in finance and marketing and cooperation in material infrastructure and common knowledge base) emerges in early entrepreneurial contexts, has illustrated how coopetitive analysis can be supportive of entrepreneurial strategies.

Drawing on a parsimonious set of theoretical antecedents (Dagnino and Padula, 2002; Dagnino and Mariani, 2007; Padula and Dagnino, 2007), we have advanced a framework in which the emergence of coopetition is linked to the configuration process of early stage entrepreneurial strategies by entrepreneurs in the pre-incubation and incubation phases. With the aim of detailing a coopetitive system of value creation, we looked at interorganizational entrepreneurial strategies that allow the firms involved to manage a partially convergent interest and goal structure and to create value by means of coopetitive advantage.

The partially convergent structure of interest and goals is epitomized by the fact that, in the case of the AlmaCube new venture ideas, entrepreneurial purposes, while clearly financially unaligned, were in fact consistent from both the material infrastructure and knowledge infrastructure perspectives. Start-ups from AlmaCube that are now competing for the same market or industry had once been incubated by the same university department, where they cooperated with each other by sharing facilities, common services and knowledge practices. Accordingly, we are able to confirm that the AlmaCube story we have told is in essence a story of an early entrepreneurial coopetition strategy for becoming start-ups from both the key financial and infrastructural perspectives. We have also found that the strategy of coopetition relates closely to underlying strategic mechanisms that can favour the growth and affirmation of nascent entrepreneurship.

By clearly exemplifying entrepreneurial coopetitive strategies, entrepreneurial initiatives in bridging the gap between the capability space and the opportunity space play a definite strategic role that is expanding the range of coopetition to early stage entrepreneurship. This study is linked to the recent budding stream of investigation of the interfaces between strategy and entrepreneurship that was termed 'strategic entrepreneurship' (Hitt *et al.*, 2001). Accordingly, in this chapter we have managed to provide some evidence on how coopetition can be the appropriate spark to initiate value creation in very early stage entrepreneurial contexts, whereby entrepreneurs have to select their strategic courses of action by capturing the right well-timed opportunities, frequently making use of a limited capability base.

NOTES

1. This was actually the very first competitive contest for business ideas ever launched by an Italian university.
2. With regard to Table 5.2, it is worth mentioning that 32 start-ups received highly specific academic incubation: 27 of the start-ups were incubated inside AlmaCube, while five of them were in the incubator at Imola.

REFERENCES

Barnett, W.P., G.A. Mischke and W. Ocasio (2000), 'The evolution of collective strategies among organizations', *Organization Studies*, **21**(2), 325–354.
Capron, L. and W. Mitchell (1998), 'Bilateral resource re-deployment and capabilities improvement following horizontal acquisitions', *Industrial and Corporate Change*, **7**(3), 453–484.
Contractor, F.J. and P. Lorange (1988), *Cooperative Strategies in International Business*, Lexington: Lexington Books.
Cooper, A.C. (1985), 'The role of incubator organizations in the founding of growth oriented firms', *Journal of Business Venturing*, **1**, 75–86.
Dagnino, G.B. (2003), *Bridging the strategy gap: Firm strategy and coevolution of capability space and opportunity space*, The Wharton School, Sol C. Snider Center for Entrepreneurial Research, Working Paper 306.
Dagnino, G.B. and M. Mariani (2007), 'Dynamic gap bridging and realized gap set development: The strategic role of the firm in the coevolution of capability space and opportunity space', in U. Cantner and F. Malerba (eds), *Innovation, industrial dynamics and structural transformation: Schumpeterian legacies*. Berlin: Springer.
Dagnino G.B. and G. Padula (2002), 'Coopetition strategy: A new kind of inter-firm dynamics for value creation', Paper presented at the *2nd European Academy of Management Conference*. Stockholm: 9–11 May.
Das, T.K. and B.S. Teng (2001), 'Trust, control and risk in strategic alliances: an integrated framework', *Organization Studies*, **22**(2), 251–283.
Doz, Y.L., P.M. Olk and P.S. Ring (2000), 'Formation processes of R&D consortia: Which path to take? Where does it lead?', *Strategic Management Journal*, **21**(3), 239–266.
Eisenhardt, K.M. (1989), 'Building theory from case study research', *Academy of Management Review*, **14**, 532–550.
Eisenhardt, K.M. and M.E. Graebner (2007), 'Theory building from cases: Opportunities and Challenges', *Academy of Management Journal*, **50**(1), 25–32.
Eisenhardt, K.M. and J.A. Martin (2000), 'Dynamic capabilities: What are they?', *Strategic Management Journal*, **21**(Special Issue 10–11), 1105–1121.
George, G., S. Zahra and D. Wood (2000), 'The effects of business-university alliances on innovative output and financial performance: A study of publicly traded biotechnology companies', *Journal of Business Venturing*, **17**, 557–590.
Gersick, C.J.G. (1988), 'Time and transition in work teams: Toward a new model of group development', *Academy of Management Journal*, **31**(1), 9–41.
Glaser, B.G. and L. Strauss (1967), *The discovery of grounded theory*, Chicago: Aldine Publishing.

Helfat, C.E. and M.A. Peteraf (2003), 'The dynamic resource-based view: Capability lifecycles', *Strategic Management Journal*, **24**(10), 997–1010.

Hitt, M.A., M.T. Dacin, E. Levitas, J.L. Arregle and A. Borza (2000), 'Partner selection in emerging and developed market contexts: Resource-based and organizational learning perspectives', *Academy of Management Journal*, **43**(3), 449–467.

Hitt, M.A., R.D. Ireland, S.M. Camp and D.L. Sexton (2001), 'Guest Editors' introduction to the special issue on strategic entrepreneurship: Entrepreneurial strategies for wealth creation', *Strategic Management Journal*, **22**(6–7), 479–491.

Jick, T. (1979), 'Mixing qualitative and quantitative methods: triangulation in action', *Administrative Science Quarterly*, **24**, 602–611.

Kirk, J. and M. Miller (1986), *Reliability and validity in qualitative research*, Beverley Hills, CA: Sage.

Kirzner, I.M. (1997), 'Entrepreneurial discovery and the competitive market process: An Austrian approach', *Journal of Economic Literature*, **35**(March), 60–85.

Kumar, N., L.W. Stern, and J.C. Anderson (1993), 'Conducting interorganizational research using key-informants', *Academy of Management Journal*, **36**(6), pp.1633–1651.

Langlois, R.N. (1995), 'Capabilities and coherence in firms and markets', in C.A. Montgomery (ed.), *Resource-based and evolutionary theories of the firm: Towards a synthesis*, Boston: Kluwer, pp.71–100.

Levinthal, D. and J. Myatt (1994), 'Co-evolution of capabilities and industry: The evolution of mutual fund processing', Special Issue, *Strategic Management Journal*, **15**(Winter), 45–62.

Lewin, A.Y. and H.W. Volberda (1999), 'Prolegomena on coevolution: A framework for research on strategy and new organizational forms', *Organization Science*, **10**(5), 519–534.

Mariani, M.M. and G.B. Dagnino (2007), 'Unveiling the modal capability lifecycle: the coevolutionary foundations of the firm's effectiveness in capturing strategic opportunities', *International Journal of Learning and Intellectual Capital*, **4**(1/2), 132–46.

Maxwell, J.A. (1996), *Qualitative research design: An interactive approach*, Thousand Oaks, CA: Sage.

Miles, M. (1979), 'Qualitative data as an attractive nuisance: The problem of analysis', *Administrative Science Quarterly*, **24**, 590–601.

Miles, M. and A.M. Huberman (1984), *Qualitative data analysis*, Beverley Hills, CA: Sage.

Miller, D. (2003), 'An asymmetry-based view of advantage: towards an attainable sustainability', *Strategic Management Journal*, **24**(10), 961–976.

Mintzberg, H. (1979), 'An Emerging Strategy of "Direct Research"', *Administrative Science Quarterly*, **24**(4), 580–89.

Mintzberg, H. and W.J. Waters (1985), 'Of Strategies, Deliberate and Emergent', *Strategic Management Journal*, **6**(3), 257–72.

Murmann, J.P. (2003), *Knowledge and competitive advantage: The coevolution of firms, technology, and national institutions in the synthetic dye industry, 1850–1914*, Cambridge, UK: Cambridge University Press.

Nelson, R.R. and S.G. Winter (1982), *An evolutionary theory of economic change*, Cambridge, MA: Belknap Press of Harvard.

Nicolau, N. and S. Birley (2003), 'Academic networks in a trichotomous categorization of university spinouts', *Journal of Business Venturing*, **18**(3), 339–359.

Oliver, A.L. (2001), 'Strategic alliances and the learning life-cycle of biotechnology firms', *Organization Studies*, **22**(3), 467–489.

Padula, G. and G.B. Dagnino (2007), 'Untangling the rise of coopetition: The intrusion of competition in a cooperative game structure', *International Studies of Management and Organization*, **37**(2), 32–52.

Penrose, E.T. (1959), *The theory of the growth of the firm*, New York: John Wiley.

Pettigrew, A.W. (1988), 'Longitudinal field research on change: theory and practice', Paper presented at the National Science Foundation Conference *Longitudinal Science Methods in Organizations*, Austin, TX.

Polanyi, M. (1962), *Personal knowledge: Towards a post-critical philosophy* (corrected ed.), Chicago: University of Chicago Press.

Roberts, E.B. and D.H. Peters (1981), 'Commercial innovation from university faculty', *Research Policy*, **10**, 108–126.

Schiemann, W.A. (2006), 'People equity: A new paradigm for measuring and managing human capital', *Human Resource Planning*, **29**(1), 34–44.

Shane, S. (2002), 'Selling university technology: Patterns from MIT', *Management Science*, **48**(1), 122–137.

Sobocinski, P. (1999), *Creating hi-tech business growth in Winsconsin: University of Winsconsin-Madison technology transfer and entrepreneurship*, Madison, WI: University of Winsconsin System Board of Regents.

Spender, J.C. (1996), 'Making knowledge the basis of a dynamic theory of the firm', *Strategic Management Journal*, **17**(Winter special issue), 45–62.

Strauss, A. (1987), *Qualitative analysis for social scientists*, Cambridge, UK: Cambridge University Press.

Teece, D.J., G. Pisano and A. Shuen (1997), 'Dynamic capabilities and strategic management', *Strategic Management Journal*, **18**(7), 509–533.

Weick, K.E. and K.H. Roberts (1993), 'Collective mind in organizations: Heedful interrelating on flight decks', *Administrative Science Quarterly*, **38**, 357–381.

Winter, S.G., C. Fang and J. Denrell (2003), 'The economics of strategic opportunity', *Strategic Management Journal*, **24**(10), 977–990.

Yin, R. (1981), 'The case study crisis: some answers', *Administrative Science Quarterly*, **26**, 58–65.

Yin, R. (1984), *Case study research*, Beverley Hills, CA: Sage.

Youndt, M.A. and S.A. Snell (2004), 'Human resource configurations, intellectual capital, and organizational performance', *Journal of Managerial Issues*, **16**(3), 337–360.

Zahra, S.A. and G. George (2002), 'Absorptive capacity: A review, reconceptualization and extension', *Academy of Management Review*, **27**(2), 185–203.

Zahra, S.A. and J.C. Hayton (2004), 'Technological entrepreneurship: Key themes and emerging research directions', in G. Corbetta, M. Huse and D. Ravasi (eds). *Crossroads of Entrepreneurship*, Berlin: Springer.

Zollo, M. and S.G. Winter (2002), 'Deliberate learning and the evolution of dynamic capabilities', *Organization Science*, **13**(3), 339–351.

Web Site

http://www.almacube.com, accessed on 22 November 2009.

6. The role of architectural players in coopetition: the case of the US defense industry

Colette Depeyre and Hervé Dumez

INTRODUCTION

In recent years, papers on coopetition have flourished. They have highlighted the fact that firms can compete in product development, marketing strategies and relationships with customers and suppliers, and, at the same time, cooperate to develop, for example, non-market strategies (defining standards, trying to capture states). Some theoretical issues, however, remain unexplored. Research programs focus almost exclusively on firms that compete and cooperate on a horizontal level; the role played by other actors – customers, regulators – has not been investigated. Yet these actors can have an architectural role in coopetitive behaviors and structures. Two phenomena are of particular interest. First, a lot of papers have dealt with coopetition between firms and a few ones with coopetition within firms; however, the interaction between both forms of coopetition in relation to horizontal and vertical dimensions has not been studied as such. For example, when a firm decides to cooperate with a competitor, it often places its own subsidiaries in competition with those of its competitors. The customers and regulators, as architects of coopetition, can try to shape this complex synchronic dimension. Second, coopetition deploys and changes over time (diachronic dimension). Firms can cooperate for a time then return to fierce competition, and vice versa. Again, it can be assumed that customers and regulators can have an impact on the successive forms of coopetition through their interactions with firms.

To try to highlight these theoretical issues, we have completed a longitudinal case study within a specific industry. It has been selected in order to see whether customers and regulators can play an architectural role in coopetition, and to explore the way external and internal coopetition can interact, and the way different types of coopetition can follow each other.

In the first section of the chapter, we shall present the theoretical issues in a more developed manner. In the second part, we shall give details of our methodological choices. Then we shall analyze three sequences of coopetition in the studied industry and highlight the theoretical issues in the conclusion.

1. THEORETICAL ISSUES

The combination of competition and cooperation is a means to create sustainable rents (Lado, Boyd and Hanlon, 1997). This is not a new discovery: it is the way trade guilds worked in ancient times. More recently, a lot of studies have been focused, for example, on strategic alliances that occur mostly between competitors (Ketchen, Snow and Hoover, 2004; Garrette, Castaner and Dussauge, 2009). Many particular industries have been investigated from a coopetitive angle: steel (Gnyawali, He and Madhavan, 2006) and telecoms (Spiegel, 2006). Yet at least three theoretical issues remain open:

1. Generally focused on coopetition developing between horizontal competitors, studies do not address the role other actors (customers, regulators) can play in the phenomenon. A connection has to be made with works on the architecture of industries. Architectures can be defined as:

   > an abstract description of the economic agents within an economic system (in terms of economic behavior and the capabilities that support the feasible range of behaviors) and the relationships among those agents in terms of a minimal set of rules governing their arrangement, interconnections, and interdependence (the rules governing exchange among economic agents). Architectures provide the contours and framework within which actors interact. (Jacobides, Knudsen and Augier, 2006, p. 1203; see also Jacobides and Billinger, 2006; Jacobides, 2007)

   Some players can leverage an architectural capacity within an industry, shaping cooperation and competition, and the role of customers and regulators can be studied in such a perspective. To what extent can they play on the architecture of an industry? In particular, in business-to-business markets, when systems (Mattson, 1973) or solutions (Tuli, Kohli and Bharadwaj, 2007; Cova and Salle, 2008) are sold and bought, the customer can try to shape competition and cooperation between its suppliers in the most effective way. Doing this, it must respect the antitrust rules and is monitored by antitrust authorities that also play an architectural role.

2. Most of the work on coopetition deals with coopetition between firms.
    A few studies are focused on coopetition within firms (Tsai, 2002;
    Luo, Slotegraaf and Pan, 2006). The issue of the interaction of exter-
    nal and internal coopetition has not been addressed although they
    appear to be linked. When a firm is vertically integrated and intends to
    design a complex system for a customer, it can rely on its own subsidi-
    aries to develop the needed subsystems, or it can organize competition
    between its subsidiaries and subsidiaries of competitors and possibly
    choose to cooperate with the latter. The customer can also influence
    the choice in requesting the firm to organize this competitive process,
    as we shall see. This synchronic complexity of coopetition, which
    plays out on the horizontal and vertical levels, has not been sufficiently
    studied. The architectural role of the customers or regulators can be
    investigated in that perspective too.
3. Coopetition is also a diachronic phenomenon. Phases of cooperation
    and phases of competition can follow one another, and usually do.
    This leads to a focus on competitive actions and reactions, defined
    as: 'purposeful and observable moves undertaken by firms in order to
    improve their competitive position vis-à-vis their competitors in the
    industry' (Gnyawali, He and Madhavan, 2006, p. 511). Coopetition
    can be seen as a succession of strategic sequences articulating coop-
    eration and competition developed at multiple levels, as put forward
    by Dumez and Jeunemaître (2006a), who speak of multidimensional
    strategic sequences. Again, it can be assumed that architects of
    coopetition can have an impact on that diachronic dimension.

2. METHODOLOGY

We aim to explore the potential architectural role of some actors while
considering the synchronic and diachronic dimensions of coopetition.

To treat the diachronic dimension of coopetition, we have chosen
to complete a longitudinal case study with a comparative dimension:
'the longitudinal comparative case method provides the opportunity to
examine continuous processes in context and to draw in the significance
of various interconnected levels of analysis' (Pettigrew, 1990, p. 271).
This study has been conducted using a narrative approach (Dumez and
Jeunemaître, 2006b) relying on sequence analysis (Abbott, 2001; Dumez
and Jeunemaître, 2006a).

To address the synchronic complexity of the coopetitive phenomena, we
have tried to visualize their vertical and horizontal dimensions in building
up templates of three types of coopetition. Each figure aims at picturing

a typical situation of coopetition during each sequence. These figures are not explanations in themselves, but a support for analysis, in the sense that Wittgenstein spoke of synopsis or 'übersichtliche Darstellung': 'a perspicuous representation produces just that understanding which consists in "seeing connections"' (Wittgenstein, 2008, §122, p. 42). The figures try to make visible the complexity of connections between horizontal and vertical cooperation and competition.

The selected case is the US defense industry. It is characterized by the production of complex systems that require the involvement of many firms – it is the industry where systems integration appeared (Sapolsky, 2003). Firms compete to become 'primes', responsible for the development of the systems. But systems are so complex that no firm can develop them on its own. They must cooperate. Therefore, coopetition is likely in the field of systems development and integration. Moreover, the customer, in a situation of a monopsony, plays a role in the shaping of the industry at the structural and the behavioral levels and it is an industry where important antitrust decisions have been made. Consequently, the case should allow the architectural roles of the customer and regulators in coopetition to be brought out, if such roles exist.

The case study relies on data extracted from firms' annual reports, official reports (Government Accountability Office – GAO, Department of Defense – DoD), reports by non-profit private organizations (Rand Corporation), press articles and interviews of staff of the firms, financial analysts and journalists. The interviews (twenty of them, two to four hours each) have been conducted from a theoretical perspective, to bring out the theories the actors use to understand what is going on in the industry and to test theories developed by the authors (Piore, 2006).

3. CASE STUDY: THREE SEQUENCES OF STRATEGIC INTERACTIONS

Analyzing the US defense industry since the end of the Second World War, we shall identify three sequences of strategic interactions, separated by two main disruptions: the end of the Cold War and the development of systems of systems at the end of the 1990s.

3.1 First Sequence: 'Imposed Coopetition'

Traditionally, different customers were in competition. Procurement was conducted independently by the Navy, the Air Force and the Army (Dombrowski and Gholz, 2006). During the Vietnam War, for instance, aircraft carriers were equipped with Phantoms designed and produced by McDonnell while the Air Force was equipped with F-104s designed and produced by Lockheed. The F-111 bomber, jointly used by the Navy and the Air Force, had been designed and produced by General Dynamics.

Each customer formulated its requirements for the weapon it needed and then organized a tender enforcing the 'winner-take-all' rule. The sequence is characterized by intense competition between suppliers. Each made its tender and the winner was considered to be the 'prime'. But the customer imposed vertical cooperation in choosing the second-tier suppliers, which were often competitors of the primes on the same or other contracts. For example, in 1962 the Navy and the Air Force selected Grumman as a supplier of General Dynamics for the production of the F-111 bomber, whereas in 1968, the Navy selected Grumman as a prime contractor for the F-14 fighter, against General Dynamics and other competitors.

At that point, the architectural role of the customer can be summarized as follows:

- it selects primes through a competitive process;
- it selects suppliers through a competitive process;
- it imposes vertical cooperation between competitors;
- and through regulation, it maintains competition with the 'winner-take-all rule'.

This way of organizing 'imposed coopetition' (Figure 6.1) – horizontal competition and vertical cooperation directly imposed by the customer – lasted until the end of the Cold War. At the beginning of the 1990s, with the collapse of the Soviet Union, the deal changed. Between 1989 and 1999, the military budget experienced a drop of about 30 per cent. As it was difficult to massively reduce staff or maintenance, the biggest cuts hit procurement: during the same period, it decreased by a half, falling from $110 billion per year to $52 billion. Moreover, as this reduction was related to the end of the Cold War, it was seen as permanent and structural, and the customer therefore strongly encouraged its suppliers to restructure. Doing this, it triggered the development a new form of coopetition.

3.2   Second Sequence: 'Structural Complementary Coopetition'

The customer modified its procurement practices after the end of the Cold War, leading to a new type of coopetition. It started by restructuring itself in limiting competition between the military forces and becoming a monopsony. Consequently, it increased its power over the industry and developed a new architectural capability. It compelled the firms to

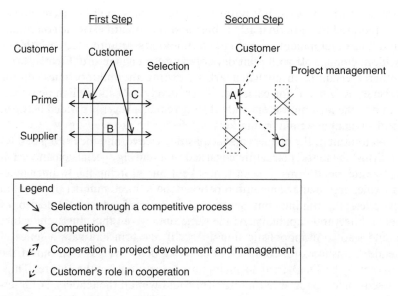

Figure 6.1 Imposed coopetition

restructure. In 1993, fifteen defense industry CEOs were invited for dinner at the Pentagon by the Defense Secretary. After dinner, everyone retired to the briefing room and the CEOs were told that the government did not want to pay for the overhead costs of so many companies. In short, the DoD needed only two competing producers for each weapons system (submarines, fighters, bombers and so on). Half of the firms were to disappear, with the government providing financial help for mergers and restructuring projects. Norman Augustine, then CEO of Martin Marietta, labelled this event the 'Last Supper'.

Consequently, firms like Vought, General Dynamics, Grumman and Rockwell, which had been major competitors, suddenly became acquisition targets. For five years, a wave of mergers and acquisitions deeply changed the industry, until in March 1998, the Antitrust Division of the Department of Justice blocked the intended acquisition of Northrop Grumman by Lockheed Martin and put an end to the mergers and acquisitions wave in the industry. Firms had to choose between three strategies: exit, specialize in defense markets, or adopt a dual strategy (operate simultaneously in civilian and military markets). Small and medium sized firms exited, often acquired by bigger ones. Most of the biggest firms chose to specialize in defense markets (for example, General Dynamics sold its civilian aircraft subsidiary, Cessna). Some firms, like Raytheon, tried to develop civilian and military strategies, relying on technologies that were used in both domains. But business did not follow: military technologies are required to be particularly robust and function in extreme conditions and the development of military technologies requires secrecy; this is seldom compatible with joint development for civilian use. Finally, firms either specialized in civilian markets, exiting the military ones, or the reverse. Raytheon, for example, progressively sold its civilian activities. Among the top contractors, only Boeing remained evenly divided between both civilian and military markets.

As a result of the mergers and acquisitions wave, and the exiting of a lot of firms, the market structure consisted of a few big specialized and vertically integrated firms. The customer kept on enforcing the 'winner-take-all' rule, organizing competition between the reduced number of potential suppliers; this minimal but fierce competition is a fundamental element of its architectural capability. At the same time, given that this architecture could lead to monopolistic situations – if one firm had won a series of tenders, unsuccessful competitors could be definitively driven out of the market – the DoD tried to maintain competition for the future. Thus, the customer made sure that no firm could win all the tenders. An interviewee compared the competitive game to major league baseball, where no team wins or loses more than two-thirds of its games. In a way, the DoD managed competition in the same way, avoiding too great a dominance by one or two players. But at the same time, the different suppliers had to vertically cooperate. Weapons systems became so technologically complicated that no prime could master the development of all the needed subsystems. As a prime, it had to subcontract to competitors parts of the job it had been selected to do. For example, in 1994, the DoD asked for tenders for a new fighter, the Joint Strike Fighter, that had to be used by the Air Force, the Navy and the Marine Corps (which asked for a short take-off and landing version). Three firms tendered: Boeing, Lockheed Martin (with Northrop Grumman and BAe Systems as its main suppliers) and McDonnell Douglas. Only Boeing and Lockheed Martin were allowed to develop a demonstrator: McDonnell Douglas was eliminated from this second round. Then in 2001, the Lockheed Martin demonstrator won the production prime contract against Boeing. In parallel, the DoD launched a project in 1994 for an unmanned aerial vehicle. One of the demonstrators submitted, the Darkstar, was a joint project between Boeing (producing wings and avionics) and Lockheed (the prime). The other demonstrator, the Global Hawk, was jointly developed by Ryan (the prime – later acquired by Northrop Grumman) and Rockwell (producing the wings). The case shows that Boeing and Lockheed could at the same time be fierce competitors for selection as primes for some projects, and vertical partners for some other projects. The situation became more complicated when

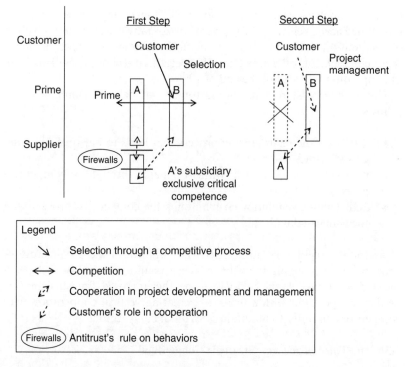

Figure 6.2   Structural complementary coopetition

Boeing acquired Rockwell in 1996. From then, Boeing had an exclusive competence in the field of wings for unmanned aerial vehicles. The competitive process could be distorted: as Boeing produced wings and avionics in the Darkstar project, its interest was to favor this one against the Global Hawk, for which it produced only the wings. It was quite simple to achieve this if the Rockwell teams – now part of Boeing – were asked to supply the Global Hawk with a deliberately inferior technology. Antitrust authorities obliged Boeing to build a 'firewall' separating the teams working on the Darkstar project and the ones working on the Global Hawk.

The decision of the DoD to deal with only a few big vertically integrated suppliers therefore created a market structure characterized by a new form of coopetition: defense firms were competing fiercely to be primes for weapon systems projects (aircraft, missiles, tanks and so on), but were cooperating on a vertical basis to have at their disposal the best subsystems. This form of coopetition was 'structural' (Figure 6.2): the DoD had promoted concentration among its suppliers, and firms were then few and vertically integrated, in a situation of monopoly regarding certain competences (Boeing, for example, concerning the wings of the unmanned aerial vehicles). Firms were horizontally in a structural position of competition and vertically in a structural position of cooperation, given their 'complementary' competences in specialized technologies. This form of coopetition lasted until the end of 1990s.

The architectural role of the customer can be now summarized as follows:

- it triggers the restructuring process that leads to big vertically integrated primes;
- it selects primes (allied with suppliers) through a competitive process;
- and through regulation, it maintains the competitive process with the winner-take-all rule.

As for the regulatory authorities, they influenced the architecture of coopetition by stopping the wave of mergers and acquisitions in 1998 at the structural level. At the behavioral one, they imposed 'firewalls' limiting vertical cooperation within firms and creating vertical cooperation with competitors, in order to maintain horizontal competition.

3.3   The Third Sequence: 'Strategic Coopetition'

Another shift in the market occurred at the end of the 1990s, with the development of 'systems of systems'. What are they?

A missile is a complex system, but it is actually only a subsystem of even more complex systems (platforms like aircraft or submarines). The missile is launched by an aircraft, can be programmed by the pilot to reach a target, and reprogrammed by a ground station to reach a new target. These complex systems already raise important issues in terms of design, interoperability, organization of the supply chain, testing and integration of the different elements (Prencipe, Davies and Hobday, 2003). But at the end of the 1990s, US forces began to try to develop systems of systems. This approach aims to gather and process information exchanged between units engaged in combat (ground vehicles, aircraft, missiles, ships and so on) and headquarters. The information has to be processed in a complex technological environment where a lot of systems are unmanned. The complexity of these 'network-centric' – rather than 'platform-centric' – systems has changed the nature of coopetition in the industry, making it more 'strategic'.

First, the customer now realizes that it is no longer able to manage such complex systems, for at least two reasons. Because of declining military budgets, the DoD has lost a lot of highly qualified people with the ability to set systems requirements and manage the competition between firms; besides, the design of these systems has become so complicated that no DoD internal team can manage it. The customer must rely on the conceptual, technical, and managerial capabilities of firms, even to define its own needs.

Second, only a few firms can develop this kind of capabilities. A hierarchy has developed among the players: a few of them, the biggest ones, are able to master the development of systems of systems; the other must content themselves with becoming second-tier suppliers developing subsystems. Third, contracts concerning systems of systems are rare and last for years.

The competitive process can be characterized as follows. Only a handful of firms are able to submit a tender concerning a system of systems. The firm that succeeds in landing the contract secures a monopolistic relationship with the customer for a long time and probably gets a sustainable competitive advantage grounded in path-dependency and lock-in. The fact that this firm works alone with the customer to define sophisticated needs and systems requirements creates an asymmetry of knowledge and trust vis-à-vis its competitors. This kind of competitive process therefore presents a risk. Once a competitor has been selected, it secures a technical and managerial monopoly for many years, while unfortunate competitors will have to exit the market or gradually lose the capabilities to be credible competitors. Thus, competition vanishes. To prevent this inadvertent production of monopoly, the customer has been trying to strategically shape coopetition.

The architectural role of the customer can be summarized as follows:

- it favors alliances;
- it selects an alliance as the Lead Systems Integrator (LSI) – or 'mega prime' – through a competitive process;
- it provides the LSI with the task of selecting suppliers through a competitive process;
- it enforces the 'winner-take-all' rule.

As for regulatory authorities, they introduced an 'Organizational Conflict of Interest' rule prohibiting vertical cooperation within the LSI and obliged it to cooperate with its competitors.

Figure 6.3 illustrates the complexity of this coopetitive type. Detailing an example can help to understand its synchronic and diachronic dimensions. Let us consider the US Army system of systems, the Future Combat Systems.

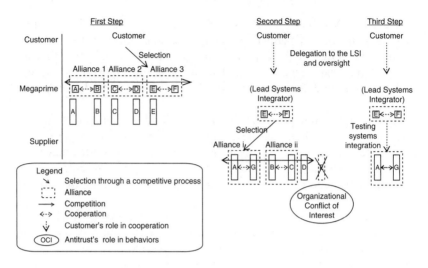

Figure 6.3   Strategic coopetition

4. THE CASE OF THE FUTURE COMBAT SYSTEMS AS 'STRATEGICALLY SHAPED COOPETITION'

The Future Combat Systems (FCS) is the system of systems launched by the DoD for the Army and the Marine Corps (Flood and Richard, 2006; Government Accountability Office, 2007). The FCS aims to modernize the conditions of ground battles. It consists of warrior equipment, sensors, unmanned and manned ground vehicles (transport, artillery, tanks, command cars, ambulances), unmanned aerial vehicles with embedded C4ISR (Command, Control, Communications, Computers, Intelligence, Surveillance and Reconnaissance), training and supportability. For the first time, the US Army no longer develops tanks, artillery vehicles, mortars and so on, separately. The idea is to get a whole system of weapons systems allowing coordination, reactivity and joint use: that is to say, a system of systems. In a few days, a force must be able to deploy anywhere in the world. The vehicles must be designed to fit transport aircraft and helicopters (no system element is allowed to weigh more than 20 tons fully combat loaded and all elements must fit within the hold of a C130J airplane). The time target is 2012–2025 and a lot of the technologies that have to be mobilized in the different systems do not exist yet. The project requires substantial resources for simulation and testing.

On 9 May 2000, the Army selected four teams to tender for the system architecture: Boeing, General Dynamics/Raytheon, Lockheed Martin and SAIC (Science Applications International Corporation). Each team had to develop two concepts. The first called for a network-centric, distributed force to include a manned command and control element and personnel carrier, a robotic direct-fire system, a robotic non-line of sight launch system and an all-weather robotic sensor system, coupled with other layered sensors. The second concept was to be the team's own design approach for a system of systems. Two things should be noted about this structure. First, only General Dynamics is a traditional supplier of the Army, and it had to team with Raytheon because of the capability this second firm has in electronics and computer science. The three other competitors are new entrants: Boeing and Lockheed Martin are aerospace companies; SAIC delivers services. None of these has ever developed a tank or a mortar. One month before the end of this first conceptual phase, Boeing and SAIC decided to join forces and finally won the 'prime' competitive process: the alliance was chosen as LSI. As such, they have been in charge (under the customer's oversight) of organizing competition among their competitors for subsystems contracts. For example, the contract for the development of manned vehicles has been given to a General Dynamics/BAe Systems team (BAe Systems was originally in the SAIC team, whereas General Dynamics was initially teamed with Raytheon).

What lessons can be drawn from this case? The development of the systems has produced a double phenomenon. On the one hand, the customer has been experiencing a capability gap. The DoD is no longer in a position to master the development of such complex systems or even to express its own needs. It must rely on the capabilities of firms. On the other hand, the firms that hold these capabilities are very few. General Dynamics has previously developed complex platforms like the Abrams tank. But it needed to team up with Raytheon to get credibility as a potential system of systems integrator (and did not succeed). The two firms (Boeing and SAIC) that got the contract are not traditional suppliers of the Army, and during the first phase, they were competitors. Then they decided to team together and this team was selected. Why did they create this alliance?

Perhaps because they are complementary. Boeing, when developing the 777, one of the greatest successes in terms of commercial aircraft, created a new method of working with customers (airlines) and suppliers: the Working Together Team (WTT). This approach consisted in involving the airlines (the customers) in designing the aircraft, so that it met their needs, and in involving the suppliers to match Boeing's requirements. Boeing thus offers a specific capability to assist its customers in formulating their needs, to design the technical architecture of very complex systems, to manage the supply chain to get subsystems designed and produced, and to test and integrate these subsystems. SAIC is an engineering firm that has resources in simulation and testing. It has also had some experience of contracting with the US Army.

But the customer may have encouraged the cooperation. As the final contract secures a monopoly for a long period, to award it to an alliance offers several advantages to the customer. As SAIC is not vertically integrated, whereas Boeing is, the final design can be less dependent on Boeing's solutions. Besides, the fact that the contract is given to an alliance keeps two firms instead of just one in the job of LSI. In the long run, these firms can become competitors again. If Boeing and SAIC have complementary capabilities in certain domains, they can learn from each other and be more inclined and better armed to compete in the future. Cooperation is incentivized by the customer at the level of the LSI to reduce the degree of dependence on the LSI and to keep the competitive game more open. For example, it was noted above that Raytheon teamed with General Dynamics to tender for the FCS. Lockheed was a competitor in this case. However, in June 2007, Raytheon, in a competition against an alliance between General Dynamics and Lockheed Martin, won a system of systems contract for the training of the US Army.

But this is only one dimension of the coopetition. Regarding the LSI contracts, the customer has adopted an Organizational Conflict of Interest rule (Gordon, 2005), which forbids the Lead Systems Integrators from taking part in the competitive process they organize in the name of the DoD for subsystems. Once the best tenders have been selected, Boeing and SAIC have to cooperate with these competitors to integrate the subsystems they are responsible for designing and producing. The customer and the regulators have shaped this complex type of coopetition.

5. DISCUSSION

Our objective was to address the architectural role of actors like customers or regulators in the synchronic and diachronic dimensions of coopetition.

The case study shows that the customer does play an architectural role in the coopetitive game the firms are engaged in. First, between sequence one and sequence two, the customer created the structural conditions of coopetition by triggering a wave of mergers and acquisitions among its suppliers. This led to the emergence of a few big vertically integrated firms, able to design and develop big systems. As systems have become more and more complex, this structural shift has had an effect on coopetition, because firms will compete to gain the prime position to develop systems but will have to cooperate on subsystems. This shows that there exist structural conditions for coopetition and the customer can have an impact on them. Second, the customer can try to influence firms at the behavioral level. During the third sequence, for instance, the customer instigated the creation of alliances among firms. This favors coopetition: to get some contracts, some firms are allied, and to get other contracts, the same firms, allied with other partners, compete. This strategy presents two main advantages for the customer. It can select the best combination of complementary capabilities (a situation of co-specialization in the sense of Teece, 1988). This is the traditional way of analyzing alliances and joint ventures. But from the customer's strategic point of view, there is another benefit. The customer can assume that the two firms, working together, will learn from each other and be able to enlarge their respective capabilities, acquiring those they missed (a sort of 'cross-acquisition of capabilities'). In encouraging alliances at the architectural level, it tries to keep the current competitive process more open and preserve the possibility of a future competition. If things turn out badly, it can create a certain reversibility in re-internalizing the systems integration capability and downgrading the firms from a position of LSI to that of classical primes. At last, the customer plays an architectural role in laying down rules and enforcing them in a certain manner. In our case, the main rule is the 'winner-take-all' one. Its role is to enhance competition between firms, and also innovation. This rule has raised fierce controversy but has been maintained through the whole period and is likely to be maintained in the future (Defense Science Board, 2008, p. 27). Strictly enforced, the rule can lead to the dying out of competitors and thus the extinction of competition. That is the reason why the customer enforces it with flexibility and sometimes forces cooperation between the winner and its competitors in order to let them survive.

The antitrust regulators have also played an architectural role. In preventing Lockheed Martin from merging with Northrop Grumman, they marked the end of the market restructuring game. At the behavioral level, they have imposed rules forcing competitors to cooperate, prohibiting some vertical internal cooperation (with firewalls and Organizational Conflict of Interest rules).

The synchronic dimension appears complex to analyze. First of all, the case study shows that different types of coopetition can develop. Three types have been isolated in the case in discussion. Some others could probably be constructed in different contexts. This suggests a need to conceptualize tools for the visualization of the diverse synchronic dimensions of coopetition. Then, the analysis leads to the establishment of a relationship between internal and external coopetition. In the first type, the customer prevents the firm selected as prime from cooperating with its subsidiaries and forces it to cooperate with those of the competitors. In the second type, the regulator obliges parts of the firm not to cooperate with the corporation and to cooperate with competitors (firewalls). In the third, the LSI's subsidiaries are excluded from the competitive bid for subsystems (Organizational Conflict of Interest). The condition for coopetition to develop is that the hierarchy within the firm be flexible, what Tuli *et al.* (2007) have called 'contingent hierarchy'.

From a diachronic perspective, it appears that coopetition evolves over time and must be analyzed as a succession of strategic actions and reactions between actors that can play an architectural role (customers, regulators) and firms in a position to compete and/or cooperate. At the beginning of the second sequence, the customer triggered a restructuring process that led to the creation of a restricted oligopoly. At the start of the third sequence, Boeing played a decisive role in the development of the system of systems approach. Each time, a strategy decided by one of the players, leading to strategic reactions by the other players, gave rise to a new type of coopetition.

CONCLUSION

This chapter has highlighted the architectural role of actors like customers or antitrust regulators in coopetitive strategies, at the structural and the behavioral level. It has also highlighted the importance of rules laid down by different actors – the customer, the regulators and the firms themselves (contingent hierarchy). It has illustrated how coopetition can evolve over time from one type to another. The case study, however, raises a theoretical issue. Most of the studies on coopetition consider that in coopetition, competition and cooperation can be analyzed at the same level. Frédéric Le Roy, in a conversation, noted that this is probably not the case: cooperation is a social phenomenon by nature, competition is not. The case study suggests that another difference does exist: competition is always a credible alternative, a constant threat, to cooperation. This is probably why the DoD prefers to appoint alliances as Lead Systems Integrators. In the future, the firms composing the alliance can become competitors again. To select an alliance is inducing cooperation to preserve the possibility of a future competition. On the contrary, the shift from competition to cooperation is far less easy. It takes a long time and many interactions to build up cooperation (Axelrod, 1984). This dissymmetry between competition and cooperation is a theoretical issue that should be addressed in future studies.

REFERENCES

Abbott, Andrew (2001) *Time Matters: On Theory and Method*, Chicago: Chicago University Press.

Axelrod, Robert (1984) *The Evolution of Cooperation*, New York: Basic Books.

Cova, Bernard and Robert Salle (2008), 'Marketing solutions in accordance to the S-D logic: Co-creating value with customer network actors', *Industrial Marketing Management*, **37**, 270–277.

Defense Science Board Task Force on Defense Industrial Structure for Transformation (2008) *Creating an Effective National Security Industrial Base for the 21st Century: An Action Plan to Address the Coming Crisis*, Washington D.C., Office of the Undersecretary of Defense for Acquisition, Technology and Logistics, July.

Dombrowski, Peter and Eugene Gholz (2006), *Buying Transformation: Technological Innovation and the Defense Industry*, New York: Columbia University Press.

Dumez, Hervé and Alain Jeunemaître (2006a), 'Multidimensional strategic sequences: A research programme proposal on coopetition', Milan, *2nd Workshop on Coopetition Strategy*, EURAM, 14–15 September.

Dumez, Hervé and Alain Jeunemaître (2006b), 'Reviving narratives in economics and management: Towards an integrated perspective of modeling, statistical inference and narratives', *European Management Review*, **3**(1), 32–43.

Flood, Scott and Paul Richard (2006), 'An assessment of the lead systems integrator concept as applied to the future combat system program', *Defense Acquisition Review Journal*, December 2005/March 2006, 357–373.

Garrette, Bernard, Xavier Castaner and Pierre Dussauge (2009), 'Horizontal alliances as an alternative to autonomous production: Product expansion mode choice in the worldwide aircraft industry 1945–2000', *Strategic Management Journal*, **30**(8), 885–894.

Gnyawali, Devi R., Jinee He and Ravindranath Madhavan (2006), 'Impact of coopetition on firm. Competitive behavior: An empirical examination', *Journal of Management*, **32**, 507–530.

Gordon, Daniel I. (2005), 'Organizational conflicts of interest: A growing integrity challenge', *Public Contract Law Journal*, **35**(1), 25–41.

Government Accountability Office (2007), *Role of Lead Systems Integrator on Future Combat Systems Poses Oversight Challenge*, Washington DC, GAO-07-38, June.

Jacobides, Michael (2007), 'Pour une approche stratégique des architectures sectorielles', *Le Libellio d'Aegis*, **3**(2), 28–34.

Jacobides, Michael and Stephan Billinger (2006), 'Designing the boundaries of the firm: From "make, buy or ally" to the dynamic benefits of vertical architecture', *Organization Science*, **17**(2), 249–261.

Jacobides, Michael, Thorbjorn Knudsen and Mie Augier (2006), 'Benefiting from innovation: Value creation, value appropriation and the role of industry architectures', *Research Policy*, **35**(8), 1200–1221.

Ketchen, David J., Charles C. Snow and Vera L. Hoover (2004), 'Research on competitive dynamics: Recent accomplishments and future challenges', *Journal of Management*, **30**(6), 779–804.

Lado, Augustine A., Nancy G. Boyd and Susan C. Hanlon (1997) 'Competition,

Cooperation, and the Search for Economic Rents', *Academy of Management Review*, **22**(1), 110–141.

Luo, Xueming, Rebecca J. Slotegraaf and Xing Pan (2006), 'Cross-functional "coopetition": The simultaneous role of cooperation and competition within firms', *Journal of Marketing*, **70**(April), 67–80.

Mattson, Lars-Gunnar (1973), 'Systems selling as a strategy on industrial markets', *Industrial Marketing Management*, **3**, 107–120.

Pettigrew, Andrew M. (1990), 'Longitudinal field research on change: Theory and practice', *Organization Science*, **1**(3), 267–292.

Piore, Michael J. (2006), 'Qualitative research: Does it fit in economics?', *European Management Review*, **3**(1), 17–23.

Prencipe, Andrea, Andrew Davies and Michael Hobday (eds) (2003), *The Business of Systems Integration*, Oxford: Oxford University Press.

Sapolsky, Harvey M. (2003), 'Inventing systems integration' in Prencipe, Andrea *et al.* (eds), *The Business of Systems Integration*, Oxford: Oxford University Press, 15–34.

Spiegel, Menahem (2006), 'Coopetition in the telecommunications industry', in Crew, Michael A. and Menahem Spiegel (eds), *Obtaining the Best from Regulation and Competition*, New York: Kluwer, 93–108.

Teece, David J. (1988), 'Capturing value from technological innovation: Integration, strategic partnering, and licensing decisions', *Interfaces*, **18**(3), 46–61.

Tsai, Wenpin (2002), 'Social structure of "coopetition" within a multiunit organization: Coordination, competition, and intraorganizational knowledge sharing', *Organization Science*, **13**(2), March–April, 179–190.

Tuli, Kapil R., Ajay K. Kohli and Sundar G. Bharadwaj (2007) 'Rethinking customer solutions: From product bundles to relational processes', *Journal of Marketing*, **71** (July), 1–17.

Wittgenstein, Ludwig (2008) *Philosophical Investigations*, 50th Anniversary Edition, Oxford: Blackwell.

7. Exploring how third-party organizations facilitate coopetition management in buyer–seller relationships

Sandro Castaldo, Guido Möllering, Monica Grosso and Fabrizio Zerbini

INTRODUCTION: COOPETITION IN STRATEGIC MARKETING RELATIONSHIPS

Conceptually as well as practically, coopetition requires the management of the tensions, if not dilemmas, resulting from the simultaneous presence of conflicting and converging goals between two parties (Brandenburger and Nalebuff, 1996). In this chapter, we look beyond the coopetitive dyad and explore the managerial option of involving a third party to deal with the challenge of developing a dyadic relationship that is both cooperative and competitive. Drawing on evidence from three successful category management projects, we are not only able to show the general plausibility of using third-party mediation for coopetition management, but we also shed some light on the conditions for successful mediation and the mechanisms that mediators use to promote cooperation within distribution channel relationships that are also competitive.

Our chapter addresses a strategic management issue but, given the empirical cases we study, we also build specifically on an extensive literature on marketing channels, which has emphasized the importance of managing relationships between sellers and buyers for over fifty years (Zerbini and Castaldo, 2007). This literature has evolved with different perspectives and interests over time, but the main themes remain the interplay of the economic and social dimensions of channel relationships and the tension between the partners' common and competing interests. The intrinsic duality of competitive and cooperative motives in distribution channels suggests that the concept of coopetition, and the managerial issues it implies, can be applied fruitfully to vertical relationships, even though the idea of coopetition arose originally in the context of horizontal relationships (Bengtsson and Kock, 2000; Brandenburger and Nalebuff, 1996).

The basic coopetitive situation in distribution channels is evident. On the one hand, both the seller (for example, a consumer good supplier) and the buyer (for example, a retailer) want to maximize the turnover and margins from sales to satisfied end consumers (Jap, 1999; Jeuland and Shugan, 1983). Hence they both benefit from realizing an optimal price–volume ratio and low channel costs. Besides this common interest in 'pie expansion', though, buyers and sellers also have competing interests in maximizing their share of the pie (Corstjens and Doyle, 1979). A classic case would be the promotion of a particular product in a chain of super-markets by offering a discount, which is intended to increase sales of the product, but makes suppliers and retailers haggle over how to split the discount. Efforts at pie expansion call for a long-term orientation and an openness that allows for learning and continuous improvement (Anderson and Narus, 1990). Efforts at maximizing one's own share of the pie, however, suggest a short-term orientation and secrecy over critical information (El-Ansary and Stern, 1972; Jap, 1999, 2001). The option to exit from a relationship and switch to another partner keeps up the com-petitive element of channel relationships whereas the benefits from loyalty support a cooperative stance.

The literature on vertical relationships has emphasized the great poten-tial resulting from a long-term, cooperative orientation (for example, Dyer and Singh, 1998; Porter, 1985; Sheth and Parvatiyar, 2000). Despite this evidence in favor of long-term relationships, however, managers still encounter serious problems in the maintenance of cooperative relation-ships (Rigby, Reichheld, and Schefter, 2002), because competing interests remain too, and can even result in highly antagonistic relationships in some cases (Jap and Ganesan, 2000). Channel relationships that are char-acterized by high levels of power asymmetry and dysfunctional conflict can become predominantly competitive, lose the benefits of collaboration and perform poorly (Brown and Day, 1981; El-Ansary, 1979; Eliashberg and Michie, 1984; Etgar, 1976; Perry, 1991).

In other words, coopetition in distribution channel relationships is more easily said than done and there is a shortage of research explaining how partners can create a productive interaction between competition and cooperation rather than a destructive one. Prior research on coopetition management more generally has focused to date on the question of how the partners in a dyad can tackle the challenge between them (Bengtsson and Kock, 2000; Brandenburger and Nalebuff, 1996). Many chapters in this book are instructive in this regard too. Our own contribution in this chapter is to suggest that a promising strategy in coopetition management is to look for help outside the dyad and to use a third party to deal with the dilemmas of simultaneous competition and cooperation. The third party would be expected to ensure that cooperation is not prevented by an entrenched competitive stance or – in the opposite case – the third party may generate some competition in relationships that have become too cooperative to generate any innovative ideas for additional value. This perspective and the possibilities it implies have not been on the agenda of coopetition research to date (see Walley, 2007).

Recent channel management initiatives offer practical insights on cooperation opportunities generated while exploiting the new sources of value creation deriving from the support of third parties external to the focal dyad within specific cooperative initiatives (Castaldo, 2007). For example, ECR is a worldwide association of suppliers and retailers specializing in the development and diffusion of interaction models and tools to improve quality and performance of the channel relationships. ECR has acted as a third party, allowing suppliers and retailers to develop cooperative program standards, such as the 'Fast Perfect Order' and the 'Continuous Replenishment Programme', which they would not be able to achieve in a dyadic interaction.

In this chapter, we provide empirical evidence for the decisive role that third parties can play in coopetition management. We analyze the conditions under which third-party mediation is promising. In particular, we look at the quality of the relationship within the dyad and the relationships between the dyad members and the third party to identify when the involvement of a third party is necessary and possible. Moreover, we investigate the main mechanisms by which a third party may intervene in the dyadic relationship between suppliers and retailers to foster coopetition management by mitigating competing tensions with cooperation. This clarifies the kind of role that the third party needs to play.

Our analysis draws on three original case studies on cooperative projects in category management. The marketing practice of category management aims at optimizing the presentation of products at the point of sale in line with customers' cognitive schemes. This involves an interpretation of sales data which increasingly cannot be undertaken by a retailer alone but is most effective when channel partners, especially suppliers, join in (Zenor, 1994). Category management projects represent the classic tension between the pie-expanding potential of the project and the pie-sharing issues arising from sharing confidential data and implementing changes.

The chapter is organized as follows. In the next section, we describe the methodology we used to analyze category management projects as examples of third-party mediation in managing coopetition within vertical relationships. After this, we give a general overview of our three cases. Next, we present our empirical findings on the conditions and mechanisms of successful third-party mediation in the projects at all stages from project initiation to implementation and review. Finally, we discuss the implications of our study for theory and practice, consider the limitations and opportunities for further research, and conclude with our main insights.

1. METHODOLOGY: A QUALITATIVE MULTIPLE CASE STUDY

Third-party involvement in coopetition management in general and in category management projects specifically is a new and complex phenomenon both in theory and practice. Hence we have chosen an exploratory, multiple case study approach and we analyze three strategic cooperative projects aimed at joint value creation that have been developed by a buyer and a seller with the intervention of a third party. Such a qualitative approach is consistent with the purpose of reaching a deep understanding of research issues (for example, Yin, 1984), such as disentangling the conditions and mechanisms that enable third parties to promote cooperation in competitive vertical relationships.

The need to access confidential information demanded a careful endorsement strategy with multiple stages. First, we decided to contact a firm that has recognized experience and expertise in acting as a third party in consumer marketing projects in Italy, where the majority of our research team was based. Our choice fell on ACNielsen, because it is one of the three leading suppliers of professional services to both buyers and sellers within the Fast Moving Consumer Goods (FMCG) sector and because we had good access to key managers in this firm. Second, with ACNielsen, we pre-selected different projects and dyads corresponding to three main criteria: recency, relevance, and mixed power balance. The recency of the cooperative project was a requirement to reduce memory biases by the respondents; the relevance of the project was estimated roughly in terms of the size of the value creation opportunity from the cooperation between the supplier and retailer; and the power balance between the buyer and the seller was considered in order to enhance the generalizability of our findings by mixing cases where the buyer, the seller, or neither of them had the upper hand (Caniëls and Gelderman, 2007). Third, we began preliminary phone dialogues with each of the companies' marketing directors to check their disposition to participate in the study. The final sample contains three cases of category management projects. They are all highly recent and relevant, involved ACNielsen as a third party, and represent three different power scenarios (see Table 7.1).[1]

Table 7.1 Different power scenarios in the three dyads studied

DYADS	RELATIVE SIZE	PRIOR RELATIONSHIP WITH MEDIATOR	POSITIONING IN THE BUSINESS	BARGAINING POWER
R-Market*	Residual FAVORING SUPPLIER	First CM project FAVORING SUPPLIER	Residual FAVORING SUPPLIER	UNBALANCED FAVORING SUPPLIER ↑
SunWash+	One of the 3 leaders	Stable and positive	One of the 3 leaders	
Iper-G*	Leader FAVORING RETAILER	Stable and positive FAVORING RETAILER	Leader FAVORING RETAILER	UNBALANCED FAVORING RETAILER ↑
Acetil+	Follower	First CM project	Follower	
S-Store South*	Leader FAVORING RETAILER	First CM Project BALANCED	Residual FAVORING SUPPLIER	BALANCED ↑
Italian Flavor+	Follower	First CM Project	Leader	

Notes:
1. In column 1, the retailer is at the top of the box and the supplier is at the bottom.
2. * indicates retailers.
3. + indicates manufacturers.

Data were collected through semi-structured, in-depth interviews and archival data on decision processes and results. Each interview was conducted by at least two investigators, lasted an hour and a half on average, and was tape-recorded and transcribed. Our analysis followed the conventional steps of multiple case study research (Bourgeois and Eisenhardt, 1988; Yin, 1984). The preliminary analysis of the verbatim transcripts consisted of a triangulation of the collected data referring to each dyad, comparing the retailer, supplier and third-party's points of view. After the analysis of each dyad, we conducted a cross-case analysis to build a general explanation that holds across the individual dyads even though every case has its unique details, too. The usual measures for ensuring reliability and validity in qualitative case study research were taken (Yin, 1984). As a further validation strategy after data collection, the identified key informants served as a check throughout the analysis process to verify our interpretations (Creswell, 2003). In an exploratory project of this kind, internal validity is more important than external validity, but generalization beyond the three cases was enhanced by controlling for the variance in power between buyers and sellers (Table 7.1).

2. CASE PRESENTATION: GENERAL BACKGROUND TO THE PROJECTS

In this section we give a brief overview of the three dyads in our sample, each of which has implemented a strategic cooperative project aimed at improving the performance of a product category, using ACNielsen as a third party in initiating and completing the project. The projects were similar in nature with respect to the kinds of consumer products and retail channels involved. Each project can also be traced from the beginning to the end through four analytically distinct phases: (1) agreement, (2) analytical phase, (3) strategic phase, and (4) implementation and review phase. The following overviews give first insights into the conditions under which the third party got involved in the category management projects.

Case I: The R-Market–SunWash Category Management Project

The first cooperative project involved the Italian division of a German retailer, R-Market, and the Italian division of a British consumer goods supplier, SunWash. R-Market operates in Italy through three main store brands and nearly 600 stores. SunWash is a leading supplier operating in the mass-consumption industry of cleaning products, including home cleaning, personal care and clothes cleaning.

Before the category management project, R-Market and SunWash already had an arm's length relationship with each other which was maintained by the supplier's key account manager and the retailer's buyers on a transactional basis, that is, ordinary sales orders and related activities. Interestingly, both parties considered their relationship long-standing and solid, but it actually resulted in poor value creation. In order to improve, the parties would have to share sensitive information, but were unwilling to do so. Nevertheless, they were both keen on a solution to increase their performance and saw the potential for ACNielsen to come in as a third party to assist them.

The persons initiating the cooperative project were in this case the retailer's market research analyst and marketing director. They did an internal analysis of product performance within the clothes cleaning category and held a number of meetings with ACNielsen, their trusted provider of data analysis services. With ACNielsen, the retailer sought to find a way to set up a category management project with the supplier. Based upon the meetings between R-Market and ACNielsen, they agreed on a large-scale collaboration project, suitable for improving the performance of the product category within the shops without requiring the retailer to disclose strategic information to SunWash pertaining to the products' performance in the market.

It is important to note the basic dilemma in this case, which applies to all other cases too: while both sides want to improve the performance of SunWash products in R-Market outlets, the retailer is not keen on giving SunWash the figures for its other suppliers, and neither would the supplier like to reveal how much it is able to sell in non-R-Market outlets. In other words, their common interest is in pie expansion but information exchange might affect their pie sharing, that is, bargaining power, negatively. ACNielsen come in because they can ensure that the two sides give and receive no more than the information required for the category management project.

Case II: The Iper-G–Acetil Category Management Project

The second project we analyzed concerns the Italian division of Iper-G, a worldwide leader in retailing, and Acetil, an Italian supplier in the pickled vegetable sector.

Iper-G has around 10 300 stores and 420 000 employees worldwide. In Italy it operates with four different store formats and around 1100 stores. Acetil is the second largest supplier in the pickled vegetable sector in Italy. Despite Acetil's outstanding performance in its sector, it is a family-run firm and it appears as a relatively small business when compared with the big multinational Iper-G.

As in the previous case, the relationship between Iper-G and Acetil was based on conventional buying–selling transactions and judged positively. However, in the years before the category management project we analyzed, performance decreased. Furthermore, Acetil perceived that the interaction with Iper-G was becoming more complex because of the organizational changes on the retailer's side that increased the number of buyers interfacing with the supplier.

The project initiator in this case was the third party, ACNielsen, which suggested the opportunity of developing a project with a retail partner to Acetil. The firm accepted the suggestion with two main objectives in mind: to increase its knowledge of a partner which was becoming more and more complex, and to improve its performance. In order to get Iper-G on board for this project, ACNielsen showed data to the retailer indicating the opportunity to improve its performance by collaborating with Acetil. We can note already that third-party mediation is not only a rescue strategy for a partnership in trouble, but also an external inspiration to enhance a relatively solid relationship.

Case III: The S-Store South–Italian Flavor Category Management Project

Finally, the third category management project we investigated involved a regional division of an Italian retailer, S-Store South, and the Italian market leader in the coffee industry, Italian Flavor.

S-Store South is the regional division of a retailer which operates prevalently in the convenience store channel, with 159 stores owned by both associate and affiliate companies. With five different kinds of outlet, its aim is to reach customers in densely populated neighborhoods. The other firm in this case, Italian Flavor, is the Italian leader in the roasting and selling of coffee, with an annual turnover of Euro 767 million and 1700 employees. Italian Flavor is recognized around the world as a symbol of Italian espresso.

Once again, the two companies in this case have a stable and positive relationship based on sales transactions and maintained by the supplier's key account manager and the retailer's buyer. The parties became aware that the performance of Italian Flavor in S-Store South outlets in this particular region of Italy was below the average of the Italian marketplace and both sides saw the opportunity to increase their returns.

In this case, the initiator of the cooperation was neither the retailer (Case I) nor the third party (Case II) but the supplier, which proposed a cooperative project to S-Store South. It turned out that the retailer was unwilling to share with Italian Flavor the information required to collaborate in increasing value creation. The parties therefore jointly decided to get a third party involved as a guarantor of the proper, neutral use of sensitive data. S-Store South suggested the trusted provider of its data analysis services, ACNielsen, for this. Italian Flavor agreed to this mediator, because ACNielsen was also one of its own data providers. The project scope and the strategic goal were defined by both parties during a series of meetings with the help of ACNielsen.

The similar background conditions of the three cases are noteworthy. They are all stable transactional relationships with room for improvement, an unwillingness to exchange sensitive information directly, and established contacts with a trusted third party. As we will see in the further analysis, these conditions are important for the projects' success.

3. EMPIRICAL FINDINGS FOR DIFFERENT PROJECT PHASES

In the following, we present the results of a detailed analysis of our interview data in order to bring out more clearly the conditions that made the category management projects necessary and possible, and to identify the mechanisms that the third party uses to perform its function of enabling cooperation in antagonistic buyer–seller relationships. We follow the sequence of the cooperative project phases: agreement, data analysis, strategy definition, and implementation and review. In each phase we shall look at the conditions of the mediated relationship and the mechanisms activated to bypass factors inhibiting collaboration.

3.1 Agreement Phase: Coming Together and Launching the Project

The first step is often the most difficult one. This general fact of life also applies to the three projects we studied. The initial move to contact a potential partner and agree on starting to cooperate on a strategic marketing project at the dyadic level is tricky, because it requires suppliers and retailers to be prepared to open up and jointly manage a portion of their marketing, sales and procurement activities (Cova and Salle, 2007). The dilemma is that while both sides may see room for improvement in the relationship, they also see the risk of exposing misaligned processes (Drupe and Gruen, 2004; Gruen and Shah, 2000), asymmetrical outcomes and opportunistic behaviors by the counterpart (for example, Morgan, Kaleka, and Gooner, 2007; Zajak and Olsen, 1993). In other words, when issues are revealed at the beginning, it may make matters worse and this can inhibit the parties' collaboration.

In our three case studies, the common situation was that the parties had a stable and positive arm's length relationship, but needed to produce the willingness to develop a much closer and deeper relationship in order to start a cooperative project. If trust is a key antecedent of cooperative interaction (Ganesan, 1994; Morgan and Hunt, 1994), then the problem of the dyads we analyzed was a necessary shift in the strength and quality of their mutual trust. The trust required for an arm's length relationship is different from the trust required when moving on to closer cooperation (for example, Lewicki, Tomlinson, and Gillespie, 2006). With distrust or very low trust at the calculative-transactional level (arm's length) it will be even more difficult to initiate the transformation to trusting cooperation at the relational-strategic level.

In this respect, the good news from our interview data is that there was no distrust in the dyads we studied, because the buyers and suppliers had good, long-standing exchange relationships with each other. This is also seen by our respondents as a requirement for embarking on a more cooperative project:

> You pointed out that there must be an approval of the mediator's choice of the counterpart, can you specify further what you mean by that? (Interviewer)
> The approval means that with many suppliers there may have been a prior issue in negotiations, that is, there are suppliers with whom we work better or worse in each product category. Therefore the approval is in some sense a way to say that there isn't a veto on the choice of the supplier . . . If I really don't have a good relationship with a given supplier, I won't choose it for the project (Interview with R-Market project leader).

> We have chosen Acetil because we already maintained good transactional relationships. It was a firm that gave us stimulus such as new promotional proposals . . . because when we start such a kind of project and exchange data . . . data for us have a value, so they can be shown only when we have a trustworthy relationship, of course concerning only the business (Interview with Iper-G project leader).

However, the existence of a long-standing relationship and the absence of distrust are not the same as having a trusting relationship (Lewicki, McAllister, and Bies, 1998). Consequently, without positive trust, ordinary transactions may be possible but there is no basis on which to establish deeper collaboration. Indeed, the absence of trust from at least one side of each dyad was an apparently insurmountable obstacle to collaboration on the project in our Case III:

> [At the beginning, we maintained] the usual relationship between industry and distribution. Those were shallow, based only on commercial aspects, on the fact that if a buyer was not satisfied, it would be difficult to maintain a good

collaboration relationship . . . Italian Flavor had already approached us, but we have always been reluctant to start this project with them (Interview with S-Store South project leader).

Under such conditions, the intervention of a third party, trusted by both other parties, can perform the mechanism of building a bridge between the supplier and the retailer. This bridging means that the third party serves as a mediator, bypassing the direct supplier–retailer relationship and thus coordinating indirectly the two parties' activities based on the trust that they have in the mediator (for example, Burt, 2000, 2001).

Consistent with this, our cases showed that the mediator was allowed to bridge the relational distance between the suppliers and retailers. Essentially, the mediator was entitled to represent each of the parties' interests on the basis that both sides of the dyads trusted them. More specifically, trust in the third party was grounded in its reputation as a competent player in the marketplace and its prior relationships with the parties as a professional service provider. The prior relationships are important, because they mean that the third party enjoyed knowledge-based trust (Lewicki and Bunker, 1996) and not just calculative trust. In other words, the parties valued working with a third party they already knew and may not have accepted in the same way an equally qualified but unfamiliar mediator. Our interviews confirm this:

There were pre-existing relationships with the parties, which were based on daily services provided in this activity . . . Over the years, I never received a call or a message sent from someone whom I didn't know (Interview with ACNielsen project leader).

ACNielsen are experts in approaching both this kind of projects and the relational problems between buyers and sellers; this is certainly a positive aspect (Interview with SunWash project leader).

ACNielsen helped to overcome the initial reluctance to collaborate, because it was expected to behave in the interest of both parties, to manage conflicts, and to engender the needed commitment (Morgan and Hunt, 1994) from both sides of the dyad. Indeed, this effect is confirmed by our data:

There were no problems with the partnership between the mediator and us or between the mediator and the counterpart . . . He does not have any reason for privileging one of the two parties . . . It was a good triangulation, we could expect high-quality work (Interview with Italian Flavor project leader).

Nielsen stimulated the willingness of both parties to begin such a project by showing us the numbers proving that the category was underperforming . . .

> Iper-G market share was really underperforming in all its store formats . . . We
> were also underperforming in hypermarkets . . . In supermarkets the situation
> for us was even worse . . . So Nielsen convinced us that we could recover this
> gap with this project (Interview with Acetil project leader).

Hence, the third party played the role of a trust bridge, because its
intervention changed the interaction pattern between the supplier and
the retailer, reinforcing this interaction as a feedback effect which enables
the trust in the third party to also be exploited within the direct supplier–
retailer interaction. Our interviewees reported the following:

> This project allowed us to enter into more strategic settings and to have a
> different dialogue, which was no longer based on the achievement of a rebate
> from a big order of volume X. Things changed, the relationships began to
> change and become more tranquil, collaborative, almost like over a meal,
> because you have managed a method and you have obtained satisfying results
> . . . Nielsen was the glue of this process (Interview with S-Store South project
> leader).

In the agreement phase of the projects we studied, it was important that
there was no distrust between the buyer and the seller and that they both
had trust in ACNielsen as the third party which could thus act as a bridge
and enhance the relationship between the buyer and the seller.

3.2   Analytical Phase: Sharing Data and Selectively Using Them

After the parties have reached an agreement on doing a category management project together, the crucial next step to make the project succeed is
to get the supplier and the retailer to share information which is required
to perform the strategic analysis that will tell them how the category performance may be improved. This sharing of information is critical to the
project success, because the supplier and the retailer usually have complementary market knowledge that is considered sensitive by both sides. We
found that, specifically, the supplier has data on how its products are performing in other retail chains, whereas the retailer knows how successful
other suppliers' products are in its own outlets. Indeed, once shared, this
knowledge could not only be used within the domain in which the parties
collaborate, but also outside the category management project in competitive bargaining at the transactional level of sales orders and discounts. Our
interviewees specifically noted that:

> It's evident that we don't have all those data related to the products . . . because
> of our economic role in the business . . . So the partner becomes relevant,

because we know the aggregated data, but when we have to reason at the single reference level, we need a knowledgeable partner (Interview with Iper-G project leader).

We don't exchange information with the suppliers, this is a company policy . . . It is Nielsen that undertakes the responsibility for managing the data for that particular project and for nothing else. That is why this role is very important to us (Interview with S-Store South project leader).

In other words, we see that in the analytical phase, the typical coopetitive tension between pie expansion (cooperation) and pie sharing (competition) as noted in the introduction is no longer abstract but becomes tangible. The parties have to move from voicing good intentions to actually making themselves vulnerable by sharing sensitive information. The question is whether the project can still succeed even if the parties in the supplier–retailer dyad are not willing to exchange information with each other, as the S-Store South project leader pointed out.

In such a context, where the willingness to give the counterpart access to sensitive information is low, the inclusion of a third party can be the solution. From our interviews, we found that in the analytical phase, similarly to the previous phase, the third party still uses, first of all, a bridging mechanism by acting as the link between the two parties. The supplier and the retailer provide the required sensitive information to ACNielsen instead of sharing it directly. In this context, the Acetil project leader mentioned the following:

During the analysis, we met just Nielsen. In this phase the retailer analyzed some data just with Nielsen, too. So we had separate meetings . . . This is because there was the need to 'clean' the data . . . [Moreover,] we never met Iper-G without Nielsen (Interview with Acetil project leader).

The third actor therefore offered the safe context within which the analysis of market data could be performed. It is very important to note, though, that the bridging mechanism which brings the parties together can only work because the third party simultaneously utilized a second mechanism aimed at conflict reduction by keeping the parties apart: the mechanism of selecting who was to be involved in which part of the analysis and what kind of data were passed on. This means that ACNielsen had the full picture and could coordinate the analysis, while the other project partners did not get to see more than they needed to. Bridging and selecting are complementary and equally important mechanisms. The parties only trusted ACNielsen to be their link, because they knew that confidentiality would be maintained:

The third party works as an interface, allowing the retailer to disentangle all the aspects related to the analysis . . . We decide the pricing policies and the promotion jointly with the supplier, but we don't obtain information about market segmentation or targeting from the supplier . . . We discuss, on a 360° basis, sharing information, but we need a neutral party which certifies the process (Interview with S-Store South project leader).

A closer look at specific practices in the strategic analysis phase reveals how carefully the third party managed the simultaneous bridging and selecting. We found that one common practice was the 'encryption' of sensitive data such as margins and sales value. This means that the third party found ways to display sensitive results, for example the superior market share of a competitor, without giving the precise figures or company names:

Figures on economic roles, sales for packaging types, sub-segments sizes and their contribution to overall volumes and margins were encrypted by reporting them in graphs where values on the axis were omitted, but relative distance of segments could still be evaluated in order to clarify the kind of role that each sub-segment played. This analysis was shown to the seller (Italian Flavor) with Nielsen always present . . . In this way we were able to share these analyses and to match them with the decisions on the strategic role of the category within each segment (Interview with S-Store South project leader).

In any case, the presence of this mediator allowed getting information that, albeit encrypted, was very useful for the analysis. I refer in particular to the margins: if we had interacted directly with R-Market, we wouldn't have been able to refer to this information (Interview with the SunWash project leader).

In this way, the parties kept control of their data but were still able to discuss results. ACNielsen brought them together but also protected them from each other by being there as a neutral third party and selecting items for the agenda. This finding is interesting since it provides insight that third parties may be allowed to perform a knowledge filtering role which is different from the brokerage role assumed in structural holes, where the mediated actors are supposed to be unaware of, or ignore, each other (for example, Burt, 1992, 1997). In our cases, the suppliers and retailers knew very well who was on the other side of the mediated relationships and that their counterparts owned the knowledge resources needed to develop and complete the cooperative project. The third party managed the information flow and analysis for the benefit of the other two parties. ACNielsen did not use the data from the two parties for its own advantage or to play them off against each other. On the contrary, the third party strengthened its own position and reputation by being trustworthy in its bridging and selecting roles during the data analysis phase.

3.3   Strategic Phase: Finding Solutions and Agreeing on Action

If sharing sensitive information can be a source of conflict in distribution channel relationships, then we can expect that it is even more difficult to reach a joint conclusion on what kind of category management activities should be undertaken, based on prior analysis. It requires strategic integration and this is the most critical issue for the success of cooperative relationships in vertical dyads (Johnson, 1999). Once again, our empirical findings confirm the basic problem of coopetition, that is, the strong need for coordination between the parties given their common interests on the one hand (Zenor, 1994) that is inhibited by conflicting goals that they have on the other hand (Dussart, 1998; Gruen and Shah, 2000; Sa Vinhas and Anderson, 2005). We find that a third party such as ACNielsen also needs to activate the bridging and selecting mechanisms in this phase of a category management project. The third party brings the other parties together for strategic decision making but it also selects the options that are considered, filtering out in advance any options that would severely disadvantage one of the parties. Moreover, by providing an established and shared data processing method, the third party adds objectivity to the cooperative process and acts as a clearing house, which is very important in supporting the day-to-day operations within the project in order to prepare major strategic decisions. The following quotation captures how the third party's neutral bridging activities lead to a positive outcome:

> We identified the standard assortment in respect of each product reference. Italian Flavor started to see some [of its] product references that were excluded from the assortment, but Italian Flavor managers were happy with this solution . . . I also was very happy when I saw the shelf. In fact, there was absolutely no forcing, because it had been managed in a really neutral way (Interview with Italian S-Store South project leader).

Our interviews were also very instructive with regard to how the selecting mechanism is applied in practice in the strategy definition phase. Here, it is important to know that the multiplexity of vertical relationships (Zerbini and Castaldo, 2007) increases when a strategic cooperative marketing project is undertaken at the same time as the competitive trading relationship at the transaction level continues. While some people from the supplier and the retailer side have meetings with the third party to integrate their marketing strategy for a category, their colleagues who are key account managers and buyers are still in an ongoing bargaining relationship with the common conflicts about value sharing. The domain of interaction between the buyer and the key account manager is different from that where knowledge should be shared for setting joint strategies of value creation. The domains need to be kept separate or the category project may be jeopardized. This means that the third party brings together the 'right' people at the strategic level, but keeps out the 'wrong' people from the transactional level. A neutral party like ACNielsen can remind the partners that they should not be distracted by current, short-term issues at the transaction level (for example, a buyer complaining about an account manager's behavior), but should focus on the strategic opportunities which warrant the exchange of some sensitive data and the effort to integrate category management initiatives. This is illustrated by the following quotation:

> ACNielsen is a subject super partes [party above the others] which guarantees that the project will proceed till the end . . . It is someone who stimulates the relationship, that is: if S-Store South don't answer me because its buyer has argued with my local seller, I can't do anything to solve the problem . . . whereas ACNielsen acts as a connector telling S-Store South: 'the project should go on because of the investments both of you have done' (Interview with Italian Flavor's category manager).

This evidence from our interviews suggests that third-party mediation succeeded in tightening relationships between suppliers and retailers, because it could manage the complexity of the relationships resulting from the tension between cooperation and competition within and across the multiple relationship levels involved. ACNielsen, as the mediating third party, was able to introduce flexibility into the relationship, because it was trusted by both partners, linked and separated them for the benefit of the project, and acted like a membrane, controlling the level of osmosis between the supplier and the retailers. This enabled the members of the dyad to decide on an integrated strategy which could be implemented in the next phase of the category management project.

3.4 Implementation and Review Phase: Broadening Commitment and Getting Results

Obviously, the successful completion of the previous phases will be in vain, unless the strategic decisions can be implemented in practice in the parties' logistics and point of sale arrangements. Once strategies have been defined, the implementation is dependent on the parties' ability to extend collaboration to other functions that have not been involved in the cooperative project before. The issue here is that these peripheral functions, for example the local buyers and sellers responsible for specific products and outlets, were not included in the project in previous phases.

They may lack the commitment to implement the changes required by the marketing functions that sponsored the cooperation in the category management project, because at the transactional buyer–seller level, entrenched competitive bargaining dominates the cooperative stance achieved at the project level. In the three cases we studied, it was critical that a wider subset of functions and actors participated unreservedly in the project's implementation. We find that this situation calls, once again, for the selecting mechanism on the part of the third party. However, in this phase it is not a matter of deciding whom to exclude, as in the previous phase, but whom to include now. In other words this selecting prepares for further bridging.

Based on our interviews, we found that the suppliers' and retailers' project leaders leveraged a key characteristic of the third party – its widespread reputation and credibility within the industry – to avoid resistance from the other functions, which are required to accept and implement the defined strategies and to offer their endorsement and commitment to the project. The following quotations underline this point:

> We need the method to be communicated to everyone, to be shared and accepted by our associates, at the level of each point of sale . . . Nielsen provided us with the method (Interview with S-Store South project leader).

> This project raises the awareness of category management not only within S-Store South, but also among the S-Store South associates . . . They have involved the associates in the process to ensure their sponsorship of the project (Interview with Italian Flavor regional account manager).

Note that the third party, ACNielsen, now becomes a mediator not between the supplier and the retailer, but between different functional levels in the suppliers' and the retailers' own organizations. By way of illustration, marketing managers would bring in an ACNielsen expert to convince their account managers that the project makes sense. And the buyer responsible for a particular outlet would rearrange the point of sale because the request 'from above' is endorsed by ACNielsen.

Finally, the implementation phase comprises also the review of the outcomes from the category management project. Has the project led to an improvement in the category performance? And can this success be attributed to the third-party involvement? Moreover, has the project led to a more cooperative stance facilitating coopetition management in the future? Our three cases show very clearly that all three questions can be answered affirmatively. While we are not able to give exact performance figures here, we know from our interviews that all three projects have resulted in superior category performance and an increase in value thanks

to the collaboration. Second, our investigation highlights that relationships between the two parties after the project have been extended beyond
the typical domain of interaction of an arm's length transactional relationship. A wider set of people and organizational functions in each firm has
now established contacts with their counterparts in the other organization, laying the ground for further collaboration and the development of
stronger trust instead of just an absence of distrust. The following quotation is very apt in this respect:

> At the end, this type of project has several benefits, it's difficult to have a nega-
> tive outcome: besides having positive consequences from a selling perspective –
> as it is better to guide certain decision[s] of the retailer instead of receiving them,
> influenced by other competitors – it also has a potential . . . because it strength-
> ens the current relationship. You interact with higher-order decisional figures,
> different from those you are used to deal with in day-by-day negotiations, one
> or two decisional levels higher, and this is an asset that can last over time . . .
> Such relationships are fundamental in the long term, when you have known and
> worked with a person, even if [at a] distance, on a project like this one, it's a big
> advantage . . . eventually when you need it – and I hope I never need it – you
> can make the call that solves even a hot issue . . . there's a relational advantage
> in dealing with these projects (Interview with the SunWash project leader).

In the implementation and review phase, we therefore find that bridging
and selecting mechanisms are still supported by the third party, but this
third party moves more into the background, providing the legitimacy for
rolling the project out into the outlets and maintaining the commitment
for it until the measurable success of the category management project
speaks for itself and strengthens the dyadic relationship as well as the
trust in the third party. While none of our cases were failures, it should
be noted that the reputation of the third party is at stake when a project
like this fails, even if the reasons lie outside the project or the mistakes
were made by the supplier or the retailer in the implementation phase at
the end.

4.   DISCUSSION

The involvement of a third party has been a neglected avenue to strategic collaboration in distribution channels (Johnson, 1999) and, more
generally, an underexplored option in coopetition management that is
not even mentioned in recent review papers (for example, Walley, 2007).
Our study underlines that further research in this area will contribute to
a better understanding of coopetition in theory as well as to enhanced
value creation opportunities in practice. We have presented three cases

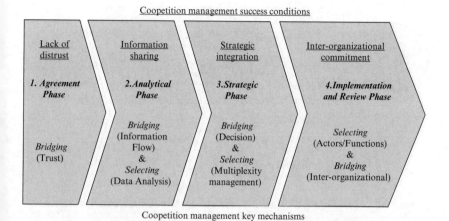

Figure 7.1 Third-party coopetition management: success conditions and key mechanisms

in cooperative category management where third-party involvement was crucial in making the projects successful. Moreover, we have preliminary evidence on the conditions and mechanisms that contributed to the successful intermediation (Figure 7.1).

First, while there may be other promising constellations, our three cases have a common pattern in the conditions that made third-party mediation necessary and promising. The following constellation was found: the parties in the supplier–retailer dyad did not distrust each other, but they had no positive trust to build on either; each of the parties in the dyad trusted, based on prior experience, in the goodwill and competence of the same third party. We can speculate that when there is open distrust between parties, they will not even agree on getting a third party involved; and if there is strong trust in the dyad already, they can manage coopetition on their own without the help of a third party. We can also infer that if the members of the dyad are supposed to deal with a third party that they do not know or trust, or if they have different ideas on who the best third party should be, then it will be more difficult to agree on a cooperative project.

Further work can draw on typologies of buyer–supplier relationships such as the one by Möllering (2003), who distinguishes, based on a cluster analysis of relationships between printers and paper suppliers in the United Kingdom, between 'traditional wary traders', 'controlled routine partners' and 'committed flexible partners'. Presumably, the first type would benefit most from the help of a third party to become more cooperative, the

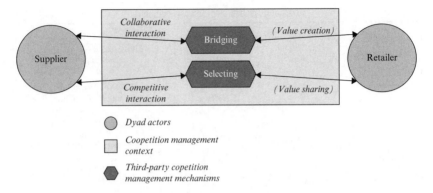

*Figure 7.2   Mechanisms of third-party coopetition management:
            separating and bridging*

second type would need the third party mainly to introduce innovative ideas in an already cooperative relationship, and the third type is already cooperating so successfully that they do not need the help of a third party. Managers considering the option of seeking help from a third party should first assess what kind of a relationship they are in and whether third-party involvement is necessary and possible.

Second, across the three cases we studied, we found two main complementary mechanisms that the third party activated (Figure 7.2): bridging and selecting. Interestingly, this means that the third party is responsible for bringing the other two parties together but also for keeping them apart in several important ways. Crucially, the third party is a trustee of sensitive information, a neutral authority in decision-making processes, and a legitimating force in generating commitment within and between the supplier and retailer organizations.

In further research, we shall need to establish in more detail the activities of the third party that are used to ensure a complementary balance between bridging and selecting. This is also a fruitful avenue for coopetition research more generally. While it is now well understood why many vertical relationships have both competitive and cooperative elements so that they can justifiably be called 'coopetitive', we do not know much about the mechanisms that can manage competition and cooperation independently but with an integrated outcome, that is, an optimal 'mix' of competition and cooperation. For example, we can study in more detail how to isolate key actors and activities that are critical for cooperative value creation from those actors and activities involved in conflicting interaction and bargaining.

Third, the use of mechanisms differs in different phases of collaboration

(Figure 7.1). For example, the isolation of cooperative and competitive parts just mentioned may be desirable in some phases, but in other phases, the isolated parts need to be brought together again. This is why in our analysis of cooperative category management projects, we distinguished between four phases: agreement, analytical, strategic, and implementation and review phases. The selecting mechanism was particularly important in the second and third phase while bridging was necessary to get the project started in the first phase and implemented in the last phase. Mostly, however, the two mechanisms complemented each other in all four phases.

The mechanisms we identified are still very broad. More research is needed to come up with a list of more detailed and additional mechanisms that third parties can activate in performing their mediating role. Further insights on this might come from literatures that we have not been able to fully integrate into this analysis yet, such as work on boundary spanners (Stamper and Johlke, 2003), conflict in project management (Butler, 1973; Cooper and Budd, 2007) and social network analysis (Kilduff and Tsai, 2003). The most fruitful approach in this regard could be to focus on 'multiplex relationships' (Zerbini and Castaldo, 2007) or 'compound relationships' (Ross and Robertson, 2007) resulting from adding a cooperative dimension to a competitive inter-organizational relationship and from creating multi-functional contacts between firms.

An exploratory study like the one reported here has some limitations. We cannot yet generalize from our three cases of successful marketing channel coopetition in Italian retail to coopetitive strategies in other value chain stages, industries and countries. The basic dilemma we have studied is fairly generic though, as is the possibility of involving a third party. Therefore, we believe that the gist of our findings is likely to be applicable to other forms of project-based strategic collaboration, for example, joint product development, and other vertical business relationships that are enabled by third parties, for example, investment projects mediated by banks.

Bearing the limitations and the preliminary nature of our findings in mind, managers can already draw some plausible practical lessons. Specifically, they should consider bringing in a third party when the conditions we observed are fulfilled: no distrust but low trust within the dyad, combined with the availability of a third party trusted by both parties. Hence, we do not propose that coopetition should *always* benefit from third-party involvement. Instead, our results answer the call for typological work in coopetition research (for example, Walley, 2007) and we suggest a basic distinction between purely dyadic coopetition and mediated coopetition.

CONCLUSIONS

In this chapter, we have conceptually explored and empirically demonstrated the key role that third parties can play in enabling coopetitive strategies. The organizational and management puzzle at hand remains that, even when there are clear economic incentives, firms often find it hard to move from simple transactions to more holistic collaboration, that is, from an established, uniplex trading relationship to an enhanced, multiplex marketing relationship (for example, Spekman and Carraway, 2006), where they use modern practices such as cooperative category management (Corsten and Kumar, 2005; Zenor, 1994). These practices require suppliers and retailers to set up additional channels of communication, to recognize common opportunities and moderate any conflicting interests, and to collaborate in generating and developing new ideas on how to organize market offerings at the point of sale according to customer needs. This goes far beyond the usual transactional responsibilities (and capabilities) of the sales managers and purchasing managers who negotiate stock orders. We hope that further research will be able to draw on our findings here and investigate the role of third parties commanding the necessary capabilities, resources and trust that are missing in the trading dyad (see also Burt and Knez, 1995; Ferrin, Dirks, and Shah, 2006). This chapter has contributed original pointers to how, with the help of third parties such as marketing service providers, inter- and intra-organizational boundaries are created and removed in order to manage the required coopetitive multiplexity in advanced relational strategies.

NOTE

1. Apart from ACNielsen, the names of the firms have been changed to guarantee their anonymity.

REFERENCES

Anderson, J.C. and J.A. Narus (1990), 'A model of distributor firm and manufacturer firm working partnerships', *Journal of Marketing*, **54**(1), 42–58.

Bengtsson, M. and S. Kock (2000), '"Coopetition" in business networks – to cooperate and compete simultaneously', *Industrial Marketing Management*, **29**(5), 411–26.

Bourgeois L.J., III and K.M. Eisenhardt (1988), 'Strategic decision processes in high velocity environments: Four cases in the microcomputer industry', *Management Science*, **34**(7), 816–35.

Brandenburger, P.M. and B.J. Nalebuff (1996), *Coopetition*, New York: Doubleday.
Brown, J.R. and R.L. Day (1981), 'Measures of manifest conflict in distribution channels', *Journal of Marketing Research*, **18**(3), 263–74.
Burt, R.S. (1992), *Structural Holes: The Social Structure of Competition*, Cambridge, MA: Harvard University Press.
Burt, R.S. (1997), 'The contingent value of social capital', *Administrative Science Quarterly*, **42**(2), 339–65.
Burt, R.S. (2000), 'The network structure of social capital', in R.I. Sutton and B.M. Staw (Eds), *Research in Organizational Behavior*, **22**, Greenwich, CT: JAI Press, pp. 345–423.
Burt, R.S. (2001), 'Structural holes versus network closure as social capital', in N. Lin, K.S. Cook and R.S. Burt (Eds), *Social Capital: Theory and Research*, Chicago, IL: Aldine de Gruyter, pp.31–56.
Burt, R.S. and M. Knez (1995), 'Kinds of third-party effects on trust', *Rationality and Society*, **7**(3), 255–292.
Butler, A.G., Jr. (1973), 'Project management: A study in organizational conflict', *Academy of Management Journal*, **16**(1), 84–101.
Caniëls, M.C.J. and C.J. Gelderman (2007), 'Power and interdependence in buyer-supplier relationships: A purchasing portfolio approach', *Industrial Marketing Management*, **36**(2), 173–182.
Castaldo, Sandro (2007), *Trust in Market Relationships*, Cheltenham, UK and Northampton, MA: Edward Elgar.
Cooper, M.J. and C.S. Budd (2007), 'Tying the pieces together: A normative framework for integrating sales and project operations', *Industrial Marketing Management*, **36**(2), 219–29.
Corsten, D. and N. Kumar (2005), 'Do suppliers benefit from collaborative relationships with large retailers? An empirical investigation of efficient consumer response adoption', *Journal of Marketing*, **69**(3), 80–94.
Corstjens, M. and P. Doyle (1979), 'Channel optimization in complex marketing systems', *Management Science*, **25**(10), 1014–1025.
Cova, B. and R. Salle (2007), 'A comprehensive approach to project marketing and the marketing of solutions', [Introduction to the special issue Project Marketing and the Marketing of Solutions] *Industrial Marketing Management*, **36**(2), 138–146.
Creswell, J.W. (2003), *Research Design: Qualitative, Quantitative and Mixed Methods Approaches*, London: Sage Publications.
Drupe, K. and T.W. Gruen (2004), 'The use of category management practices to obtain a sustainable competitive advantage in the fast-moving-consumer-goods industry', *Journal of Business and Industrial Marketing*, **19**(7), 444–459.
Dussart, C. (1998), 'Category management: Strengths, limits and developments', *European Management Journal*, **16**(1), 50–62.
Dyer, J.H. and H. Singh (1998), 'The relational view: Cooperative strategy and sources of interorganizational competitive advantage', *Academy of Management Review*, **23**(4), 660–679.
El-Ansary, A.I. (1979), 'Perspectives on channel system performance', in R.F. Lusch and P.H. Zinszer (Eds), *Contemporary Issues in Marketing Channels*, Norman, OK: The University of Oklahoma Printing Services.
El-Ansary, A.I. and L.W. Stern (1972), 'Power measurement in the distribution channel', *Journal of Marketing Research*, **9**(1), 47–52.

Eliashberg, J. and D.A. Michie (1984), 'Multiple business goals sets as determinants of marketing channel conflict: An empirical study', *Journal of Marketing Research*, **21**(1), 75–88.

Etgar, M. (1976), 'Channel domination and countervailing power in distributive channels', *Journal of Marketing Research*, **13**(3), 254–62.

Ferrin, D.L., K.T. Dirks and P.P. Shah (2006), 'Direct and indirect effects of third-party relationships', *Journal of Applied Psychology*, **91**(4), 870–883.

Ganesan, S. (1994), 'Determinants of long-term orientation in buyer–seller relationships', *Journal of Marketing*, **58**(2), 1–19.

Gruen, T.W. and R.H. Shah (2000), 'Determinants and outcomes of plan objectivity and implementation in category management relationships', *Journal of Retailing*, **76**(4), 483–510.

Jap, S.D. (1999), 'Pie-expansion efforts: Collaboration processes in buyer–seller relationships', *Journal of Marketing Research*, **36**(4), 461–475.

Jap, S.D. (2001), '"Pie sharing" in complex collaboration contexts', *Journal of Marketing Research*, **38**(1), 86–99.

Jap, S.D. and S. Ganesan (2000), 'Control mechanism and the relationship life cycle: Implications for safeguarding specific investments and developing commitment', *Journal of Marketing Research*, **37**(2), 227–245.

Jeuland, A.P. and S.M. Shugan (1983), 'Managing channel profits', *Marketing Science*, **2**(3), 239–272.

Johnson, J.L. (1999), 'Strategic integration in industrial distribution channels: Managing the interfirm relationship as a strategic asset', *Journal of the Academy of Marketing Science*, **27**(1), 4–18.

Kilduff, M. and W. Tsai (2003), *Social Networks and Organizations*, London: Sage.

Lewicki, R.J. and B.B. Bunker (1996), 'Developing and maintaining trust in work relationships', in Roderick M. Kramer and Tom R. Tyler (Eds), *Trust in Organizations*, Thousand Oaks, CA: Sage, pp.114–139.

Lewicki, R.J., D.J. McAllister and R.J. Bies (1998), 'Trust and distrust: New relationships', *Academy of Management Review*, **23**(3), 438–458.

Lewicki, R.J., E.C. Tomlinson and N. Gillespie (2006), 'Models of interpersonal trust development: Theoretical approaches, empirical evidence, and future directions', *Journal of Management*, **32**(6), 991–1022.

Möllering, G. (2003), 'A typology of supplier relations: From determinism to pluralism in inter-firm empirical research', *Journal of Purchasing and Supply Management*, **9**(1), 31–41.

Morgan, N.A., A. Kaleka and R. Gooner (2007), 'Focal supplier opportunism in supermarket retailer category management', *Journal of Operations Management*, **25**(2), 512–527.

Morgan, R.M. and S.D. Hunt (1994), 'The commitment–trust theory of relationship marketing', *Journal of Marketing*, **58**(3), 20–39.

Perry, M.A.T. (1991), 'Channel member conflict and performance: A proposed model and research agenda', *International Review of Retail, Distribution and Consumer Research*, **1**(2), 233–252.

Porter, M. (1985), *Competitive Advantage*, New York: Free Press.

Rigby, D.K., F.F. Reichheld and P. Schefter (2002), 'Avoid the four perils of CRM', *Harvard Business Review*, **80**(2), 101–109.

Ross, W.T. and D.C. Robertson (2007), 'Compound relationships between firms', *Journal of Marketing*, **71**(3), 108–123.

Sa Vinhas, A. and E. Anderson (2005), 'How potential conflict drives channel structure: Concurrent (direct and indirect) channels', *Journal of Marketing Research*, **42**(4), 507–515.
Sheth, J.N. and A. Parvatiyar (2000), *Handbook of Relationship Marketing*, Thousand Oaks, CA: Sage Publications.
Spekman, R.E. and R. Carraway (2006), 'Making the transition to collaborative buyer–seller relationships: An emerging framework', *Industrial Marketing Management*, **35**(1), 10–19.
Stamper, C.L. and M.C. Johlke (2003), 'The impact of perceived organizational support on the relationship between boundary spanner role stress and work outcomes', *Journal of Management*, **29**(4), 569–588.
Walley, K. (2007), 'Coopetition: An introduction to the subject and an agenda for research', *International Studies of Management and Organization*, **37**(2), 11–31.
Yin, R.K. (1984), *Case Study Research: Design and Method*, Beverly Hills, CA: Sage.
Zajak, E.J. and C.P. Olsen (1993), 'From transaction cost to transactional value analysis: Implications for the study of interorganizational strategies', *Journal of Management Studies*, **36**(7), 941–954.
Zenor, M.J. (1994), 'The profit benefits of category management', *Journal of Marketing Research*, **31**(2), 202–213.
Zerbini, F. and S. Castaldo (2007), 'Stay in or get out the Janus? The maintenance of multiplex relationships between buyers and sellers', *Industrial Marketing Management*, **36**(7), 941–954.

8. Coopetition among nature-based tourism firms: competition at local level and cooperation at destination level

Ossi Pesämaa and Per-Erik Eriksson

INTRODUCTION

In tourism we often find situations where firms compete at a local level and simultaneously cooperate at a destination level to outperform other destinations (Pesämaa and Hair, 2007, 2008). This situation of combining competition and cooperation by differentiating business activities at different levels is known as coopetition (Brandenburger and Nalebuff, 1996). Various examples from the tourism literature emphasize different aspects of this dilemma. One coopetitive advantage seems to exist in sharing informational platforms (Belleflamme and Neysen, 2006) or marketing activities at a destination level (Grängsjö, 2003), but in all other aspects remaining competititors. Also, organizational aspects of coopetition are recognized in the tourism literature. Wang and Krakover (2008) argue that firms are diversifying among different types of relationships by independently controlling close relationships but organizing themselves in webs of interdependent activities when relationships are more distant from customers. We therefore claim that tourism firms focus too much on competition at a local level instead of cooperating locally and competing against each other at a destinations level.

Coopetition is especially significant in tourism, since the place (that is, a geographical area) is the basis for the attraction through which the destination is developed. These attractions can be both man-made and natural. Recall that one theoretical idea of coopetition is that long-term strategic cooperative objectives should dominate competition, which is mostly derived by short-term financial interests (Wang and Krakover, 2008). This idea of coopetition can be challenging in tourism, especially when it is dominated by many small firms offering a variety of different products. The coopetitive issue in tourism is also prevalent and relevant from the perspective of a nature-based destination, because it involves elements of social, ethical and environmental issues (Cohen, 1984; Huybers and Bennett, 2003). These issues emanate from the fact that many nature-based attractions, as physical places, encompass local cultures and heritages giving certain rights to locals. Understandably, tension emerges as commercial competitive interests confront established local cooperative rules. One challenge is thus to balance short-term financial aspects (for example, customer needs) with long-term interest in trying to preserve local rights and maintain rules and obligations on how to exert control over nature and how to take action in local development. One key question in such discussion is how much and what type of fishing and hunting to permit, who to give permission to and to what extent to allow exploitation of, for example, the river, forest and mountains. Coopetition from the perspective of balancing commercial development with public interest thus goes into the heart of community development programs. Individual interests needs to be negotiated against shared interests. Sometimes the outcome of this negotiation is that individual interests benefit from those that are shared.

Thus, tourism businesses are in part interdependent and in part competing against each other. We did not find any studies that elaborated on this social dilemma and proposed a strategic direction for developing programs to deal with this issue. According to Lado, Boyd and Hanlon (1997), game theory provides a useful conceptual lens for examining simultaneous competition and cooperation, explaining the behavior of firms (players) in inter-firm relationships (games). Game theory can then be a useful tool to analyze and predict actors' interdependent decisions.

In this chapter, a game-theoretic simulation is used to elucidate two different strategies of cooperating or competing and discuss their consequences. These consequences are investigated by elaboration of different behavior strategies and different perspectives of risk. Specifically, we ask what rationale justifies cooperation in nature-based tourism destinations. Do the actors prefer a decision to cooperate in favor of competition based on their perspective of risk?

1.   COMPETITION, COOPERATION AND COOPETITION

Neoclassical economic theory describes competition as different structures within an industry. This theory of competition as a state, normally in equilibrium (Hunt, 2000) can be defined as a condition of tension between different actors, derived by a conflict of interest between them when they try to pursue their goals (Anderson, 1988). Bengtsson and Kock (1999) analyze competition beyond mere structural characteristics. Instead of treating it as a static condition in an industry, it is merely a dynamic interactive process where perceptions and experience affect organizational actions and interactions (Zajac and Olsen, 1993). This process symbolizes the constant struggle for comparative advantages in resources, generating marketplace positions of competitive advantage and thereby superior financial performance (Hunt, 2000).

Competitive behavior refers to actors' self-interest in favor of common interests (Bengtsson and Kock, 1999), which is a rather individualistic perspective (Ghoshal and Moran, 1996). In game theory, competitive behavior provides a useful point of departure for understanding interfirm relationships. Game-theoretic literatures provide a broad span of different competitive behaviors which all elaborate on different reasons for competing. In game theory, we find that defection from cooperation and opportunistic behavior are synonyms but have different emphases (for example, Hill, 1990; Khanna, Gulati and Nohria, 1998; Lado, Boyd and Hanlon, 1997). Moreover we find that defection is derived from self-interest wherein the actor is maximizing outcomes (Axelrod, 1984). Opportunistic behavior refers to parties taking advantage of non-contractible or non-specified aspects of a contract to increase their own benefits at the expense of other parties (Landry and Trudel, 1998). Other related concepts exemplify competitive behavior as being cheating, shirking, distorting information, misleading partners and providing substandard products (Das and Teng, 1998). From this point, competitive behavior is used as a synonym for defecting, acting opportunistically and other similar concepts.

Cooperation, on the other hand, includes contradictory elements in relation to competitive behavior. In strategic management (Lado, Boyd and Hanlon, 1997) and marketing (Bengtsson and Kock, 2000; Ylimaz and Hunt, 2001) cooperation emanates from the search for someone sharing the same interests and from the participation of the other actors' goals and interests. The idea of cooperation is therefore a search for calculated outcomes which are mostly expressed in the selection and execution of shared decisions and goals (Lado, Boyd and Hanlon, 1997; Ylimaz and Hunt, 2001). In opposition to competition, which is derived from conflicting interests, Bengtsson and Kock (2000) state that cooperative relationships consist of friendliness due to common interests. Thus, a precondition for cooperation is the participation of individuals in collective actions to achieve common goals (Bengtsson and Kock, 2000). Therefore, cooperation necessarily involves interdependencies between actors (Ouchi, 1980). Whereas competition is related to conflict, cooperation is related to harmony, since trust and mutuality result in harmonious relationships (Bengtsson and Kock, 1999). Contrary to competitive behavior, which is derived from a focus on self-interest, cooperative behavior is related to collectivism and concern for the needs of other parties and outcomes in interactions (Ghoshal and Moran, 1996; Wilkinson and Young, 2002). Cooperative behavior is characterized by being truthful (for example, honest dealing, fair play and complying with agreements) and showing commitment by making efforts (Das and Teng, 1998). In this chapter, competition and cooperation are treated as opposites, which is normal in game theory.

The neoclassical focus on competition is argued to be obsolete by many authors, though too much focus on cooperation may also be harmful, since it may lead to laziness and stagnation or even opportunism (Eriksson, 2008a). Placing too much unwarranted trust in an untested partner can expose an organization to grave damage (Parkhe, 1998). There is a danger that collaborative relationships become the objective rather than a suitable medium for achieving the overriding goal, that is, improved business performance (Cox and Thompson, 1997). Accordingly, developing a relationship should be based on a sound business case, not on a utopian ideal of working better together. Therefore, a suitable balance between cooperation and competition seems pertinent (Eriksson, 2008a), since cooperation is required to enhance coordination of activities, joint problem solving and transaction of specific investments (Uzzi, 1997), and competition is generally important for the effectiveness of the relationship (Bengtsson and Kock, 1999). If cooperation involves interdependencies between actors (Ouchi, 1980) and competition stimulates conflict mechanisms (Teece, 1992), coopetition recognizes the importance of balancing these two paradoxical concepts (Eriksson, 2008b). Analyzed from a game-theoretical perspective, Brandenburger and Nalebuff (1996) gave birth to this new concept. Coopetition is foremost cooperation when baking a cake by expanding the total amount of rewards and resources available and competition when dividing the rewards and resources (Brandenburger and Nalebuff, 1996). Many authors (such as Lado, Boyd and Hanlon, 1997; Wilkinson and Young, 2002) apply these ideas by analyzing coopetition using game theory, often with an application of the Prisoner's Dilemma game involving decisions of cooperation and competition.

1.1   Towards Coopetition in Tourism

Despite the advantages cooperation seems to offer, most cooperative efforts end up in failure (Park and Russo, 1996). One conclusion based on this is that cooperation does not come easily if there are no clear incentives.

The difficulty of cooperating under poor incentives is especially present in nature-based tourism destinations (Huybers and Bennett, 2003). In a small local economy, there is much cooperative effort. The only incentive to cooperate might be long-term survival. The social dilemma in which the individual's interest is interdependent on others' interests, along with poor incentives to cooperate, become the foundation of conflicting interests here. One interest is that of 'self' and the second is that of 'others'.

'Self' interest concerns the interest of 'my' profit, 'my' reputation, 'my' financing, 'my' effort and 'my' responsibility. These are all important in forming the interest of 'self'. Being reluctant to take an active role of cooperation is probably the result of having the perception of making too many sacrifices with regard to rights and freedom in favor of others (Anderson and Weitz, 1992). The interest of 'self' in combination with being averse to cooperation could also be the result of feeling strongly independent (Park and Folkman, 1997) and believing that independent local competition, rather than collective goals, stresses competitiveness.

Too much focus on 'self' interests (non-cooperation) generates collective failures (Olson, 1965). The opposite interest – 'our' (cooperation) – in tourism is at a destination level caring for 'our' tourism bureau (if public), 'our' roads, 'our' website, 'our' logotype, 'our' wilderness, 'our' waters, 'our' nature, 'our' hunting and 'our' fishing privileges. It might appear far-fetched to ask the independent firm or manager to care for 'our' roads, but collective lobbying activities are sometimes more effective than trying to obtain such change independently. This interest of 'ours' is especially present in the example of nature-based tourism destinations. The individual who is aware of 'our' interest realizes that cooperation is beneficial or at least necessary for long-term survival. Neglecting destination-specific interests (our interests), is the same as ignoring part of the base for attracting guests.

2.   THE PRISONER'S DILEMMA IN NATURE-BASED TOURISM DESTINATIONS

Simulation in game theory refers to the evaluation of situations (Axelrod, 1984) by visualizing and exploring the minds of other actors (Romp, 1997). The exploratory advantage helps to structure empirically complicated situations (Parkhe, 1993) such as establishing nature-based tourism destinations. By elaborating on different scenarios of the counterpart's behavior orientation and the risk of the strategic situation (Parkhe, 1993), possible explanations or even predictions occur (Zagare, 1984). Prisoner's Dilemma (PD) is the most analyzed game-theoretic situation (Axelrod,

1984; Zagare, 1984). It triggers scholars and practitioners to find different solutions to resolve the dilemma. PD consists of a situation where two actors are caught in a dilemma represented by alternatives that will yield different outcomes (pay-offs) depending on what risk each actor is willing to take.

Game theory can be applied to an individual problem (a single round game), or to a series of problems (a repeated game). In a repeated game, the weight (W) of every decision (also called the discount parameter) as well as the length of the game (the number of repeated rounds) affect the players' decision making (Axelrod, 1984). The discount parameter is a useful tool to subdivide the total value of the decisions. For instance, the weight of the second decision could be half as important as the first and the third half as important as the second. In this case the discount parameter would be 0.5 (Axelrod, 1984).

The game in this chapter is divided into two parts: one single game and one repeated game with two strategic situations. Assumptions regarding pay-offs in the simulated PD are presented in Figure 8.1 and also illustrated in a tree diagram (see Figure 8.2). The PD is later analyzed according to different perceptions of risk. The scenario contains a case of two actors choosing either to cooperate or defect (compete) in a situation with identical information.

Assumptions are directly derived from general requirements for the Prisoner's Dilemma where $T>R>P>S$ (Axelrod, 1984; Zagare, 1984). The proposed scenario also includes the element of survival by tailoring the assumptions so that $R> (T+S)/2$. In other words, if $R+R$ is larger than $T+S$ there is an incentive to cooperate, because switching the formula to

		Actor 2	
		Cooperate	Defect
Actor 1	Cooperate	$R_2 = 8$ $R_1 = 8$	$T_2 = 9$ $S_1 = 1$
	Defect	$S_2 = 1$ $T_1 = 9$	$P_2 = 3$ $P_1 = 3$

R = Reward for mutual cooperation   T = Temptation to defect
S = Sucker's pay-off   P = Punishment for mutual defection

Figure 8.1   Pay-offs of the PD game

R<(T + S)/2 would by turns give incentives to defect (T) or to forgive the other party. The scores in the selected game are not empirically derived, but cover assumptions necessary for the behavior orientation strategies used.

3.   BEHAVIORAL ORIENTATION TO COOPERATE OR DEFECT IN A PD GAME

Behavioral orientation refers to individual strategies in a game which aims to reflect a real situation. Behavior orientations reflect assumptions of how the actor perceives the situation according to his or her independent perceptions but also how s/he believes the confronting actor will behave. Every strategy will be given an abbreviated attribute.

As the behavior orientation refers to a certain strategy, including specific assumptions, every change of the assumptions also has the effect of creating a whole new game. There are several different strategies that a decision maker can undertake in repeated games. We offer the most basic strategies in Table 8.1.

The definitions in Table 8.1 indicate that establishing agreements or

Table 8.1   Behavior orientation and definition

Behavior orientation strategy	Name	Definition	Study
Notorious defector	ND	ND will always defect to ensure not being trapped by someone else's defection and/or to ensure a minimum gain.	Axelrod, 1984
Tit-for-tat	TFT	TFT is a strategy in which actor obediently follows the most recent move of the partner.	Axelrod, 1984; Outkin, 2002
Mutant strategy	MS	A powerful strategy, where the actor is exploring different ways of finding high pay-offs through trial and error.	Axelrod, 1984
Notorious cooperator	NC	Strong ties of kinship or culture facilitate notorious cooperation through altruism or respecting common rules because of the risk of collective punishment.	Adler, 2001; Axelrod, 1984, 1997

relationships, without including some kind of punishment for those break-ing the agreement, will risk exploitation by a notorious defector (ND), who always chooses to defect. The Tit-for-tat (TFT) strategy operates on a reciprocity basis. Being oriented by TFT has the consequence that if Actor 1 defects, Actor 2 follows with defection in order to adapt to the prevalent behavior of the game (Outkin, 2002). TFT is probably the most popular and most quoted strategy in game theory.

> TIT FOR TAT's robust success in infinite repeated games is based on its com-bination of being nice, retaliatory, forgiving and clear. Its niceness prevents it from getting into unnecessary trouble. Its retaliation discourages the other side from persisting whenever defection is tried. Its forgiveness helps restore mutual cooperation. And its clarity makes it intelligible to the other actor, thereby elic-iting long-term cooperation (Axelrod, 1984: 54).

Mutant strategy (MS) is a risky way of finding a solution to the problem; but in itself also increases the chances of getting high pay-offs. At the end of the repeated games, the behavior orientation of MS actors is characterized by defection, since this actor tries to finish the game with the highest pay-off (T) when it is impossible to retaliate. In kinships or safe environments, where strong ties have been established between the actors (Adler, 2001; Axelrod, 1997; Sally, 2001), altruism or avoiding defection is appropriate or even necessary (for example, in your own family or neighborhood), result-ing in notorious cooperation (NC). Unexpected defection may result in the quick collective punishment of discrediting reputation by action where, for example, a dominant actor (for example, locomotive company) actively works to limit such behavior (Axelrod, 1984). Another reason for choosing cooperation can be that the survival of the other actor is important for your own survival. The pay-off is then not accounted for in terms of how well or how much you may win. Instead, success is just accounted for in terms of survival. If the cooperative partner vanishes then it means that both partners have to 'close shop'. In fact, tourism is such an industry, since one business cannot be attractive enough because tourists want safety, pleasure, a myriad of shopping alternatives, different activities and so on. If one or several shops close, then part of the attractiveness also diminishes.

4. GAME SIMULATION

This section describes two different games: a single round game and a repeated game (see Figure 8.1 for the assumptions regarding pay-offs). Figure 8.2 views all possible outcomes of both games. It is common to illus-trate sequential games with tree illustrations. The game is characterized as

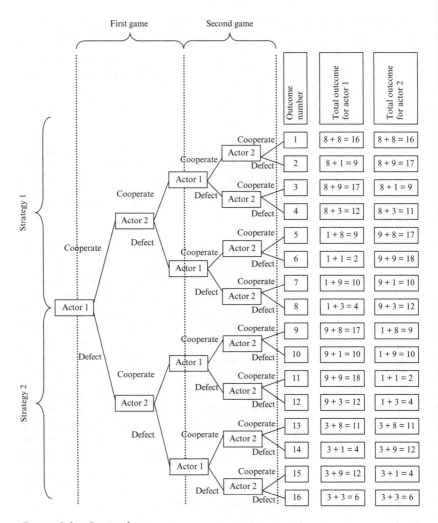

Figure 8.2　Derived outcomes

one of imperfect information, which means that the actors are not aware of each other's choices in the current round of the game. Both players act independently within each round, but in the second round they act on the basis of the other actor's previous move (that is, the decisions made in the first round are known to both actors in the second round). Tree diagrams illustrate paths accurately as well as the total value of executed decisions. The illustrations thus show the history of alternative decision-making strategies. When collecting evidence of experiences, this is one way to express and discuss the issue. In the game, the discount parameter is w=1, which means that every decision is worth the same.

5. ANALYZING THE RESULTS

Analysis of the single as well as the repeated game is divided into two different mathematical principles according to different views on risk (optimistic or pessimistic).

5.1 Analyzing the Single Round Game

As the PD in Figure 8.1 reveals, each actor has two main decision options: to cooperate or to defect. The two general mathematical principles adopted from Grubbström (1977) involve a pessimistic and an optimistic estimation of the outcomes – see Table 8.2. The first view refers to Wald's criterion, which aims to explore the outcomes from a pessimistic perspective. The pessimistic decision maker is risk averse and looks to minimize the risks (maximin) by trying to avoid the worst outcomes. The second view, Hurwicz's criterion, is a more optimistic and risky approach, trying to achieve the highest pay-off (maximax). This view concentrates on achieving the best outcomes (Grubbström, 1977).

- Regarding the minimizing strategy, the Wald criterion, the actor will choose the highest (3) of the low values, which in this simple game means to defect.
- The maximizing strategy, Hurwicz's criterion, suggests that the actor will choose the value which yields the highest score (9). In this example the actor will also defect.

5.2 Analysis of Results in the Repeated Game

The analyses from the repeated game are based on the same scores as expressed in Figure 8.1 and illustrated in Figure 8.2. These analyses reveal

Table 8.2 Outcomes analyzed in a single game

	Lowest score Wald's criterion	Highest score Hurwicz's criterion
Cooperate	1	8
Defect	3	9

Table 8.3   Categories of strategy selected by each actor in two games

Outcome	Game 1		Game 2		Behavior orientation	
	Actor 1	Actor 2	Actor 1	Actor 2	Strategy Actor 1	Strategy Actor 2
1	8	8	8	8	NC/ TFT/MS	NC/ TFT/MS
2	8	8	1	9	NC/ TFT/MS	MS
3	8	8	9	1	MS	NC/ TFT/MS
4	8	8	3	3	MS	MS
5	1	9	8	8	NC/MS	MS
6	1	9	1	9	NC	ND/MS
7	1	9	9	1	TFT/MS	MS
8	1	9	3	3	TFT/MS	ND/MS
9	9	1	8	8	MS	NC/MS
10	9	1	1	9	MS	TFT/MS
11	9	1	9	1	ND/MS	NC
12	9	1	3	3	ND/MS	TFT/MS
13	3	3	8	8	MS	MS
14	3	3	1	9	MS	ND/MS
15	3	3	9	1	ND/MS	MS
16	3	3	3	3	ND/MS	ND/MS

Table 8.4   Analysis of simulated behavior orientation in two games

	Min	Max	Wald Pessimistic view	Hurwicz Optimistic View
Notorious defector (ND)	6	18	6	18
Tit-for-tat (TFT)	4	16	4	16
Mutant strategy (MS)	4	18	4	18
Notorious cooperator (NC)	2	16	2	16

a specific kind of pattern in behavior and thus manifest the strategy the actors employ. Hence, each outcome also represents behavior orientation, derived from Figure 8.2 and further analyzed as a category of strategy in Table 8.3. Each type of behavior orientation is categorized on the basis of the pattern that the actors demonstrate while executing cooperative decisions. In Table 8.4, each category also receives a minimum and maximum score. These are all-important for completing the analysis.

The result of the analyses presented in Table 8.4 is that notorious defection (ND) is the most rational strategy no matter which criterion is used to evaluate the benefits while also considering the risks. Consequently, in the simulated game, defection is the most rational behavior, whether the player is optimistic or pessimistic.

CONCLUSIONS

The questions we addressed in this chapter were: what rationale justifies cooperation in nature-based tourism destinations? Do the actors prefer a decision to cooperate in favor of competition based on their perspective of risk? This chapter uses some logic to build a conceptual understanding of coopetition, in which the actors compete and cooperate simultaneously. Initially the chapter demonstrates that competition and cooperation are at odds with each other, partly because 'my' incentives are stronger than 'our' incentives while competing at a firm level (my) and cooperating at a destination level (our). The dilemma is that coopetition based on cooperation at a destination level and competition at a local level is vital for the long-term success of the tourism firms. However, game simulation tells us that cooperation is not easy to establish when actors are behaving rationally. In fact, the dominant strategy, which outperforms all other strategies in finite repeated games, is defection (Zagare, 1984), which in a way breaks the rationale of coopetition, where the benefits of cooperation are assumed to dominate those of competition (Wang and Krakover, 2008). This may also explain why Park and Russo (1996) found in their historical archive study that most cooperation efforts become failures and Olson (1965) noted that focus on the self also runs the risk of a collective failure. Results of the simulated game corroborate that establishing cooperation is a difficult task and there is in fact no rational justification for cooperating in a single or finite repeated game – see Table 8.2. The results of the game simulation show that defection is rational no matter which risk orientation the actor has.

Furthermore, trusting the corresponding person is a risky task, which also goes with the argument of Jones and Wicks (1999) that trust is a matter of risk. Trust is indeed considered as a degree rather than an absolute measure which is conducive to cooperation (Zaheer, McEvily and Perrone, 1998). These results cannot corroborate that trust is a degree, but depending on what behavior orientation a person has, the risk is always there if the actor confronts a person oriented by notorious defection (ND), which means that trust is always a risky task. In infinite repeated games, however, trust and familiarity breed cooperation. Axelrod (1984) labels experiences 'tit-for-tat' in his scenarios, whereas Gulati (1995) prefers to use the concept of familiarity. These results have the implication that being familiar and knowing the partner also generate knowledge of what to expect, which further breeds trust and cooperation through increased behavior predictability (Das and Teng, 1998). In infinite repeated games, tit-for-tat is the most successful and rational strategy (Axelrod, 1984). In reality, inter-organizational relationships are often informal and based on trust, making them correspond better to an infinite repeated game than a finite repeated game (Eriksson, 2007).

The emphasis on risk may also revisit some of the literature on coopetition and on the issue of establishing nature-based tourism destinations. The major assumption of this chapter has been that the two goals of competing and cooperating are at odds with one another. We also framed that the interest of the 'self' is interdependent with 'our' interest (Hardin, 1968). Therefore we propose that the interest of the 'self' is best obtained simultaneously with interest of 'ours' through establishing common goals (Park and Folkman, 1997) coordinated from one point (that is, a hierarchical strategic network or transport company). Having both goals coordinated from the same point may possibly increase the likelihood that both will be achieved to a higher degree than if the responsibilities are divided and differentially placed in the absence of a hierarchy. Strategic hierarchical networks or transport companies[1] have perhaps the reputation and resources needed to take such responsibility. Organizing from one point is here proposed as one way of solving these conflicting interests practically. Firms are then cooperating at a destination level in order to be better able to compete against other network of firms at other destinations. This separation usually takes the form of coopetition, in which temporary or lasting goals, operations and activities are beneficial for both parties despite being in the midst of competition. In this way, coopetition in nature-based tourism destinations is typically characterized by cooperation when baking the cake (the destination) and competing when dividing it (attracting tourists when they have arrived), as suggested by Brandenburger and Nalebuff (1996).

Furthermore, it would be beneficial to have a counselling aspect in a hierarchical strategic network or transport company, in which it is possible to control processes of trust by having the instrument to punish undesired behavior. In reality, there are no distinct and isolated games (Brandenburger and Nalebuff, 1996). Hence, what happens in one game (relationship) can therefore have consequences in another game. Cooperation can therefore be facilitated in a particular game if a third party (for example, a transport company) has the power to punish a defecting player later in another game. Since nature-based tourism destinations consist of a network of players, this situation of several connected games is much more comparable to reality than an isolated game. Cooperation is also a matter of awareness of how an intended decision will affect the outcome. Since awareness of this interdependence in making the destination competitive is low in tourism, there is a strong incentive to coordinate some activities from a network level and thus sustain the structure of local competition at another level. Game-theoretic reasoning can also be useful in increasing the actors' awareness that their decisions are dependent on other actors' decisions. Thus, the 'negative' results of the game situation can in reality be more positive, both through punishing a third party and by an infinite length of game.

A contribution of this chapter is that practitioners and scholars can use the quite simple mathematical principles (regarding perception of risk) to elaborate on different strategic options. These principles clarify rules, conditions and terms characterizing different situations. Since practical situations involve many unknown and hidden variables, these principles may help to estimate the risks of different scenarios and to establish mechanisms by which managers can establish rules of thumb. Complex situations surrounding individual decision making limit the opportunities to be rational (Romp, 1997). Simulated games extend the opportunity to manage complexity and enable every individual actor to be more aware of the consequences of their actions. Since increasing complexity fosters cooperation (Kirchkamp, 2000), tools specifically designed to simulate complex outcomes of alternative decisions to cooperate or compete should be highly relevant.

NOTE

1. See, for example, www.ironrangeresources.org and www.sveaskog.se, respectively.

REFERENCES

Adler, P.S. (2001), 'Market, Hierarchy and Trust', *Organizational Science*, **12**(2), 215–234.
Anderson, A. (1988), *Konkurrensanalys och Marknadsagerande*, Kungälv: Goterna.
Anderson, E. and B. Weitz (1992), 'The Use of Pledges to Build and Sustain Commitment in Distribution Channels', *Journal of Marketing Research*, **24**, 18–34.
Axelrod, R. (1984), *The Evolution of Cooperation*, New York: Basic Books.
Axelrod, R. (1997), *The Complexity of Cooperation*, Princeton: Princeton University Press.
Belleflamme, P. and N. Neysen. (2006). 'Coopetition in Infomediation: General Analysis and Application to e-Tourism', *2nd Workshop on Coopetition Strategy*, Milan, Italy, 14–15 September.

180 *Coopetition*

Bengtsson, M. and S. Kock (1999), 'Cooperation and Competition in Relationships between Competitors in Business Networks', *Journal of Business and Industrial Marketing*, **14**(3), 178–193.

Bengtsson, M. and S. Kock (2000), 'Coopetition in Business Networks – To Cooperate and Compete Simultaneously', *Industrial Marketing Management*, **29**(5), 411–426.

Brandenburger, A. and B. Nalebuff (1996), *Coopetition*, New York: Doubleday.

Cohen, E. (1984), 'The Sociology of Tourism: Approaches, Issues, and Findings', *Annual Review of Sociology*, **10**, 373–392.

Cox, A. and I. Thompson (1997), 'Fit for Purpose Contractual Relations: Determining a Theoretical Framework for Construction Projects', *Europe Journal of Purchasing and Supply Management*, **3**(3), 127–135.

Das, T. and B.-S. Teng (1998), 'Between Trust and Control: Developing Confidence in Partner Cooperation in Alliances', *Academy of Management Review*, **23**(3), 491–512.

Eriksson, P.E. (2007), 'Cooperation and Partnering in Facilities Construction – Empirical Application of Prisoner's Dilemma', *Facilities*, **25**(1/2), 7–19.

Eriksson, P.E. (2008a), 'Achieving Suitable Coopetition in Buyer–Supplier Relationships: The Case of AstraZeneca', *Journal of Business to Business Marketing*, **15**(4), 425–54.

Eriksson, P.E. (2008b), 'Procurement Effects on Coopetition in Client–Contractor Relationships', *Journal of Construction Engineering and Management*, **134**(2), 103–111.

Ghoshal, S. and P. Moran (1996), 'Bad for Practice: A Critique of the Transaction Cost Theory', *Academy of Management Review*, **21**(1), 13–47.

Grängsjö, Y. (2003), 'Destination Networking: Coopetition in Peripheral Surroundings', *International Journal of Physical Distribution and Logistics Management*, **33**(5), 427–448.

Grubbström, R. (1977), *Besluts- och Spelteori med Tillämpningar*, Lund: Studentlitteratur.

Gulati, R. (1995), 'Does Familiarity Breed Trust? The Implications of Repeated Ties for Contractual Choice in Alliances', *The Academy of Management Journal*, **38**(1), 85–112.

Hardin, G. (1968), 'The Tragedy of the Commons', *Science Magazine*, **162**, 1243–1248.

Hill, C. (1990), 'Cooperation, Opportunism, and the Invisible Hand: Implications for Transaction Cost Theory', *The Academy of Management Review*, **15**(3), 500–513.

Hunt, S. (2000), *A General Theory of Competition*, Thousand Oaks: Sage Publications.

Huybers, T. and J. Bennett (2003), 'Inter-Firm Cooperation at Nature-Based Tourism Destinations', *Journal of Socio-Economics*, **32**, 571–587.

Jones, T.M. and A.C. Wicks (1999), 'Convergent Stakeholder Theory', *The Academy of Management Review*, **24**(2), 206–221.

Khanna, T., R. Gulati and N. Nohria (1998), 'The Dynamics of Learning Alliances: Competition, Cooperation, and Relative Scope', *Strategic Management Journal*, **19**(3), 193–210.

Kirchkamp, O. (2000), 'Spatial Evolution of Automata in the Prisoners' Dilemma', *Journal of Economic Behavior*, **43**, 239–262.

Lado, A., N. Boyd and S. Hanlon (1997), 'Competition, Cooperation, and the

Search for Economic Rents: A Syncretic Model', *Academy of Management Review*, **22**(1), 110–141.

Landry, S. and Y. Trudel (1998), 'Just-In-Time Supply: Cooperation, Competition, and Abuse', *Competitiveness Review*, **8**(1), 37–45.

Olson, M. (1965), *The Logic of Collective Action*, Cambridge, MA: Harvard University Press.

Ouchi, W. (1980), 'Markets, Bureaucracies, and Clans', *Administrative Science Quarterly*, **25**(1), 129–141.

Outkin, A.V. (2002), 'Cooperation and Local Interactions in the Prisoners' Dilemma Game', *Journal of Economic Behavior and Organization*, **52**(4), 481–503.

Park, C.L. and S. Folkman (1997), 'Meaning in the Context of Stress and Coping', *Review of General Psychology*, **1**(2), 115–144.

Park, S.H. and M.V. Russo (1996), 'When Competition Eclipses Cooperation: An Event History Analysis of Joint Ventures', *Management Science*, **42**(6), 875–890.

Parkhe, A. (1993), 'Strategic Alliance Structuring', *Academy of Management Journal*, **36**(4), 794–809.

Parkhe, A. (1998), 'Building Trust in International Alliances', *Journal of World Business*, **33**(4), 417–438.

Pesämaa, O. and J.F. Hair Jr, (2007), 'More Than Friendship is Required: An Empirical Test of Cooperative Firm Strategies', *Management Decision*, **45**(3), 602–615.

Pesämaa, O. and J.F. Hair Jr, (2008), 'Cooperative Strategies for Improving the Tourism Industry in Remote Geographic Regions: An Addition to Trust and Commitment Theory with One Key Mediating Construct', *Scandinavian Journal of Hospitality and Tourism*, **8**(1), 48–61.

Romp, G. (1997), *Game Theory: Introduction and Applications*, Oxford: Oxford University Press.

Sally, D. (2001), 'On Sympathy and Games', *Journal of Economic Behavior and Organization*, **44**, 1–30.

Teece, D. (1992), 'Competition, Cooperation, and Innovation: Organizational Arrangements for Regimes of Rapid Technological Progress', *Journal of Economic Behavior and Organization*, **18**, 1–25.

Uzzi, B. (1997), 'Social Structure and Competition in Interfirm Networks: The Paradox of Embeddedness', *Administrative Science Quarterly*, **42**(1), 35–67.

Wang, Y. and S. Krakover (2008), 'Destination Marketing: Competition, Cooperation or Coopetition', *International Journal of Contemporary Hospitality Management*, **20**(2), 126–141.

Wilkinson, I. and L. Young (2002), 'On Cooperating Firms, Relations and Networks', *Journal of Business Research*, **55**(2), 123–132.

Ylimaz, C. and S.D. Hunt (2001), 'Salesperson Cooperation: The Influence of Relational Task, Organizational, and Personal Factors', *Journal of the Academy of Marketing Science*, **29**(4), 335–357.

Zagare, F. (1984), *Game Theory: Concepts and Applications*, Beverly Hills, CA: Sage Publications.

Zaheer, A., B. McEvily and V. Perrone (1998), 'Does Trust Matter? Exploring the Effects of Interorganizational and Interpersonal Trust on Performance', *Organization Science*, **9**(2), 141–159.

Zajac, E.J. and C.P. Olsen (1993), 'From Transaction Cost to Transactional Value Analysis: Implication for the Study of Interorganizational Strategies', *Journal of Management Studies*, **30**(1), 131–145.

Electronic Sources

www.ironrangeresources.org, accessed on 22 November 2009.
www.sveaskog.se, accessed on 22 November 2009.

PART III

Coopetition strategies at the aggregate level

9. Coopetition within an oligopoly: impacts of a disruptive strategy

Pierre Roy and Saïd Yami

INTRODUCTION

The strategic literature identifies the oligopolistic market configuration as an appropriate context in which to question the dialectics between individual and collective fates characterizing firms (Astley, 1984). Indeed, the oligopolistic interdependence is binding on firms and creates collective interests exceeding those specific to each firm (Pennings, 1981). The emergence of the concept of coopetition deals precisely with this relational paradox (Brandenburger and Nalebuff, 1996).

In this research, we investigate a firm's deviance from a collective fate in an oligopoly and the competitive implications of such a move on the coopetitive relation between dominant firms. To be precise, we wonder about the impacts of the introduction of a disruptive strategy (Hamel and Prahalad, 1994) within an oligopoly. In this regard, we study the case of UGC's unlimited access card launched in March 2000 in the French movie theater sector. This event characterizes a disruptive strategy individually carried out by one of the dominant firms and which goes against the collective interests of the oligopoly (composed of Gaumont, Pathé and UGC).

In this chapter, we first present the theoretical background, mobilizing the concepts of collective strategy, coopetition and disruptive strategy. Then we explain the methodological aspects of our study and the empirical context. The third part is devoted to the treatment of the case from a longitudinal perspective.

1. THEORETICAL BACKGROUND

1.1 Oligopoly and Interdependence

The starting point of our research is linked to the following statement: the contemporary economy privileges more and more the oligopolistic form.

One of the direct consequences of this statement is the existence of a strong interdependence linking firms within the same industry. Indeed, in an oligopolistic context, an organization must necessarily consider the actions of other organizations.

Such a situation refers to the horizontal type of interdependence in the typology suggested by Pennings (1981). The author defined it in these terms: 'horizontal interdependence exists when all members of an organization-set compete with each other in obtaining similar resources and disposing of similar goods and services' (p.434). Within an oligopoly, firms indeed have comparable resources and appreciably target the same customers in the market. These firms develop interdependence from their repeated interaction at the same time in the provisioning market and the market where goods and services are sold to the customers.

According to Pennings (1981), horizontal interdependence generates uncertainty for firms within an oligopolistic context since in this case the interdependence is recognized by firms. Also, according to Bresser and Harl (1986), interdependence between firms can generate problems of uncertainty during the decision-making process, in so far as the leaders are conscious of the interdependencies of the firm and consequently have difficulty in controlling the probable activities of the other organizations (Pfeffer and Salancik, 1978; Pennings, 1981).

The awareness of the interdependence between competitive firms assumes the latency of collusive behaviours between firms (Stigler, 1964), more or less tacit according to specific cases. The reciprocal knowledge of oligopoly members can indeed lead to the coordination of certain axes of their policy (for example price or innovation). The economic literature identifies several factors leading to coordinated policies between competitive firms. Hay and Kelley (1974) list seven factors: a small number of actors, a high degree of concentration, homogeneity of products, inelastic demand, a functioning by invitation to tender, an irregular demand and the presence of high fixed costs. These parameters encourage firms to coordinate their strategies in the market in order to reduce uncertainty (Bresser and Harl, 1986).

1.2   From Interdependence to Coopetition

Oligopolistic interdependence thus constitutes an appropriate ground for the realization of a collective fate for the few firms leading the industry. This leads us to pay attention to the ambiguous nature of contemporary competitive relations and, therefore, to consider the engagement of collective action on the market. Astley (1984: 533) thus evokes the intrinsically antagonistic character of oligopolistic relations:

coalitions – such as those established in oligopolistic practice – are seen as mixed-motive games. Although such interaction appears to be cooperative, it is seen, more or less, as an antagonistic, tongue-in-cheek, short term cooperation designed to allow each organization to improve its own long term competitive position.

Precisely this question is discussed in strategic management literature and brings a new perspective on contemporary competitive relations. Indeed, the traditional dichotomy between competition and cooperation is no longer appropriate for understanding inter-firm relations. The concept of 'coopetition' (Brandenburger and Nalebuff 1996) and its early developments focused mainly on the definition and the understanding of the nature of this ambiguity (Lado, Boyd and Hanlon, 1997; Bengtsson and Kock, 2000; Gnyawali and Madhavan, 2001; Dagnino and Padula, 2002; Lecocq and Yami, 2002). The current challenge for scholars is to investigate various empirical contexts in order to discuss its key success factors and drivers (Gnyawali, He and Madhavan, 2007).

The main problem of this emerging stream of research is the lack of a convincing theoretical background. We think that literature on collective strategy (Astley and Fombrun, 1983) could allow us to deal with two main issues of coopetition: the ambiguous nature of firms' relations and the voluntaristic dimension of this kind of strategy. According to Astley and Fombrun (1983: 578), collective strategies are defined as 'the common mobilization of resources and the formulation of the action within communities of organizations'. Among the issues relative to this approach, the question of mixing collective and individual strategies is critical.

Furthermore, the postulate of coopetitive relations between firms (Brandenburger and Nalebuff, 1996) suggests that a collective strategy is necessarily confronted in due course with individual 'deviances', that is, attempts of firms to pursue individual interests to the detriment of the collective. Thus, the main question is not whether these egoistic behaviours will appear, but more if the collective of firms can manage them, that is, survive in spite of the individualistic moves.

In an oligopoly, the question of the interdependence of actors arises in a crucial way in terms of choice between individual and collective fates (Bresser and Harl, 1986), but also in terms of profit or loss for the actor who chooses the satisfaction of individual interests instead of collective ones. Our objective is to highlight the implications of an individual behaviour (that is in contravention to the standards accepted collectively) on the way the collective functions and the nature of inter-firm relations. Thus, the concept of disruptive strategy offers an appropriate illustration of a pure individual move in the competitive landscape.

1.3   The Impacts of a Disruptive Strategy

The concept of 'strategic innovation' or 'disruptive strategy' (Hamel, 1996, 1998a, 1998b, 2000) characterizes the 'disturbing' dimension of such an individual behaviour. This conception contrasts with the traditional approaches to strategy which dominated the field in the 1970s and the 1980s, that is to say, approaches privileging a rather defensive or adaptive logic. Indeed, based on the concept of strategic intent (Hamel and Prahalad, 1989), disruptive strategy corresponds to a voluntarist behaviour of the firm, the key success factors lying in its 'core competences', independently of the sector in which it is immersed, and its will to revolutionize the market (Hamel, 1996). Thus, the disruptive strategy is 'the ability [of a firm] to re-conceive existing models of the industry in a way to create a new value for customers' (Hamel, 1996). It also expresses a way to enter into competition in a fundamentally different way in an existing industry (Charitou and Markides, 2003).

Until now, the literature on disruptive strategies has considered the question of competitive implications either from the perspective of the sector and its stakeholders (regeneration of the activity, reformulation of competitive rules of the game, creation of a new value for the customer and so on) or from the disrupter's point of view (profits associated with the move, pre-emption of the market, obsolescence of competition, management of the new economic model and so on).

The intermediate level, that is, the implications of a disruptive strategy on interfirm relations inside a collective such as an oligopoly, has not been investigated. According to us, three critical issues should be tackled at this interorganizational level (oligopoly):

1. Is it rewarding for a firm to conduct an individual strategy within a collective structure such as an oligopoly? In other words, what are the impacts in terms of profits and losses attached to this type of deviating behaviour?
2. How does a collective of firms react to deviating behavior from one of them?
3. What happens to the collective of firms after such a dissension from one of its members?

The next sections of this chapter explore these three questions related to the implications of a disruptive strategy within a collective of firms, using the case study of the unlimited access card in the French movie theater sector.

2. RESEARCH METHOD

Our research is based on an in-depth longitudinal case study. The case study proves to be a relevant option since the studied phenomenon is dynamic and implies several dimensions (Eisenhardt, 1989; Yin, 1994).

Two types of data were collected. Firstly, the accumulation of primary data was achieved through 40 interviews between February and December 2004 with different stakeholders within the industry. The sample included different points of view, namely managers from the three industry stages (production, distribution and screening), representatives of public authorities and members of professional associations. The discursive material was completely transcribed into 474 pages, anonymized and thematically coded according to the procedure suggested by Miles and Huberman (1994). The thematic dictionary includes 30 items dealing with the evolution of the sector and firms' competitive behaviours. The second type of data is secondary. They are both qualitative (press articles, public studies and reports and so on) and quantitative (statistical series, in particular those produced by the CNC[1]).

The recent transformation of the motion picture industry constitutes an appropriate context for studying firms' strategic behaviours (Prahalad and Hamel, 1994). Showing movies is the activity located downstream of the motion picture industry. Thus, it follows the activities of movie production and distribution. Movie theaters appeared at the end of the 19th century thanks to the Lumière brothers. The sector experienced four life cycle stages over the last century: start (1895–1909), growth (1909–1947), maturity (1947–1957) and decline (1957–1992).

Since 1993,[2] the sector has seen some regeneration due to the creation of 'multiplex' cinemas. This new generation of movie theaters provides significantly improved value to the customer in terms of size and quality, a broad choice of films and schedules, additional services, a new geographical location and so on. The new equipment, coupled with a broader range of movies, stimulated the demand curve which grew from 116 million admissions in 1992 to 194.8 million in 2004 (up by 67.9 per cent). The growth was mainly profitable to the multiplex operators, who reinforced their market power (that is, the Gaumont-Pathé-UGC oligopoly).

The movie theater's sector offers an interesting illustration of the studied phenomenon – individual behaviour within a collective strategy – through the launch (March 2000) of the unlimited access card by one of the oligopoly members (see Box 9.1). UGC's strategy represents a disruption within an industry with public involvement, and competitive initiatives are usually limited by the presence of institutions (trade union and trade association lobbies). Indeed, the launch of the unlimited access card

---

BOX 9.1   THE PRINCIPLE OF UGC'S UNLIMITED ACCESS CARD

The initiative taken in March 2000 by UGC to set up a subscription system at the cinema (inspired by an English experiment in Virgin Cinemas) was a bombshell for the profession. With this system, for a monthly charge of €15, any movie goer can have a card giving unlimited access to all the UGC theatres for one year. Each visit provides a ticket which is used as a basis for the distribution of the receipts. The distributors are paid a fixed price of €5, corresponding to the average receipt in 2000.

---

turns the movie theatre experience into a common consumption good, in so far as the price can be discounted. The logic of subscription penetrates a sector that has always rejected commercial practices. For this reason, the unlimited access card characterizes not only an economic but also a cultural disruption. Last but not least, the unlimited access card illustrates a betrayal by UGC of the interests of the oligopoly.

3.   CASE STUDY ANALYSIS

3.1   A Study of Collective and Individual Behaviors

To appreciate the individual behavior compared to the collective fate, we identified four stages within the competitive sequence.

3.1.1   Origins of the collective strategy (before 1993)

Gaumont (created in 1895) and Pathé (1896) led the sector for more than a century; UGC (1946) has been a major player for half a century. These three firms have progressively developed close competitive relations, oscillating between pure confrontation (creation of new theaters, price wars, competition in film supply, marketing tools) and cooperation in different periods and places. This is especially true of Gaumont and Pathé, which merged their screening activities between 1967 and 1982. As concerns UGC, its relations with the two other market leaders can be seen as more competitive or in terms of market avoidance. This is because UGC had belonged to the opposite coalition during the 1980s (Gaumont and Pathé versus UGC and Parafrance).

Generally speaking, the close links between the three firms are also explained by the proximity of their leaders, particularly in the case of Gaumont and Pathé since the two companies were directed (before the merger of their theaters in 2001) by two brothers, respectively Nicolas and Jerôme Seydoux. Lastly, the three firms have a simultaneous and historical presence in the different stages of the industry chain. This confers a common identity as producer-distributor-screener and a strong dependence on them by the French industry.

The difficulties faced by movie theatres between the end of the 1980s and the following decade stimulated the collective fate within the oligopoly. The structural crisis of the sector resulted in a fall of admissions by almost 34 per cent between 1985 and 1992, with, in parallel, the closing of more than 800 theaters in France. During this period, the sector faced new threats such as the emergence of substitutes (VCR, a TV channel focused on cinema – Canal+). In addition, the range of films proposed to movie goers was unsatisfactory in terms of content and form (lack of entertainment effect, absence of massive blockbusters).

For movie screener, this resulted in threatening environmental conditions and a strong uncertainty about their survival. Consequently, the emergence of a collective strategy constituted a way to manage environmental turbulence (Emery and Trist, 1965; Bresser and Harl, 1986; Bresser, 1988). The emergence of these collective strategies took place within the two strategic groups located at the extremities of the competitive landscape: independent movies and/or art house cinemas on the one hand (alliances, networks of theaters), and members of the oligopoly on the other hand.

The difficulties faced by the sector constitute the first contextual element supporting the emergence of a collective strategy between Gaumont, Pathé and UGC. The second one concerns the introduction in Europe of a new concept of theater, the multiplex, characterizing a remedy for the industry crisis. The literature also considers that the advent of a technical change can support the emergence of a collective strategy (Carney, 1987). Lastly, a third factor justified the rise of a collective strategy: the increasing gap between strategic groups. Indeed, the diffusion of the multiplexes in the French market accentuated the difference between the firms having a solid financial base and owners with limited financial resources.

3.1.2 Reinforcement of the collective fate (1993–2000)

The collective strategy concerns the members of an oligopoly, that is to say it is based on informal relations and collusive behaviors. The proximity of CEOs suggests information exchanges, in particular within the framework of the central trade association of the sector: the FNCF. Within this federation, CEOs of the leading companies[3] meet several times per year. The objective of these meetings is to discuss problems shared by members of the strategic group (supply, seasonal variation of demand, commercial deals, laws, future prospects for the sector, technological developments).

The collective fate is illustrated by different elements. Initially, the transformation of theaters raises the fundamental question of the profitability of the investments. Indeed, the investments required (between 7 and 30 million euros per multiplex) imply a high capital intensity for the firms. Also, satisfying the individual interests of each operator leads to a collective logic consisting of the spatial distribution of new capacity to allow a return on investments for all firms. This strategy, which satisfies collective interests, was already part of the large firms' policy, but it was amplified by the introduction of the multiplex. Oligopoly members implemented this avoidance policy by exchanging assets at the beginning of the 1990s and by sharing the market in terms of cities.

Beyond the requirements of economic profitability of investments, the collective strategy within the oligopoly also satisfies another aim: to keep potential entrants away from the emerging French multiplex market. The protection of a collective rent and broader interests (control of the outlets to ensure the diffusion of their own productions) suggests more cooperation between the dominant firms (Dollinger, 1990). The geographical avoidance acts as an entry barrier for foreign firms, in particular American firms such as UCI, Warner and AMC. Therefore, the collective strategy is partly defensive (Butler and Carney, 1986).

3.1.3   The end of the collective fate? (March 2000)

The emergence of a collective strategy within the oligopoly is directly related to the exhibition sector's evolution during the 1990s and in particular the diffusion of the multiplexes. Facing these changes, the dominant firms took part in a collective construction of a 'new market'. The strategic literature insists that the collective is subject to the temptation of its participants to be free from the collective fate in order to achieve individual strategies. The specific literature about coopetition offers a particularly relevant metaphor for this phenomenon: 'business is cooperation when it comes to creating a pie and competition when it comes to dividing it up' (Brandenburger and Nalebuff, 1996: 4).

UGC's unlimited access card illustrates perfectly this will to be freed from the collective fate and to pursue its own interests following a collective construction of the market. UGC's move on a price dimension constitutes some kind of a betrayal of the collective interest, since UGC tries to profit alone from the demand growth resulting from collective market regeneration. The unlimited access card represents a disruption of the collectively accepted standards ('an admission at a fixed price'; geographic distribution of the French firms).

Among the motivations of UGC, the first lies in pursuing the stimulation of a demand that responded positively to the rejuvenation of movie theaters during the 1990s. The introduction of multiplexes calls for other competitive actions, especially on price. The unlimited access card clearly represents aggression towards other participants in the market and especially oligopoly members. At the marketing level, the operation is connected with a differentiation strategy. Lastly, UGC's move must be considered with its dominant position on the Parisian market in mind. In Paris, there is tough competition between UGC and Gaumont. In this respect, the card aims to boost admissions to UGC's Parisian cinemas.

3.1.4 Building a new collective fate (since 2001)

UGC's move produced several reactions from the other two members of the oligopoly. The first lay in expressing opposition to the unlimited access card by lobbying with public authorities (CNC, Ministry of Culture). The failure of this move led Pathé, and especially Gaumont, to strike back by imitating UGC's card. In the oligopolistic context of interdependence, the reaction of Gaumont and Pathé was unavoidable in order to preserve their respective competitive positions. However, with these two firms, the commercialization of an unlimited access card was carried out 'reluctantly' because the principle of this card went against the culture of the two companies.

Consequently, the collective fate of the three firms remains, since they are proposing unlimited access cards and sharing new common problems associated with this system (accounting management of the card, profitability of the operation, opposition of the independent theaters). By the mechanism of competitive imitation, UGC constrained Gaumont and Pathé to integrate into a 'new common fate', following a direction that UGC had chosen.

However, UGC's betrayal led to a complete reformulation of the way the collective functions. Indeed, the distinctive strategy precipitated the merger of Pathé and Gaumont under the EuroPalaces label, announced in December 2000 (nine months after UGC's aggression). In the light of the events, it seems hard not to interpret the creation of EuroPalaces as a 'punishment' inflicted on UGC. In other words, the individual move of a firm reinforces the solidarity between the two 'victims'. Since then, the duopolization of the sector seems to support a certain stability in the competitive game, as depicted in literature.

3.2 Case Study Implications

To tackle the implications of UGC's move, we take a look at three categories of interests: those at the level of the movie theater sector, those at the level of the collective strategy, and finally those at the individual level of each firm.

Concerning the whole sector, UGC's offensive creates two contrary effects. The first one is positive and lies in the stimulation of demand due to the unlimited access card. The increased admission rate induced by the card benefits all industry actors because of the mechanism of taxes taken on admissions and transferred as subsidies to the whole industry. The second effect for the industry is negative. It concerns the deterioration of the commercial margin of admissions due to a 'low cost' logic.

At the level of the collective of market leaders, the individual move of UGC and its mimetic reactions have ambiguous effects. On the one hand, the commercialization of an unlimited subscription system reinforces the market power of dominant firms (increased attractivity, increased negotiation power with suppliers, increased legitimacy towards the public authorities). On the other hand, the card generates disadvantages such as a 'loss of earnings' on unlimited access card admissions compared to 'full fare' admissions, and the creation of opponents to the system (lobbying by some industry stakeholders).

Lastly, in terms of particular interests, we can draw up an assessment of the individual action of UGC for each firm. The discussion on the profits and losses of each firm leads us to introduce a second hierarchy, namely the geographical distinction between national and Parisian markets. UGC obtained an essential profit from its individualism, since the firm increased its position in the highly strategic Parisian market. However, UGC suffered a setback through the loss of its leadership at the national level following the merger of Gaumont and Pathé (see Table 9.1).

Concerning the two 'victims' of UGC's behaviour, the implications are specific to each firm. For Gaumont, the aggression of UGC was stronger, as stated earlier, because of the tough Parisian competition

Table 9.1   Evolution of the competitive positions

	1992	1999	2004
Admissions France	116 million	153.6 million	194.8 million
Position (market share)[1]	1. UGC (14.8%)	1. UGC (17.6%)	1. EuroPalaces (22%)
	2. Gaumont (11.4%)	2. Gaumont (13.8%)	2. UGC (16.5%)
	3. Pathé (7.3%)	3. Pathé (11.7%)	3. CGR (9%)

Note: [1] Market shares calculated in terms of volume of admissions (France).

between Gaumont and UGC. Also, Gaumont lost market share in Paris (between four and five points) due to UGC's pre-emption of the potential market associated with the unlimited card. If Gaumont benefited indirectly through the merger with Pathé, the conditions of the merger (34 per cent of the capital held by Gaumont against 66 per cent by Pathé) highlight the influence of Pathé on the new structure. Pathé managed to avoid difficulties and to improve its position within the oligopoly. If the turn of events allowed Gaumont to solve its difficulties, it especially allowed Pathé, through the creation of EuroPalaces, to become head of the sector. Figure 9.1 summarizes the history of competitive relations within the oligopoly.

This case study provides several insights related to our three research questions.

The first question was: is it rewarding for a firm to conduct an individual strategy within a collective structure such as an oligopoly? At first, the case study reveals that the deviating firm (UGC) is rewarded by its behaviour: increase of its market share, pre-emption of the unlimited subscription market and image benefits. However, this individual competitive move then leads to negative consequences for UGC, namely the loss of its leadership after the merger of Pathé and Gaumont. We interpret this event as a kind of reprisal. Thus, this first result suggests that a firm intending to introduce a disruptive strategy should be aware of the short-term and long-term impacts of this kind of strategy. The question raised here is the management of the period after the introduction of the disruptive strategy in terms of relations between firms in a dominant collective position.

The merger of Gaumont and Pathé and the interpretation we make of this event brings insights to our second question, namely: how does a collective of firms react to deviating behavior from one of them? The case suggests that a move away from the collective fate in a triopoly can induce a reinforcement of solidarity between the two 'victims'. The 'betrayal' by UGC of oligopolistic interests leads to the reconfiguration of the collective: the triopoly becomes a duopoly. Consequently, it seems that privileging the satisfaction of the individual interests can lead to an alliance of other oligopoly members responding to the free rider. In this situation, freeing from the collective fate is a double-edged strategy: it certainly generates profits, but it also induces retaliation from other members of the collective, in particular in a different field of competition (that is, on financial capacities).

Our third question related to the survival of the collective in the case of dissension from a member. In particular, the triopoly did not resist the introduction of a disruptive strategy. The survival of the collective requires

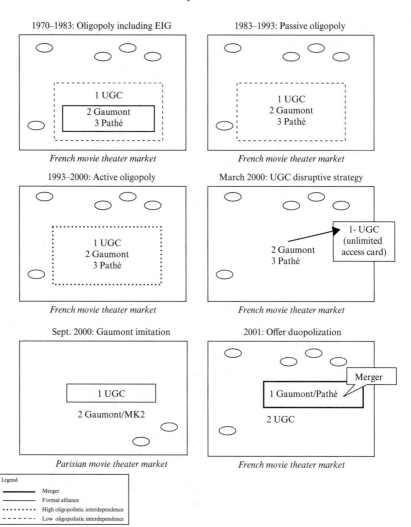

1970–1983: Oligopoly including EIG

French movie theater market

1 UGC
2 Gaumont
3 Pathé

1983–1993: Passive oligopoly

French movie theater market

1 UGC
2 Gaumont
3 Pathé

1993–2000: Active oligopoly

French movie theater market

1 UGC
2 Gaumont
3 Pathé

March 2000: UGC disruptive strategy

French movie theater market

2 Gaumont
3 Pathé

1- UGC (unlimited access card)

Sept. 2000: Gaumont imitation

Parisian movie theater market

1 UGC

2 Gaumont/MK2

2001: Offer duopolization

French movie theater market

Merger

1 Gaumont/Pathé

2 UGC

Legend
——— Merger
——— Formal alliance
· · · · · · High oligopolistic interdependence
- - - - - Low oligopolistic interdependence

Note: MK stands for Marin Karmitz (the founder of the firm).

Figure 9.1   Navigating between individual and collective fates within the oligopoly

the redefinition of its conditions (transformation into a duopoly). Thus, the case shows that oligopoly (see Figure 9.1) is not a static structure but, on the contrary, it evolves over time according to firms' behaviors. The management of the coopetitive relation between dominant firms redefines the boundaries of the oligopoly and the nature of the links within it (in terms of degree of formalization).

CONCLUSION

This research offers a relevant illustration of the fundamentally ambiguous character of contemporary competition. On the one hand, it enables description of the way in which firms' behaviors oscillate through time between the satisfaction of particular interests and respect towards collective interests resulting from a situation of horizontal interdependence (Pennings, 1981). Dominant firms are committed in coopetitive relations where collective logics (facing a common threat, limiting rivalry by mechanisms of avoidance and so on) articulate with individual logics (initiative of UGC).

If we consider this result, coopetition appears as a balance between competition and cooperation where the latter is considered the norm. However, if we adopt a fine-grained analysis, this sequence is more complex. The two sides of the relationship are simultaneously combined by dominant firms if we take into account the different reference markets. Thus, coopetition appears as a complex relationship between firms which assumes the definition of the parameters of the relationship, namely the relevant reference market(s) and the structure and dynamics of a collective of firms. In this respect, the inter-organizational level of analysis helped us to clarify the coopetitive relation. Thus, we believe that this intermediate level of analysis is accurate and promising for understanding the dynamics of coopetition.

Moreover, our questioning leads to the idea that a disruptive strategy tends to accentuate the relational ambiguity within an oligopoly. Indeed, the two dimensions of coopetition are reinforced by the disruptive strategy: it exacerbates rivalry between firms (in particular in the highly strategic Parisian market), but it also implies more cooperation through the duopolization of the sector. This insight is original in so far as the existing literature on disruptive strategy is especially focused on the competitive side and not that much on the cooperative consequences of a disruption.

Thus, we are convinced that coopetition constitutes a third paradigm next to competition and cooperation. Indeed, a coopetitive relationship is more than just a continuum between these two opposites, as was predominant in early literature. The next challenge is to deepen the concept of coopetition and to build a new framework based on the intrinsic duality of the relationship.

NOTES

1. CNC: Centre National de la Cinématographie (reference institution for the French cinema industry).
2. The first French multiplex was opened in June 1993 near Toulon by Pathé.
3. Those with at least 450 000 admissions/year.

REFERENCES

Astley, W. (1984), 'Toward an Appreciation of Collective Strategy', *Academy of Management Review*, **9**(3), 526–535.
Astley, W. and C. Fombrun (1983), 'Collective Strategy: Social Ecology of Organizational Environments', *Academy of Management Review*, **8**(4), 576–587.
Bengtsson, M. and S. Kock (2000), 'Coopetition in Business Networks – to Cooperate and Compete Simultaneously', *Industrial Marketing Management*, **29**, 411–426.
Brandenburger, A. and B. Nalebuff (1996), *Coopetition*, New York: Doubleday.
Bresser, R. (1988), 'Matching Collective and Competitive Strategies', *Strategic Management Journal*, **9**, 375–385.
Bresser, R. and J. Harl (1986), 'Collective Strategy: Vice or Virtue?', *Academy of Management Review*, **11**(2), 408–427.
Butler, R. and M. Carney (1986), 'Strategy and Strategic Choice: The Case of Telecommunications', *Strategic Management Journal*, **7**, 161–177.
Carney, M. (1987), 'The Strategy and Structure of Collective Action', *Organization Studies*, **8**(4), 341–362.
Charitou, C. and C. Markides (2003), 'Responses to Disruptive Strategic Innovation', *Sloan Management Review*, **44**(2), 55–63.
CNC (Centre National de la Cinématographie), www.cnc.fr.
Dagnino, G.B. and G. Padula (2002), 'Coopetition Strategy: A New Kind of Interfirm Dynamics for Value Creation', Paper presented at the *2nd Annual Conference of EURAM*, Stockholm, 9–11 May.
Dollinger, M. (1990), 'The Evolution of Collective Strategies in Fragmented Industries', *Academy of Management Review*, **15**(2), 266–285.
Eisenhardt, K. (1989), 'Building Theories from Case Study Research', *Academy of Management Review*, **14**(4), 532–550.
Emery, F. and E. Trist (1965), 'The Causal Texture of Organizational Environments', *Human Relations*, **18**, 21–32.
Gnyawali, D.R., J. He and R. Madhavan (2007), 'Coopetition: Promises and Challenges', in C. Wankel (ed.), *Handbook of 21st Century Management*, London: Sage.
Gnyawali, D.R. and R. Madhavan (2001), 'Cooperative Networks and Competitive Dynamics: A Structural Embeddedness Perspective', *Academy of Management Review*, **26**(3), 431–445.
Hamel, G. (1996), 'Strategy as Revolution', *Harvard Business Review*, July–August, 69–82.
Hamel, G. (1998a), 'The Challenge Today: Changing the Rules of the Game', *Business Strategy Review*, **9**(2), 19–26.

Hamel, G. (1998b), 'Strategy Innovation and the Quest for Value', *Sloan Management Review*, **39**(2), 7–14.

Hamel, G. (2000), *Leading the Revolution*, Boston, MA: Harvard Business School Press.

Hamel, G. and C.K. Prahalad (1989), 'Strategic Intent', *Harvard Business Review*, **67**(3), 63–77.

Hamel, G. and C.K. Prahalad (1994), *Competing for the Future*, Boston, MA: Harvard Business School Press.

Hay, G.A. and D. Kelley (1974), 'An Empirical Survey of Price Fixing Conspiracies', *Journal of Law and Economics*, **17**, 13–38.

Lado, A.A., N. Boyd and S.C. Hanlon (1997), 'Competition, Cooperation, and the Search for Economic Rents: A Syncretic Model', *Academy of Management Review*, **22**(1), 110–141.

Lecocq, X. and S. Yami (2002), 'From Value Chain to Value Networks: Toward a New Strategic Model', in S.M. Lundan (ed.), *Network Knowledge in International Business*, Cheltenham, UK and Northampton, MA: Edward Elgar, pp.9–27.

Miles M.B. and A.M. Huberman (1994), *Qualitative Data Analysis*, Newbury Park, CA: Sage.

Pennings J. (1981), 'Strategically Interdependant Organizations', in P. Nystrom, W. Starbuck (eds), *Handbook of Organizational Design*, vol. 1, Oxford: Oxford University Press, pp.433–455.

Pfeffer J. and G.R. Salancik (1978), *The External Control of Organizations: A Resource Dependence Perspective*, New York, Harper and Row.

Prahalad, C.K. and G. Hamel (1994), 'Strategy as a Field of Study: Why Search for a New Paradigm?', *Strategic Management Journal*, **15**, Special Issue, 5–16.

Stigler G.J. (1964), 'A Theory of Oligopoly', *Journal of Political Economy*, **72**, 44–61.

Yin, R. (1994), *Case Study Research: Design and Methods*, London: Sage.

10. Strategic management of coopetitive relationships in CoPS-related industries

Thomas Herzog

INTRODUCTION

> So how is it that two fierce competitors can work together in developing a family of engines? – That's the question I'm asked most often indeed.
> E. Schoenholz, Vice President Marketing, Engine Alliance

The increasingly complicated structures and rules of a near globalised economy today confront companies with a situation of accelerated market dynamics, intensified competition and ever-increasing product demands. Given these challenges, interorganisational arrangements have become the centre of interest. At present, they represent the make-up of economic reality and the inherent subject of strategic decisions, and manifest themselves through alliances, networks, clusters and joint ventures, and in many other ways. Not least because of their obvious popularity and presence in business practice, interfirm forms of organisation have received significant attention from management research, though the forms of interaction have mostly been characterised and analysed as purely cooperative constellations. It turns out, however, that even those arrangements made with quite cooperative intentions also always exhibit a more or less pronounced momentum of competition.

This means that cooperation only rarely implies an absolute suppression of competition, but instead causes a shift in the relational structure between the two forms of interdependence. In this view, interorganisational relations are usually marked by a multifaceted and complicated tension between forces of competition and cooperation. For the economic success of a business and the respective management of interfirm relations as a genuinely strategic challenge in the sense of establishing 'relational capability . . . as a strategic asset' (Lorenzoni and Lipparini 1999), coping with this competitive–cooperative dialectic is absolutely crucial. Companies tend to no longer have to make the decision of *either* competition *or* cooperation, but instead have to deal with central questions regarding effectiveness-oriented management of the tensions between the two antagonists in their interdependent and simultaneous appearance. In this regard, however, coopetitive constellations seem to have become too unique and complicated for it to be possible to align them mechanically along the linear continuum between the two poles of pure competition or pure cooperation, and thus a fundamental rethinking of conventional patterns of strategic behaviour is needed. Correspondingly, the significance of the management of coopetitive tensions as a new challenge has been pointed out on several occasions (Lerch, Sydow and Wilhelm 2007; Sydow and Möllering 2004; Funder 2000); however, systematic and in-depth work on this issue is only slowly beginning. For even though the relevance of a sound scientific analysis of the practice-induced phenomenon of coopetition has been identified by the relevant scientific community, the current state of research in many respects contains much inaccuracy. In fact, only a few scattered empirical samples offer deeper insight into how individual organisations operate in this field of tension between competition and cooperation in specific contexts.

This extensive lack of insight, which exposes coopetition as a clearly under-researched topic (Mariani 2007), must be noted to a similar extent for the industrial field of complex products and services (CoPS) examined in this chapter, 'in which companies have found it necessary or even essential to partner with their competitors to remain in key markets and activities' (Bokulich 2002), and which represents, due to its distinctively developed competitive and cooperative structural forces, a promising point of departure for an examination of coopetitive constellations from a corporate actor level perspective. Drawing on the empirical example of the global civil aircraft engine industry as an archetypal CoPS context (as subsequently characterised in the following section), this contribution aims to examine *why* and *how* strategic action unfolds under coopetitive conditions and to gain a more profound insight as to how companies that are linked in many ways to global networks and closely bound to their competitors by far-reaching cooperation agreements, cope with the coopetitive tension that occurs.

1.   RESEARCH DESIGN

1.1   Methodology

In the presented research (as part of a more extensively pursued study on coopetition management in complex industries) an actor-centred focal firm approach has been chosen, placing a global aircraft engine manufacturer in the centre of an elaborate network of interorganisational relationships among the remaining engine producing companies, which are characterised by strong coopetitive forces. The high degree of the focal firm's network centrality, with its subsequent role as a major binding actor within the industry, makes the company an excellent object for the examination of coopetition issues. Under these circumstances, where a sustaining theoretical and empirical body of coopetition strategy research is to date underdeveloped and substantial information on the research area is still limited, discovery must be the major aim and focus of research efforts. To this end, Gummesson (2002) suggests the use of a qualitative or interpretative research approach which is capable of yielding significant levels of data rich in informants' perceptions and experiences. This form of data is beneficial in identifying new contextual variables, themes and processes in the area of coopetition strategy. Within that interpretive paradigm, a grounded theory approach seemed to be most adequate for obtaining answers to the research questions under scrutiny. This methodology uses a systematic set of procedures to gain new inductively derived cognitions and insights about the phenomenon that is effectively grounded in the empirical data. Methodologies based on grounded theory are therefore very suitable for analysis of the way individuals and social entities resolve particular problems in particular areas. In this specific coopetition context, the approach allows organisational learning on how corporate managers meaningfully represent the world in which they live, how they act on the basis of certain meanings and how these meanings come into existence in processes of coopetitive interactions.

As there is no ex ante standard method for data collection within the grounded theory approach, the choice has been determined by the research interest and the potential access possibilities in the empirical field. Considering the strengths and weaknesses of each data collection technique, data collection combined four domains of empirical sources (in order of relevance):

1. Problem-centred interviews (according to Witzel 2000) with 38 managers of the focal firm engaged in different corporate functions within global joint aircraft engine programmes based on interorganisational risk-and-revenue-sharing agreements (primary source of data, average duration of each interview 72 minutes);
2. Selected documentary and archival data from corporate files;
3. Selected aerospace and aircraft engine industry publications;
4. Informal discussions with other (non-focal firm) industry experts.

The main focus of data collection and analysis has been on determining empirically relevant data categories depicting the specific structural, contextual and interactional influences of coopetition. Particularly interesting was thus the specific set of conditions within which interaction strategies were used to manage, handle, carry out and respond to coopetition and also the patterns of interaction which were directed at responding to coopetition as it exists under a specific set of perceived conditions. The tape-recorded interviews were entirely transcribed and analysed following the theoretical coding procedures suggested by the grounded theory approach (Strauss and Corbin 1990). During ongoing analysis, code notes, theoretical memos and logical diagrams were used to help extract potential relationships between categories identified from the textual material. Computer-aided qualitative data analysis software was employed to assist throughout the data analysis process.

1.2 Empirical Context

Complex products and systems (CoPS) are defined as high-cost, engineering-intensive products, systems and constructs for business-to-business applications; the term 'complex' is used to reflect the characteristics of the elements involved and the depth and breadth of the necessary technological knowledge and skills (Mitchell and Singh 1996; Prencipe 2000). Unlike most mass-produced consumption goods, CoPS are made up of a huge number of interconnected, customised parts, including subsystems, components and control units, designed in a hierarchical and modular manner, mostly tailor-made for specific customers (Hobday 1998). CoPS usually differ widely in kind and variety and often belong to a broad spectrum of technological fields. So, by way of example, aircraft engines are typical CoPS representatives, with a huge number of subsystems and components (more than 40000 individual parts per engine). Considering their specific characteristics, the development and production of CoPS confront companies with two major challenges:

1. The capacity to produce and implement numerous different systemically interacting modules, components and parts, including relevant state-of-the-art technologies.
2. Coping with the major financial and coordinating costs needed to establish organisational structures and integrative processes that meet the complex requirements of product realisation.

These technological and commercial requirements are considered to be too vast to be managed entirely within a single-firm organisation.

External sources must be integrated beyond the companies' boundaries and tight interorganisational cooperation is inevitable for market success (Prencipe 2004). Indeed, CoPS mostly exist only as collective combinations in the form of dense production and coordination networks which usually take the form of interorganisational projects embedded in these networks (Davies and Hobday 2005; Hobday 1998). In relation to a 'markets-as-networks' approach (McLoughlin and Horan 2002), jet engine producers need mechanisms for the strategically relevant creation of organisational effectiveness as means of achieving competitive advantage. In this context, strategic priorities require a focus on the following: processes of interorganisational coordination and foundation for successful collective product realisation, and interactional competence for 'collaborating in, bidding for, and executing projects' (Hobday 1998). The strategic goal of organisational effectiveness is thus reached through effectively 'relating' to the environment and gaining an advantageous position within a certain network context (Håkansson and Snehota 1989). Due to their specific resource demands and high entry barriers, CoPS industries typically exhibit oligopolistic market structures and only a relatively small and transparent circle of involved protagonists (Choung and Hwang 2007; Moody and Dodgson 2006; Hobday 1998). In an analogous vein, Schreyögg (1984) considers the circular interdependence of the protagonists to be the essential defining characteristic of oligopolies, which means that the influence of the decisions made by one market participant on the others is significant and mutual. In contrast to a market situation with pure competition, in an oligopoly, competition does not manifest itself through anonymous, compelling forces (or as deterministically understood 'forces of gravitation'), but in a quite individual way which tends to result in a direct strategic interaction between the competitors and thereby the simultaneous occurrence of competition and cooperation constellations. Against this background, Astley (1984) also explicitly notes the intrinsically antagonistic character of oligopolistic protagonists' interrelationships and describes 'coalitions such as those established in oligopolistic practice . . . as mixed-motive games. Although such interaction appears to be cooperative, it is seen, more or less, as an antagonistic . . . short term cooperation designed to allow each organisation to improve its own long term competitive position'. The same holds true for the empirical field of aircraft engines, where the oligopolistic industry structure forces the few interdependent manufacturers to choose among each other to cooperate closely in certain engine programmes on the one hand, despite being serious competitors in other engine programmes and related business areas of the value chain on the other. Similarly Clarke-Hill, Li and Davies (2003) also clearly point out that '[t]he strategic issue is not to choose between competition or co-operation, but to manage the tension between the two. It is their contradictory duality that forms the unity of this paradoxical relationship and the complex business reality.' Thus the strategic management of coopetition in resource-intensive CoPS industries demonstrates the effectiveness-oriented design of the organisational inter-action behaviour primarily determined by the tension between cooperative and competitive industry forces.

2. COOPETITION IN THE CIVIL AIRCRAFT ENGINE INDUSTRY

2.1 Structural Duality as Antecedent for Coopetitive Relationships

For each large commercial aircraft programme, two Original Equipment Manufacturers (OEMs) are generally selected by the airframer (at present Boeing or Airbus) to design, develop and certify an engine programme. Engines are generally sold separately from aircraft, giving the customer (airlines, cargo operators, leasing companies or corporate customers) a choice regarding which engine to buy based on technical capability and operational and economic considerations (including spare parts and main-tenance costs). As a consequence, competition in the jet engines market takes place at two different levels. First, engines compete in order to be certified for a given aircraft type under development and second, when airlines buying the aircraft select one of the available certified engines or when airlines decide on the acquisition of aircraft with different engines (whether or not the specific aircraft offers an engine choice option). In the first case, engines compete in technical and commercial terms to power the specific aircraft type selected by the aircraft producers; in the second, they also compete on technical and commercial grounds to be selected by the client (passenger or cargo airlines). Indeed, the demand for engines derives from the demand for aircraft. In this sense, an engine is a complementary product to the aircraft, the sale of the one being of no value without the sale of the other. In defining the relevant engine product markets, one also needs to take into account competition between the types of aircraft that final buyers consider.

Despite fierce competitive forces, a major characteristic of the aircraft engine industry is the common establishment of so-called 'Risk and Revenue Sharing Partnerships' (RRSPs) – close interfirm collaborative project agreements among competitors in order to jointly design, develop and manufacture new engine programmes after being selected by air-craft producers. Although harsh competitors in the market, cooperation benefits prevail, as such arrangements are driven by the necessity of the OEMs to spread the inherent financial risks (for example, potential market failure) and substantial costs associated with new engine development, and to benefit from competition among manufacturers that supply similar modules and components. Partnership members, on the other hand, benefit from a share of the engine programme's revenues. RRSPs commit to funding not only their own costs but a portion of the total costs for research and development of a new aircraft engine as well as manufacturing and other costs (including entry fees paid by OEMs to aircraft manufacturers). Similarly, all RRSPs are liable for penalties and liabilities incurred as a result of production delays or defective engine parts. In return for taking over costs and risks, RRSPs receive a share of revenues from the sale of the engines and spare parts in accordance with the relevant RRSP agreement. Generally, RRSPs are entered into for a specific engine programme and run for its whole lifetime (40 years on average). While OEMs command the largest share of RRSPs, engine module manufacturers typically have programme shares of 5–30 per cent (depending on the technology provided) and are responsible for the supply of technologically advanced engine modules. Profit margins on the sales of new engine platforms are usually low or negative (particularly at the beginning of a new programme), owing to significant research and development costs and high concessions typically offered to clients. Depending on the number of OEMs competing for the production of the jet engine for any given application, the size of the engine programme and the number of orders, OEMs and their RRSP partners generally accept lower or negative margins on the sale of new engines to boost the development of a substantial installed base of engines and thereby to subsequently secure the promising spare parts and maintenance, repair and overhaul (MRO) business, which is the primary source of business model profitability in the commercial aircraft engine market. Spare part sales throughout the maturity phase of the product life cycle usually provide for high margins (Commission of the European Union 2001).

After the competitive initial bidding phase and the cooperative product realisation through RRSPs, the lucrative maintenance market is once again marked by intense competition, focussing mainly on technological capacities, quality, duration of maintenance procedures, supply reliability and price, being influenced by different kinds of warranty contracts or maintenance agreements. Here, the field of suppliers differs greatly from the new deal market. The market for civil jet engine maintenance continues to be dominated by the large jet engine manufacturers. Additionally, some of the larger airlines have assumed corresponding MRO competence and maintain their fleets in their own maintenance enterprises. However, in the face of the required cost cuts and competence concentration, most airlines outsource their maintenance to other jet engine manufacturers, to the maintenance departments of other large airlines, or to independent maintenance suppliers, this last group being made up mostly of manufacturers of engine modules and components. Through their development and assembly of new jet engines, these manufacturers have been able to acquire extensive technological know-how, which puts them in the position of supplying maintenance services to the market in direct competition with their former partners – the OEMs – and with their products.

The most important industry specifics are recapitulated briefly here. The products are complex, with high capital and technology intensity, substantial market entry barriers, oligopolistic supply and demand and two levels of engine selection competition. It is necessary to form multiple risk and revenue sharing partnerships among the few market competitors, which gives an ambiguous picture of two dominating structural effects: harsh competition among engine manufacturers throughout the initial bidding phase and the hard-fought profitable maintenance business, with simultaneously close cooperation within the same engine programme through extensive risk and revenue sharing. Each market participant finds itself, within that determining framework, being challenged to manage the tension between cooperative and competitive behaviour properly in order to continually participate in the market.

2.2 Partly Intertwined Business Models Shaping Coopetition Dynamics

As can be seen from the structural industry characteristics described above, coopetition among interacting engine makers occurs in the first instance within a single engine programme alongside its value chain, which can be split up into various phases. The so-called 'pre-phase' at the beginning of every RRSP consists of heavy-duty negotiations prior to the final decision to participate in an engine programme and to gain an attractive risk and revenue share. That general participation agreement – the most important milestone of the engine programme – is followed by an engineering-intensive development phase, comprising systems design, prototyping, testing and engine certification, the subsequent batch production and product sales phase, and then the maintenance market at the end of the engine programme life cycle.

It has been shown that this business model obviously envisions huge investments in the early programme phases, producing a highly negative cash flow for quite a long time, which is a prerequisite to benefiting from the highly profitable post-purchase maintenance and spare parts provision in the later stages of the product life cycle, thus generating an overall

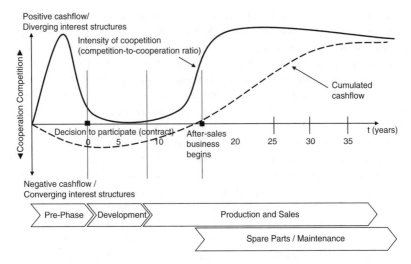

*Figure 10.1   Coopetitive business model with alternating competition-to-
cooperation ratio throughout the value chain of an engine
programme*

positive return on investment for programme participants after decades on
the bottom line. As a consequence, the intensity of competition and cooperation and the related interest structure of the engine makers involved
alters significantly throughout the value chain phases (Figure 10.1).
The pre-phase is characterised by intense competition for involvement
in aircraft engine programmes among engine module and component
manufacturers, some of which are highly specialised and may offer directly
competing technologies, and from the OEMs themselves, who may choose
to source components in-house, thus overriding the participation interests
of others. Once the decision on programme participation has been made
(parties entering the risk and revenue partnership with negotiated shares),
competition intensity slumps and gives rise to cooperative efforts in the
development phase.

During product realisation of aircraft engines as CoPS, there are
extremely demanding technological challenges, with short time to market
and exorbitantly high contract penalties on programme delay. Thus, a
solution-oriented, cooperative atmosphere, the reduction of conflict and
the maximisation of synergies are essential in this phase to meet system
specifications and objectives on time. The same holds true for the early
phase of batch production and sales, where joint capacity building and
marketing efforts to foster new engine orders are of paramount interest for
each programme participant. After approximately 15 years and advanced

product maturity, (depending on the respective programme) the cooperative paradigm again changes into a competitive one with the entry of the
attractive, high-margin after-sales business. Whereas the new engine programme has been designed, built and sold with combined interfirm efforts,
in the after-sales phase – as shown – each participating RRSP offers its
services and tries to generate business independently and on its own, thus
switching to direct and heavyweight competition with each other.

This makes it quite clear that the connected business models of the interacting jet engine manufacturers are based on a 'partly divergent interest
structure', which has been identified by Padula and Dagnino (2007) as a
central conceptual foundation of coopetition. Furthermore, each RRSP is
simultaneously engaged in a variety of such engine programmes covering
different stages throughout the value chain, thus establishing a balanced
product portfolio continuously covering several product life cycle (PLC)
phases – the late stages to generate cash flow, which is needed and used
to finance present and future investment in ongoing and upcoming programme participations in the early stages (Figure 10.2).

As a consequence, the individual RRSP programme participant, being
involved in multiple engine programmes at different stages of the value
chain and thus simultaneously covering different competition intensities
and contradictory interest structures, is challenged with the necessity of
managing multiple coopetitive arrangements in parallel (Figure 10.3).

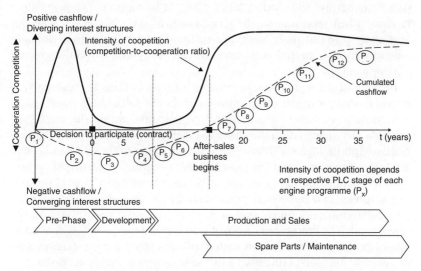

*Figure 10.2   Multiple different product life cycle stages in parallel within a
company's engine programme portfolio*

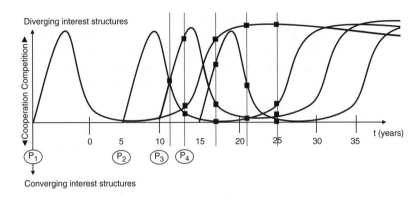

Figure 10.3   *Multiple-point coopetition through varying intensities of coopetition occurring simultaneously at different product life cycle stages within a company's engine programme portfolio*

3.   DISCUSSING COOPETITION STRATEGIES

Similar to CoPS itself, the industry structure and inherent business logic turn out to be quite complex in nature, as outlined previously. A comprehensive understanding of these antagonistic mechanisms is considered to be essential to get a clear picture of the conditions and influence under which coopetitive interaction takes place. It is important to keep them in mind when returning to the second aim of this chapter, to consider how coopetition in those multifaceted interfirm relationships is actually managed by civil aircraft engine companies in a typical CoPS-determined environment.

Because of the wide range of coopetitive relationships through participation in various engine programmes at different value chain stages, there is a strategic dilemma for the RRSP participants: within the same programme and organisation they have to juggle with alternating and diametrically opposite logics of behavioural interaction. On the one hand, there are tough negotiations in the pre-phase for programme participation and cut-throat competition in the post-sales market, combined with close (and as frictionless and effective as possible) technical and administrative interfirm collaboration requirements in the product realisation phase on the other hand. The literature on coopetition increasingly indicates that companies in coopetitive situations with partly divergent interest structures do not expose themselves directly to this schizophrenia, but instead strive to separate the distinctly contradictory logics of conduct in a manner that makes them manageable and proves consistent within the overall strategic alignment (Brandes *et al.* 2007; Walley 2007; Bengtsson and Kock 2000). A similar behaviour can be attested in the RRSP civil aircraft engine business. There is strong evidence that coopeting firms install proper organisational and managerial processes – as a consequence of the necessity to manage this set of simultaneously diverging interests – to separate the contradictory behavioural logics of competition and cooperation, thus resolving this dilemma of mingled interest structures through establishing clear-cut, non-ambiguous – *either* competitive-type, *or* cooperative-type – segregations. As already shown, there are highly competitive phases in the very early and the late phases of the engine programme value chain, interrupted by the closely cooperative and goal-oriented product realisation phase.

Whereas the competitive phases of the early and late phases are characterised by a relatively high degree of strategic freedom and independent decision making, the cooperation phase is very much bound to interorganisational coordination and adaptation. Although it needs to be able to follow and enforce its individual (strategic) business interests through pursuing intense competition, the company has a strong interest in ensuring that competition intensity does not harm the progress and efficiency of the important (and time critical) cooperative product realisation efforts. To achieve that, the engine companies apply a firewall strategy which separates the unfriendly competitive phase from the protectable cooperative phase. Thus, the overall strategy aims at avoiding behavioural conflict, through separating and protecting the cooperative block against negative spillover effects by the competitive paradigm, be it from other programme participations or from the competitive side of the same programme. In the course of organisation, companies correspondingly set up personnel, spatial and organisational firewalls, where exchange and information flow among phases is strictly inhibited or contractually regulated. The 'premarketing team' engages in fierce negotiations with potential RRSP candidates over bidding in the pre-phase and remains strictly bound to the paradigm of competition. In contrast, the programme manager and technical staff involved in the product realisation phase within the framework of the RRSP cooperate with the same company as efficiently as possible. The effect of separating these two functions, both spatially and in terms of personnel, is that despite a coopetitive constellation at the company level, no individual in either organisation actually has to deal with this intricate conflict of simultaneous competition and cooperation (Figure 10.4).

Thus, for any company involved, coopetition management arises from the need to avoid coopetitive structures at an organisational level. The tangled conglomerate of converging and diverging interests naturally resulting from different interaction episodes is separated into its

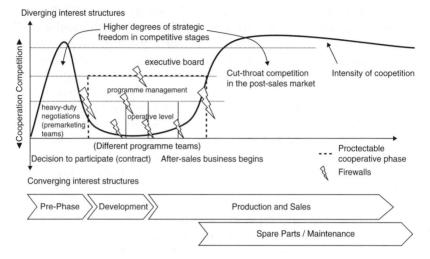

Figure 10.4   Segregation of diverging interest structures through the erection of organisational firewalls

competitive and cooperative elements, and this allows the company to manoeuvre without contradiction in each predominant paradigm, even though, from an overall firm-level perspective, the situation of coopetition remains unchanged.

CONCLUSION

Starting out from the question as to why coopetitive structures occur and how strategic behaviour is designed concretely under coopetitive conditions, or how companies cope with coopetitive tensions, this chapter has given a brief overview of the civil aircraft engine industry as a typical CoPS context. It has thus attempted to show how structural factors, and especially product characteristics, determine multifaceted interacting business models on the basis of partly divergent interest structures; it thereby aims to account for the occurrence of coopetitive business relations. Consequently, an aircraft engine manufacturer's ability to strategically manage that coopetitive tension between simultaneous cooperative and competitive forces – which appears to be crucial for its competitiveness and survival – leaves aircraft engine makers hardly any other choice than to accept constellations of simultaneous competition and cooperation with the same interaction partner. However, companies are not completely at the mercy of this contradictory and, in the sense of effectiveness-oriented management, difficult to handle situation, but instead have developed strategies which allow for a lasting modus vivendi within coopetitive interactions.

The second aim of this chapter is to create an understanding that companies are apparently eager to resolve the dichotomy of coopetitive interaction on a company level through a meta strategy of avoidance. By strictly segregating the coopetitive network of connections into their purely competitive and purely cooperative elements, and inhibiting mutual influence through the installation of effective firewalls, no one on the interaction level actually has to cope with the problematic role conflict between friend and foe, and staff can thus fully concentrate on the behavioural paradigm dominant in their corresponding sector – even though the situation of coopetition between two companies remains intact. So in the context which we have examined, the strategic management of coopetition (in the portrayed sense of an effectiveness-oriented design of the field of tension between competition and cooperation) takes the form of dissolving this tension. Or to put it briefly: effectively managing coopetition means *suppressing* coopetition.

Applying suitable qualitative and quantitative approaches, future research should further examine whether, under what conditions and in what form, these structural antecedents and resulting interactional behaviours occur in other empirical contexts (including non-CoPS industries). Furthermore, there is a need for a much more detailed examination of the segregational tool of firewalls as an exciting and apparently central mechanism within the field of strategic coopetition management; this has been widely neglected so far in this stream of research.

REFERENCES

Astley, W. (1984), 'Toward an Appreciation of Collective Strategy', *The Academy of Management Review*, **9**(3), 526–535.

Bengtsson, M. and S. Kock (2000), 'Coopetition in Business Networks – to Cooperate and Compete Simultaneously', *Industrial Marketing Management*, **29**, 411–426.

Bokulich, F. (2002), 'Collaborating with the enemy', *Aerospace Engineering*, **10**, 32–33.

Brandes, O., S., Brege, P. Brehmer, and J. Lilliecreutz, (2007), 'Chambre Separée in Product Development: Vertically Mediated Coopetition in the Automotive Supply Chain', *International Journal of Automotive Technology and Management*, **7**(2/3), 168–183.

Choung, J. and H. Hwang (2007), 'Developing the Complex System in Korea: The Case Study of TDX and CDMA Telecom System', *International Journal of Technological Learning, Innovation and Development*, **1**(2), 204–225.

Clarke-Hill, C., H. Li and B. Davies (2003), 'The Paradox of Co-operation and Competition in Strategic Alliances: Towards a Multi-Paradigm Approach', *Management Research News*, **26**(1), 1–20.

Commission of the European Union (2001), *Regulation (EEC) No 4064/89 Merger Procedure. Case No COMP/M.2220 – General Electric/Honeywell*, Brussels.

Davies, A. and M. Hobday (2005), *The Business of Projects: Managing Innovation in Complex Products and Systems*, Cambridge, UK: Cambridge University Press.

Funder, M. (2000), 'Konkurrenz und Kooperation in Organisationsnetzwerken', in M. Funder, H. Peter and G. Reber (eds), *Entwicklungstrends in der Unternehmensreorganisation: Internationalisierung, Dezentralisierung, Flexibilisierung*, Linz, Austria: Universitätsverlag Rudolf Trauner, pp. 111–132.

Gummesson, E. (2002), 'Practical Value of Adequate Marketing Management Theory', *European Journal of Marketing*, **36**(3), 325–350.

Håkansson, H. and I. Snehota (1989), 'No Business is an Island: The Network Concept of Business Strategy', *Scandinavian Journal of Management*, **5**(3), 187–200.

Hobday, M. (1998), 'Product Complexity, Innovation and Industrial Organisation', *Research Policy*, **26**(6), 689–710.

Lerch, F., J. Sydow and M. Wilhelm (2007), 'Wenn Wettbewerber zu Kooperationspartnern (gemacht) werden: Einsichten aus zwei Netzwerken in einem Cluster optischer Technologien', in G. Schreyögg and J. Sydow (eds), *Kooperation und Konkurrenz*, Managementforschung 17, Wiesbaden, Germany: Gabler, pp. 207–255.

Lorenzoni, G. and A. Lipparini (1999), 'The Leveraging of Interfirm Relationships as a Distinctive Organisational Capability: A Longitudinal Study', *Strategic Management Journal*, **20**(4), 317–338.

Mariani, M. (2007), 'Coopetition as an Emergent Strategy: Empirical Evidence from an Italian Consortium of Opera Houses', *International Studies of Management and Organization*, **37**(2), 97–126.

McLoughlin, D. and C. Horan (2002), 'Markets-as-Networks: Notes on a Unique Understanding', *Journal of Business Research*, **55**(7), 535–43.

Mitchell, W. and K. Singh (1996), 'Survival of Businesses Using Collaborative Relationships to Commercialize Complex Goods', *Strategic Management Journal*, **17**(3), 169–195.

Moody, J. and M. Dodgson (2006), 'Managing Complex Collaborative Projects: Lessons from the Development of a New Satellite', *The Journal of Technology Transfer*, **31**(5), 568–588.

Padula, G. and G. Dagnino (2007), 'Untangling the Rise of Coopetition: The Intrusion of Competition in a Cooperative Game Structure', *International Studies of Management and Organization*, **37**(2), 32–52.

Prencipe, A. (1997), 'Technological Competencies and Product's Evolutionary Dynamics: A Case Study from the Aero-Engine Industry', *Research Policy*, **25**(8), 1261–1276.

Prencipe, A. (2000), 'Breadth and Depth of Technological Capabilities in CoPS: The Case of the Aircraft Engine Control System', *Research Policy*, **29**(7–8), 895–911.

Prencipe, A. (2004), 'Corporate Strategy and Systems Integration Capabilities: Managing Networks in Complex System Industries', in A. Prencipe, A. Davies and M. Hobday (eds), *The Business of Systems Integration*, Oxford, UK: Oxford University Press, pp. 114–132.

Schreyögg, G. (1984), *Unternehmensstrategie: Grundfragen einer Theorie strategischer Unternehmensführung*, Nuremberg and Erlangen, Germany: Walter de Gruyter.

Strauss, A. and J. Corbin (1990), *Basics of Qualitative Research: Grounded Theory Procedures and Techniques*, Newbury Park, CA: Sage.

Sydow, J. and G. Möllering (2004), *Produktion in Netzwerken: Make, Buy and Cooperate*, Munich, Germany: Vahlen.

Walley, K. (2007), 'Coopetition: An Introduction to the Subject and an Agenda for Research', *International Studies of Management and Organization*, **37**(2), 11–31.

Witzel, A. (2000), 'The Problem-Centered Interview', *Forum: Qualitative Social Research*, **1**(1), available at: http://www.qualitative-research.et/index.php/fqs/article/viewArticle/1132/2521, accessed 11 November 2009.

11. Coopetition dynamics in convergent industries: designing scope connections to combine heterogeneous resources

Fabio Ancarani and Michele Costabile

INTRODUCTION

During the last few years, competition has radically changed due to the increase of unconventional players (mainly inter- or cross-industry) that have redrawn the landscape of many industries. Boundaries are increasingly fading among hi-tech industries (for example, the ICT – Wirtz, 2001) as well as among hi-touch[1] and hi-tech industries: nutriceutics (also called the 'functional food' industry), edutainment, cosmeceutics and genetics diagnostics are just a sample of the emerging convergent markets.

This dynamic is so innovative that many neologisms have been coined to describe it: hypercompetition (D'Aveni, 1994), coopetition (Nalebuff and Brandenburger, 1996), business ecosystems (Moore, 1996), blur economy (Davis and Meyer, 1998) and convergence (Collins, Bane and Bradley, 1997; Yoffie, 1997; Wirtz, 2001). Convergence and coopetition are the terms most commonly used by scholars and by the business community.

As regards coopetition, as is well known, it is the result of different types of strategic interactions (from alliances to joint ventures) between companies that compete and collaborate at the same time. Coopetition has recently attracted increasing interest from the academic community, which has devoted some special issues to the subject (*Revue Francaise de Gestion*, special issue 2007; *International Studies of Management and Organization*, special issue 2007; *Management Research*, special issue 2008). Many contributions focus on the dynamics of coopetition strategies (Dagnino, Le Roy and Yami, 2007; Le Roy and Yami, 2007; Padula and Dagnino, 2007) and on related competences (Prévot, 2007), on the role of the customer (Depeyre and Dumez, 2007), on innovation and R&D (Baumard, 2007;

Blanchot and Fort, 2007) and on the changing role of industry boundaries (Baglieri *et al.*, 2008).

As regards convergence, this phenomenon is fast becoming a hot topic for both academics and executives. A scan of the popular business press during 2001–06 yielded at least 58 articles on this topic: 29 in *Financial Times*, 15 in *The Wall Street Journal*, 10 in *Business Week* and 4 in *The Economist*. Convergence is a process by which the boundaries across industries, markets and customer experiences become blurred, resulting in new business opportunities to improve customer value and generate competitive advantage. As a consequence of convergence, firms (even competitors) which are heterogeneous go beyond the boundaries of their original industries and gradually combine products and markets previously separated. Some forms of cross- and inter-industry competition have existed in the past, but they were rare and not the rule, as is becoming the case today in convergent markets. Similarly, where it was unusual for a high number of competitors to come from outside the industry in the past, in convergence, it is becoming the standard form of competition. And finally, where products, companies and boundaries were well defined in the past, now competition is ruled by the hybrid imperative: hybrid innovative products, bundled packages that cannot be ascribed to a conventional single industry and symbols or experience that customers can find across different product categories. Similarly, cooperation between competitors was a common practice in the past, but recently the number of strategic interactions as well as agreements between competitors has increased significantly and become the rule rather than the exception.

To master convergence, firms should widen the scope of their resources and competences and exercise different strategic options. The most common is to create a web of alliances, even with competitors (coopetition), and/or continually resort to acquisitions in order to absorb or combine heterogeneous resources that fit the new 'convergent' markets.

As a consequence, connections between firms – ranging from strategic alliances to equity partnerships up to mergers and acquisitions (for example, Hamel, 1991; Grant and Baden-Fuller, 1995; Zollo, Reuer and Singh, 2002; Butler and Gill, 2003; Reuer, 2004) – are critical. We define scope connections as any kind of agreement – whether equity or non-equity based – devoted to widening the scope of resources needed to design hybrid value propositions. Such connections have heterogeneous outcomes, as only some are successful and many fail (Dussauge, Garrette and Mitchell, 2000; Sleuwaegen *et al.*, 2003).

In this chapter, we contend that in order to increase the success rate of these scope connections, it is critical to better understand the process of widening and combining heterogeneous resources, and even before that to detect the very essence of coopetition and convergence and its drivers.

Indeed, the process of combination of heterogeneous resources is becoming a top priority in the executive agenda as well as a relevant stream of academic research (Bell, den Ouden and Ziggers, 2006). With particular reference to alliances, Doz (1996) strongly suggested looking inside the 'black box' of a strategic alliance so as to understand better its possible outcome. Dussauge, Garrette and Mitchell (2000) proposed a distinction between scale alliances, that is, alliances among competing firms aimed at increasing economies of scale in production and marketing, and link alliances, that is, alliances devoted to increasing the knowledge base of competing firms. In this chapter, following Doz (1996), we look inside the 'black box' of the connection, even though we acknowledge the importance of the structure of the connection as well (Hennart, 2006). With a similar perspective, Heimericks and Duysters (2007) recently proposed a model of alliance capability as a higher-order resource built upon a firm's previous experience. They define such a capability mainly by considering the 'learning mechanisms' and a set of functions, tools, control processes and external parties, all occurring in a successful alliance.

Focusing on scope alliances, in our chapter we indicate a new issue. We argue that the process of widening and combining heterogeneous resources is successful only if the combinative capabilities among partner companies are relatively homogeneous. In other terms, the hypotheses that we have explored using a grounded theory approach (Glaser and Strauss, 1967) are that in scope connections – with alliances being one of them – firms should be able to balance a high degree of heterogeneity among technological, commercial and operational resources with a high degree of homogeneity among combinative capabilities. Heterogeneity of the former is required in order to foster hybrid innovation; homogeneity of the latter is the condition under which heterogeneous resources and competences can be effectively combined.

Looking at this in more detail, we hold that connecting partners should be relatively homogeneous in terms of language, values, visions of business and market evolution, and time horizons; that is, the essential elements of combinative capabilities (Henderson and Clark, 1990; Van den Bosch, Volberda and de Boer, 1999; Draulans, de Man and Volberda, 2003).

We review some of the most important studies on convergence and connections between firms and we develop some hypotheses on the success of scope alliances in convergent industries (section 1). A brief comparison is subsequently made between the experiences of some highly visible firms (section 2), namely, Symbian, Innéov Fermeté (Nestlé-L'Oréal) and Kodak.

In conclusion, we discuss the case studies and present some implications regarding the managerial approach that firms should adopt to combine their heterogeneous resources in order to expand the market domain and lead to competitive convergence; we highlight also some directions for future research (section 3).

1. BACKGROUND STUDIES AND HYPOTHESIS DEVELOPMENT

Convergence is the driving force behind the proliferation of many 'hybrid' products and the rise of new blurred markets. In spite of the multifaceted nature of convergence, very few studies have analysed it from a broad perspective. The seminal stream of research on convergence has analysed its drivers by focusing on the most visible one: technology. Later scholars have focused on competitive dynamics and customer evolution as the main drivers of convergence.

We present a brief review of the studies on convergence, highlighting a three-stage evolution of the literature and arguing for the complementarity of the different perspectives:

Stage 1: When convergence was first studied, strategic management scholars gave mainly technological explanations of the phenomenon (Bradley, Hausman and Nolan, 1993; Collins, Bane and Bradley, 1997; Yoffie, 1997). The convergence processes and the industry evolution dynamics were examined by referring to the central role of (digital) technological developments as the only relevant driver.

Stage 2: Later interpretations of convergence showed the driving role of competition (Prahalad and Hamel, 1994; Hamel, 1996; Chakravarty, 1997; Wirtz, 2001). The increasingly fast competitive dynamics – defined as 'hypercompetition' (D'Aveni, 1994) – put great pressure on managerial efforts to maintain growth rates consistent with financial market expectations. As a consequence, many firms have been forced to migrate from their traditional businesses and converge in contiguous or contestable businesses where they can operate with higher margins and bolder growth rates. Prahalad and Hamel (1994), Hamel (1996) and Hamel and Prahalad (1996) use the 'driving convergence' concept, showing that the firm with 'out of bounds' strategies is at the head of the convergence processes among industries.

Stage 3: Recent studies put the customer at the centre of the convergence processes. Many scholars have identified evolving customer

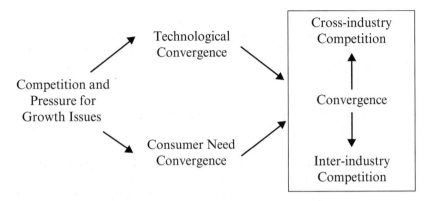

Figure 11.1   Convergence and its drivers: a conceptual framework

needs and expectations as the real drivers of convergence, with
technology considered as an enabler (O'Driscoll, Reibstein and
Shankar, 2002; Ratliff 2002; Wind and Mahajan, 2002; Ancarani
and Shankar, 2003; Shankar, O' Driscoll and Reibstein, 2003).

Combining the three main research streams on convergence, we can conclude that a complementary approach is required. Figure 11.1 shows our
complementary framework, highlighting the visible face of convergence
and the driving role of pressure for growth and competition, technology
and customer evolution. As a consequence, to compete in convergent industries, firms must develop new and hybrid product offerings that are valued
by customers, enabled by technology and of a nature that will set them
apart from conventional competitors. But to design hybrid value propositions, a broader set of resources and competences is needed. The more
hybrid the value propositions to be designed are, the more intense is the
need to broaden the set of resources and competences to be deployed. This
is the explanation of the growing relationships between firms, ranging from
strategic alliances to equity partnerships up to mergers and acquisitions.

In convergent markets, scope connections represent one of the principal ways of increasing resource heterogeneity. Particularly in convergent
industries, strategic alliances are considered an indispensable mechanism
for learning (Kogut and Zander, 1992) and increasing the resource endowment of allied firms. Dyer and Singh (1998) consider the firm's relational
strategy and its ability to leverage interfirm relationships as a crucial
organizational capability (Lorenzoni and Lipparini, 1999).

Many scholars considered learning alliances as a way of increasing
resource heterogeneity and focused mainly on hi-tech sectors, international

markets (Hamel, Doz and Prahalad, 1989; Hamel, 1991) and networks of firms (Khanna, Gulati and Nohria, 1998).

Dussauge, Garrette and Mitchell (2000), as mentioned before, studied the differences in the outcomes of link and scale alliances. Scale alliances are made in order to obtain higher efficiency in production, marketing and R&D. In these kinds of alliances, the firms accumulate symmetric knowledge to achieve scale effects. Link alliances, instead, are made in order to increase the knowledge base of the partner firms by combining asymmetric knowledge. Empirical evidence demonstrates that it is very difficult to make link alliances work when partners come from the same industry. Although these partners are prepared to share knowledge since they have a common knowledge base, creating new knowledge might be very difficult.

Sakakibara (1997) proposes a distinction between cost-sharing and skill-sharing R&D collaborative projects. Koza and Lewin (1998), instead, distinguish between firms' attempts to exploit existing capabilities and their attempts to explore new opportunities. Both authors assume that the more industries are stable, the more firms aim to exploit existing capabilities and pursue cost-sharing projects, while in fast-changing industries, like the convergent ones, firms mainly aim to explore new capabilities and skill-sharing projects.

To sum up, for firms competing in convergent businesses, the main purpose of scope connections is to increase resource heterogeneity in order to expand the competencies needed to develop and manage hybrid product offerings, and to widen the scope of business growth opportunities.

However, increasing resource heterogeneity through interfirm connections must also consider the issue of complementarity (Teece, 1986) and integration. Henderson and Clark (1990) develop the concept of 'architectural innovation' to define the capacity of firms to combine existing components in a new way. Kogut and Zander (1992) stress the importance of combinative capability in generating innovation, starting from existing knowledge. Grant (1996) points out that it is important for individual firms as well as networks of firms to be able to integrate knowledge in order to achieve sustainable competitive advantages, especially in very dynamic contexts. Finally, in the dynamic capability stream of research, Teece, Pisano and Shuen (1997) emphasize that it is important for management to coordinate firm-based capabilities with those acquired outside the company. As a consequence, any kind of scope connection seems to need a 'common platform' consisting of a set of relatively homogeneous capabilities aimed at combining heterogeneous and complementary competences, thus unleashing the vital forces of innovation.

In particular, Lane and Lubatkin (1998) distinguish between basic knowledge (general and fundamental to a given area of knowledge or business) and specialized knowledge (consolidated in the operational routine) and put forward the theory that a firm has a greater potential to learn from the partners within an alliance if its basic knowledge is similar, even though it possesses different specialized knowledge. The authors further maintain that the similarity must also include the organizational structures (for example, formalization and centralization) as well as the remuneration and incentive policies. Finally, Lane and Lubatkin point out that as long as there are interfirm relationships characterized by profitable and mutual exchanges of knowledge, there has to be a high degree of homogeneity in the 'dominant logic'. This expression, taken from the original definition of Prahalad and Bettis (1986), is meant to refer to the way firms apply specialized knowledge in defining and pursuing business objectives and therefore the visions regarding the business and the business models adopted.

The literature review shows the combination of resources in scope connections to be a critical issue. The empirical evidence reveals that connections formed to combine heterogeneous resources do not always achieve the expected results. The same evidence provides some suggestions for better understanding the drivers of success and managing them by acting on two levels:

1. At the first level, there are the technological, commercial and operational competences that should be heterogeneous and complementary and thus generate hybrid offers consistent with the new directions – or even only with the options – that the convergence process opens up;
2. At the second level, there are combinative or integrative capabilities (architectural, according to Henderson and Clark, 1990), to which each firm in the scope connection should try to contribute through homogeneous resources.

The case studies we present in the next section provide relevant insights about the many faces of convergence as well as the need to balance heterogeneity in competences on the one side and combinative or integrative capabilities on the other.

2. SCOPE CONNECTIONS IN CONVERGENT INDUSTRIES: A MULTIPLE CASE STUDY

2.1 Methodology

Since the convergence phenomenon is relatively new, we explored our hypothesis with a grounded theory approach (Glaser and Strauss, 1967) and we resorted to the analysis of highly visible case studies: this represents a methodological approach suited to starting a process of theory building (Eisenhardt, 1989). Following Yin (1994) we decided to focus on three cases of highly visible scope connections, thus developing a multiple case study. The three cases are: Innéov Fermeté, Symbian and Kodak.

We chose the cases by looking at firms involved both in business to consumer markets (Innéov Fermeté and Kodak) and in business-to-business markets (Symbian). The case studies refer to industries considered as convergent, but not all the firms and the scope connections seem to be fully successful. The partial success or failure of the firms we studied allows us to better explore the differential drivers of their behaviour and the relative outcomes. Last but not least, the case selection has been driven by the search for different kinds of structural connections: some involving only two firms (Innéov), some involving many players (Kodak and Symbian).

Both direct interviews with managers and secondary data were collected: as regards Innéov, the informant was the Communication Director in Italy, with whom many interviews were conducted. She provided us with internal data, as well as with industry reports. As regards Symbian, we conducted interviews with experts (venture capitalists) and managers in the telecoms industry (the sales and competitor manager of Nokia and the person responsible for VAS – value added services – and for TIM (Telecom Italia Mobile) and we relied on secondary data and sources. As regards Kodak, we conducted interviews with the Italian Marketing Manager and we collected secondary data and relied on other public sources.

2.2 Case Studies

2.2.1 Innéov Fermeté
Nutriceutics are the ultimate nutritional food integrators produced through the combined efforts in nutrition and cosmetics research. The intersection of cosmetics and nutritional sciences aims at improving physical appearance by working from inside the body outwards. However, the driver of the emergence of these products can be traced back not only to 'really new' scientific and technological paradigms but also to the attempt to meet the evolving needs of an emerging market segment willing to improve wellness through daily consumption. In fact, consumers increasingly want to combine several benefits in one product (nutrition, personal care and physical appearance) in addition to the symbolic value of health and beauty.

Nutricosmetics can be considered as an emblematic case of customer-based convergence. In fact, a new segment of customers is asking for a hybrid bundle of benefits that can be created only by resorting to heterogeneous resources and competences – these competences are scattered among the food, cosmetics and parapharmaceutical industries.

Innéov Fermeté was the result of a long-term effort of L'Oréal and Nestlé to find the right synergy between their endowment of resources. In June 2002, they set up the Laboratoires Innéov, a 50–50 joint venture with headquarters in Paris and branches worldwide.

From the outset, the roles of L'Oréal and Nestlé were clearly stated as regards the strategies, research management and technical and business operations. Nestlé's contribution is fundamental as regards food and nutrition, the choice of raw materials, galenics and bio-assimilation research. It also deals with legal and regulatory matters as well as production methods. L'Oréal contributes its know-how in dermatological research. It evaluates the biological effects of active ingredients and manages the distribution channels, in particular, pharmacies that now represent the only kind of retail outlets selling Innéov products.

Innéov Fermeté, the first product, together with the more recent Innéov Trico Masse, Solaire and CelluStretch, is a nutritional supplement skin redensifier especially designed for ageing skin resulting from hormone changes. The product improves skin tone thanks to the association of lacto-lycopene, soy isoflavons and vitamin C. Although the technology used is more advanced than the industry average, the product is not 'really new' from the technological point of view. The three principal components are well known and can be easily extracted from tomatoes, soy and citrus fruit. Rival firms are also aware of the beneficial effects these elements have on the body. However, the Nestlé-L'Oréal joint venture and the processes of combining heterogeneous resources led to the creation of a high-quality product sold at an extremely competitive price.

The positioning strategy aims to fill the formerly empty space of the new hybrid market by leveraging on the pharmacy channel. The marketing policy proved to be particularly effective and the product became the market leader in just three months.

The product's success was due to the ability to plan the marketing strategy and combining firm-specific and complementary expertises well in their R&D functions to create a new, hybrid product. Moreover, the R&D technical staff as well as the marketing and sales staff worked closely together, highlighting the importance of both interfirm and interfunctional integration. In general, the case study demonstrates that the two firms brought considerable heterogeneous competences to the alliance, resulting from their very different backgrounds. However, the relative homogeneity of the visions regarding the convergence dynamics certainly played an important role in the way the technological, operational and commercial competences of the two firms were combined and integrated. In particular, some similarities in the strategic vision of the two firms (focusing on the brand, recognizing new customer needs and integrating marketing and R&D, internationalization, leadership strategy based on first mover advantage, range and depth of each firm's product range) are reinforced since each partner has a financial stake in the joint venture.[2] Nestlé brought to the Innéov partnership its international experience, its legal expertise and R&D know-how in the food industry. L'Oréal brought its long-standing experience in the pharmaceutical distribution channel (thanks to a considerable shareholder participation in Sanofi-Sybthelabo) and in the R&D of the cosmetics industry. The two companies are fully aware of the emerging need for hybrid products able to offer cosmetic effects through caring nutrition with natural elements. The shared vision of convergence dynamic is one of the driving forces of Innéov's success.

2.2.2 Symbian (versus Microsoft)[3]

Founded in 1998, Symbian is a joint venture among Nokia, Sony-Ericsson, Motorola, Matsushita, Siemens and Psion (a British IT firm producing handheld computers and software OS) set up to develop an operating system (OS) for third-generation mobile equipment (3G). The Symbian OS was the first mover in this emerging market. Although Nokia, Ericsson and Motorola are direct competitors in the mobile telephone market, they are partners and collaborate in the software market – specifically in the operating systems – for mobile telephones. Symbian directly competes with the late mover Microsoft, which launched the Stinger system, Smartphone and also a number of new releases of the version of its own Windows operating system for mobile equipment (Windows Mobile).

The producers of mobile equipment had to form an alliance with Psion, an English producer of portable microcomputers that use the EPOC operating system (developed by Psion) in order to acquire the complementary competences in the IT sector. After Symbian was founded, it underwent many organizational changes due to the complex interaction with its member firms, which were at the same time partners and competitors. From the standpoint of the first-level stakeholders, for example, many new alliances have been made as well as important licensing contracts: in 1999, Matsushita (Panasonic); in 2000, Sony, Sanyo and Kenwood; in 2001, Fujitsu and Siemens; in 2002, Siemens and Sony-Ericsson. From the standpoint of innovation, in 2000 Ericsson launched the first mobile telephone using Symbian software while Nokia launched the 9210 Communicator, a hybrid between a mobile telephone and computer, also using Symbian software. In the first half of 2002, Nokia launched the

7650, the first telephone with Symbian software OS v6.1 that incorporated advanced functions like digital photography and multimedia message services (MMS).

Over the years, however, Symbian has had to face increasing competition from Microsoft. The colossus of Redmond, which had previously only focused on the traditional PC business, had gradually changed its strategic vision from 'a computer on every desk and in every home' to 'empower people through great software every time, any place and every device'. The change in Microsoft's vision was followed by some very consistent strategic choices:

1. It developed collaboration and partnership agreements with the leading European and North American mobile telephone operators, from Vodafone to AT&T, in order to form a link with firms that had the real contact with the final consumer and to break the customer brand loyalty to mobile equipment producers, first and foremost Nokia. In this connection, the launch of the Vodaphone–Microsoft mobile telephone in France in 2003 was emblematic.
2. It reinforced its partnership with the producers of computer hardware, particularly with the producers of PDAs (personal digital assistants) like HP-Compaq, Casio and Sanyo, by adopting the same successful strategy in the struggle to dominate PC operating systems, ensuring at the same time a large market share in the systems for hybrid devices more like PCs than telephones.
3. It launched a large number of products on the market, from Windows CE to Windows Pocket PC, from Stinger to Microsoft Smartphone and Windows Mobile, with the twofold aim of trying out different solutions and barring the way for its competitors.

Microsoft's strategy caused Symbian serious problems and brought to the surface problems that had been simmering within the alliance due to the direct competition among most of the partners. As a result, the entire alliance has faced many changes in the recent past. Motorola withdrew from the Symbian alliance in September 2003 and subsequently formed an alliance with Microsoft (and even Linux) and Psion withdrew in February 2004. Nokia acquired the shares in both firms and today holds the majority stake (63 per cent) in the alliance, reducing its span of resource and competence heterogeneity. Nokia's growing importance within the alliance was not welcomed by the other partners. Nowadays, Symbian is an open source software platform.

At the competitive level, the situation is very uncertain. In the United States, Microsoft and Palm seem to hold the dominant position. Symbian is the market leader in Europe, but it will be the growing Asian market that might tilt the balance.

The next few years will show whether Symbian and Microsoft can co-exist in the market or whether one or the other will win out in the end. However, what is certain is that the 'Symbian connection' has combined the competences of a large bunch of firms coming from the same industry (telecommunications) with only one firm (Psion) coming from the IT industry. The vision of convergence in the mobile ICT sector does not seem to be quite homogeneous. In fact, in the Odin project – a joint sub-project between Motorola and Psion – Motorola wanted a pocket-sized product whereas Psion wanted a bigger object that could process a large amount of data. This different vision was affected by differences in combinative capabilities shaped by the original industry mindset: telecommunications on the one hand and IT on the other.

So far, the issue of designing a really hybrid product and the underlying bundle of resources and competences has not been appropriately managed by the 'Symbian connection' since it is quite evident that other companies are on the leading edge (for example, BlackBerry, Google Android, iPhone).

2.2.3 Kodak[4]

At the turn of the 21st century, the photography industry underwent a profound change with the rapid success of digital technology. At the same time, customers were searching for convergent consumption experiences and customer scope economies – from the camera to the printer. The main players in the new business were the manufacturers of digital printers (for example, HP) and products for ICT and consumer electronics in general (for example, Sony) or multipurpose mobile telephones (for example, Nokia). Under this scenario, the incumbent leaders (Eastman Kodak, Fuji Photo and Agfa-Gevaert), traditionally tied to the chemical core business, began looking for a new marketing strategy that would allow them to maintain their position, or at least survive the upheaval in the industry.

In fact, Eastman Kodak had thirty years of experience in digital cameras. In 1975 it developed the first digital camera, which weighed more than six kilos and recorded on a magnetic tape. Although the company resumed developing digital cameras in the early 1990s to accompany roll films, it failed to pay enough attention to the new convergent market.

Kodak turnover that had reached the record level of $16bn in 1996, gradually dropped to $13.23bn in 2001 and $12.83bn in 2002. During this tough period, Kodak reacted fiercely by adopting a wide range of competitive strategies developed by the new CEO, Daniel Carp.

Daniel Carp, who had worked at Kodak for thirty-four years and had a marketing background, was the first CEO since George Eastman with no background in chemistry or engineering. In 2003 he launched and coordinated a plan to bring about Kodak's digital turnaround. This was an epoch-making event for a traditional chemicals company like Kodak that, in fact, made 50 per cent of its profits from the conventional photography business. Carp's first choice was by far the most representative: he decided he would not invest even a dollar in research and development on roll films. At the same time, he reduced the dividends by 72 per cent in order to finance an aggressive acquisition strategy so that Kodak could compete in three important business areas based on digital technology: consumer photography, commercial printing and medical imaging technology. The restructuring plan also included replacing fifteen top managers with new ones who had consolidated experience in the digital technology business and came from companies such as GE, HP and Lexmark.

In late 2004, one year after the turnaround, the global demand for roll films and roll film prints decreased more than expected (-16 per cent), but the success of digital-related products exceeded all expectations ($+36$ per cent instead of the expected 26 per cent) with a positive net result. Today Kodak is the world's fourth largest producer of digital cameras after Sony Corp., Canon Inc. and Olympus Corp. This result was obtained by adopting different strategies, not the least of which were a great number of scope connections that, since the start of the digital convergence, Kodak formed to obtain the new hybrid capabilities required to successfully compete in the market. The following lists only the most important:

1. In 1996, Kodak and Sanyo Electric Co. Ltd formed a global joint venture, the SK Display Corporation, to produce OLED (Organic Light Emitting Diode) screens used in equipment for the consumer market such as photocameras and portable photocameras.
2. In 1997, Kodak stipulated collaboration agreements with Intel and Adobe Systems to acquire capabilities designed to simplify and integrate the process of manipulation, printing and sending digital photographs from personal computers with the final customer in mind.
3. In 1998, Kodak acquired the business of medical imaging from Imation. In the same year, it acquired PictureVision, a small firm, and PhotoNet, which specialized in online digital printing.
4. In 2000, Kodak formed a joint venture with Hewlett-Packard to develop equipment for digital photography.
5. In 2001, the company formed an alliance with Lexmark to produce printers with the Kodak trademark.

6. In 2004, the company announced an agreement with China Putian, one of China's largest telecommunications companies, to promote the sale of the company's mobile phones in the 900 roll film and digital photography stores in China.
7. In 2005, Kodak and Barco, the leading company in protection systems for digital cinema, formed a joint venture aimed at expanding their respective capabilities and serving the global digital cinema market.
8. In the last few years, Kodak, in collaboration with AT&T Wireless, Cingular Wireless, Verizon Wireless, Orange and Nokia, has developed scalable and flexible solutions to managing the images on cell phones equipped with telecameras.

Thanks to the strategic alliances formed in the photography industry for the consumer market, Kodak is trying to develop its capabilities throughout the entire photographic process, from the time a photograph is taken to the time it is printed. To be more specific:

1. Kodak gives retail outlets its material and printers, in particular, Easyshare, which can be directly connected to the camera without needing a personal computer. In the second half of 2005, as many as six leading companies, including Olympus and Nikon, agreed to produce digital cameras compatible with Easyshare, which had sold one million products a year after being launched.
2. In an increasing number of retail outlets, Kodak is setting up stands where customers can insert the memory cards of their digital cameras, modify the images and print them independently or in a photographic laboratory that often has the same stands.
3. As early as 2001, Kodak had acquired Ofoto.com. Today it has 15 million subscribers worldwide and allows them to create virtual albums (via the Internet) free of charge and to print pictures (upon payment) and use them for mini personalized gadgets. Kodak also provides a service enabling mobile phone owners to organize their pictures. Moreover, the Kodak Mobile Service, launched in the United States in 2003 and in Europe in 2004, allows camera phone owners to share, store and, above all, print their photographs by connecting to its website[5] or directly from their mobile phone. The service can be accessed by the most popular mobile devices.
4. Recently Kodak has also launched EasyShare Printer DockPlus, which not only reads the memory cards of camera phones but also permits wireless access to all mobiles that have infrared portals.

3. DISCUSSION, DIRECTIONS FOR FUTURE RESEARCH AND MANAGERIAL IMPLICATIONS

Facing convergence is a relatively new and complex task and no 'easy recipes' for success are available. However, thanks to the literature review and the evidence from these case studies, a conceptual framework for detecting and managing convergence is emerging. The framework is highlighted in Figure 11.2. The figure shows the three drivers of convergence and some common components that are mainly related to 'substitution' and 'integration' dynamics.

With regard to technology, we found that the enabling forces of convergence are related to the growing opportunities to use different technologies to generate the same benefit for the customer (substitution dynamics). At the same time, we are looking at increasing technological integration deriving from interoperability and standard compatibility (for example, hybrid office machines, multimedia mobile devices and so on). Both substitution and integration dynamics (sometimes combined) enable a process of convergence between industries and firms.

With regard to the customers, we found that the evolution of their requirements has a pulling effect on convergence because of the growing dematerialization of expected value, with symbols and experiences that are easy to buy as the 'augmented' component (Levitt, 1960) of many different products, from many different industries (substitution dynamics and interindustry competition drivers). Moreover, the 'pull to converge' depends on the increasing search for scope economies that customers request by buying bundled offers (Wirtz, 2001) or hybrid products (integration dynamics and cross-industry competition drivers).

With regard to competition, we found that a strong push to converge

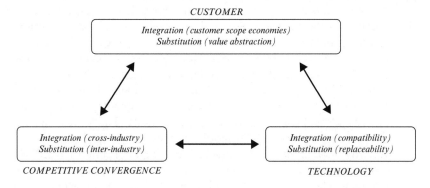

Figure 11.2   The many faces of convergence

comes from a firm's struggle for growth that leads to its entrance as a newcomer in contiguous markets (integration dynamics) or to a widening of the scope of competition, by working on the emotional (symbolic and experiential) components of the value proposition (substitution dynamics).

Future research should leverage on this model and test it, developing appropriate measures of industry convergence which are still lacking.

The managerial implications of such a conceptualization involve two strategic processes: intelligence (detection) and management (action) of convergence dynamics. In relation to intelligence, it is necessary to develop a complete understanding of the enabling, pulling and pushing drivers. With regard to the management issue, scope connections play a critical role.

Based on a literature review and empirical evidence presented through the case studies, we can highlight some implications for the design and management of scope connections, thus shedding a new light on coopetition dynamics. Here is a summary of these highlights:

1. Convergence has many faces and none of them can be disregarded. Competition in convergent business is not only played out on the technological ground, but also involves competitive and marketing issues (Gambardella and Torrisi, 1998). As a consequence, the strategic answer to convergence is not limited to the widening of technological backgrounds but is also related to the ability to effectively combine heterogeneous resources. And considering some resources like knowledge and market relationships, it is quite evident that their combination is more difficult than technology integration and/or combination. We can, therefore, argue that success in convergent business depends on the capacity to master the complementary evolution – widening and hybridizing – of technological, commercial and operational competences.

2. Since the organic evolution of firm resources is a long-term process while convergence could be very rapid, scope connection is one of the most efficient options to widen the resource endowments needed to create the hybrid and innovative value propositions required by convergence.

3. Scope connections represent an effective answer to convergence since they allow the combination of heterogeneous competences, counterbalanced by the risk of exposing the partnering firms to a 'heterogeneity paradox'. Particularly, the more heterogeneous the resources, the more difficult is their integration. Coopetition dynamics should consider this paradox and its possible solutions.

4. The solution to the paradox is not linked to the search for an optimal level of heterogeneity but also depends on the process of combination and integration of heterogeneous competences. In this respect, a critical role is played by the degree of homogeneity of the 'combinative capabilities' that must be devoted to the integration of technological, commercial and operative competences.

Focusing on the heterogeneity paradox, we propose a new conceptual framework for understanding the differential outcomes of interfirm connections, between coopetition and convergence dynamics.

Figure 11.3 presents four different outcomes of such connections considering two dimensions: the degree of heterogeneity of competences (technological, operative and commercial) and the degree of homogeneity between the partnering firms' 'combinative capabilities'. In this figure, we can find the following conditions:

● high heterogeneity of competences and low homogeneity of combinative capabilities. The outcome is a scope alliance with high innovation potential but also with a high risk of failure because of the difficulties of integration of competences belonging to the partners;
● high heterogeneity of competences and relatively homogeneous combinative capabilities. The outcome is a scope alliance with a high chance of success, since the innovation potential of the resource diversity is

Heterogeneous **Technological, operational and competitive competences** **Homogeneous**	Scope alliances with high chance of success Innéov Fermeté	Scope alliances with high potential for innovation but high risk of failure Kodak
	Scale alliances with high chance of success	Hybrid alliances with difficult innovation or integration Symbian
	Homogeneous **Combinative capabilities**	Heterogeneous

Figure 11.3   A taxonomy of company connections and their outcomes

supported by the integration process. As a consequence, the widening of the resource endowment will be likely to produce a relevant flow of new and hybrid offerings fitting the convergence dynamics;

- low heterogeneity of both competences and combinative capabilities. The outcome is a typically successful scale alliance aimed at the deployment of similar competences in order to reach a higher operative efficiency;
- low heterogeneity of capabilities and low homogeneity of combinative capabilities. The outcome is a scale alliance at risk of integration or a scope alliance that does not produce the expected results in terms of hybridization of the capabilities and innovative offering.

Referring to the cases we analysed in this paper, Innéov Fermeté can be considered as a successful scope alliance case on the basis of its capability of combining heterogeneous resources through relatively homogeneous combinative capabilities. In the case of Symbian, instead, the combinative capabilities of the partners seem to be relatively heterogeneous, whereas their resources and competences are relatively homogenous, due to the common telco background of the vast majority of partnering firms. This fact, as discussed above, has created some problems for the coalition regarding its alignment on strategic objectives, and therefore, the combination and integration process. Finally, in the case of Kodak, the competences of the companies involved seem to be relatively heterogeneous, while the combinative capabilities seem to be heterogeneous as well. The controversial evidence stemming from the scrutiny of its financial and market performances does not allow us to express a clear judgement on the success of Kodak's scope connections.

Ultimately, we can derive some further managerial implications concerning the way to master the critical combination of heterogeneous competences in a scope connection. In this regard, we argue that it is important to focus on the main components of the combinative capabilities (Van den Bosch, Volberda and de Boer, 1999): values, languages, visions, rhythms and goals. All these elements need a preliminary inter-company assessment in order to verify:

- the degree of language compatibility;
- the value consonance;
- the goal convergence;
- the degree of shared visions about the business evolution;
- the 'synchronicity' in the time pacing.

234 *Coopetition*

This issue should be further investigated by future research and empirically tested.

Based on a careful study of the matrix shown in Figure 11.3, we highlight one further managerial implication of our study: the opportunity to solve the heterogeneity paradox through a dual governance model. In this model, technological, commercial and operative competences should be selected in every partner company and should be put in the alliance on the basis of their heterogeneity and complementarity, in order to foster creativity and hybrid innovation. Combinative capabilities should, however, be as homogeneous as possible. In particular, partnering companies should have consonant and convergent values and strategic goals, use common or compatible languages, and be driven by a homogeneous vision of the business scenarios and of the role that every partner should play. Last but not least, they should share the time pacing regarding the execution plan of the convergent strategy.

The quest for competitive advantage in convergent industries is a very difficult task and scope connections are one of the most critical options a firm can pursue: their execution is as critical as their design, and correctly addressing the issue of the process of combination seems to be the first important step. Future research should devote as much time and effort to the strategic design as to the execution issue.

NOTES

1. 'Hi-touch' is marketing jargon to identify those products with a very low tech content and that need 'physical inspection' to be evaluated. They are sometimes also called 'touch and feel'.
2. Among the documentary material, reference is made also to research publications, namely to Gavetti, Henderson and Giorgi (2003) and Sawhney, Balasubramanian and Krishnan (2004).
3. The case study is based on interviews with the managers involved in the Symbian alliance. Additional information was taken from secondary sources (the business press and academic publications) including the contributions of Ancarani and Shankar (2003).
4. The Kodak case has been prepared on the basis of documental material and some personal interviews with managers in the company.
5. www.kodakmobile.eu.com, accessed on 25 November 2009.

REFERENCES

Ancarani, F. and V. Shankar (2003), 'Symbian: Customer Interaction through Collaboration and Competition in a Convergent Industry', *Journal of Interactive Marketing*, **17**(1), 56–76.

Baglieri, D., G.B. Dagnino, M.S. Giarratana and I. Gutierrez (2008), 'Stretching the Boundaries of Coopetition', *Management Research*, **6**(3), 157–164.

Baumard, P. (2007), 'Les strategies d'innovation des grandes firmes face à la coopétition', *Revue Francaise de Gestion*, **33**(176), 135–146.

Bell, J., B. den Ouden and G. Ziggers (2006), 'Dynamics of Cooperation: At the Brink of Irrelevance', *Journal of Management Studies*, **43**(7), 1607–1619.

Blanchot F. and F. Fort (2007), 'Coopétition et alliances en R&D', *Revue Française de Gestion*, **33**(176), 163–182.

Bradley, S.P., J.A. Hausman, R.L. Nolan (eds) (1993), *Globalization, Technology and Competition: The Fusion of Computers and Telecommunications in the 1990s*, Boston, MA: Harvard Business School Press.

Brandenburger, A.M. and B.J. Nalebuff (1996), *Coopetition*, London: Harper Collins.

Butler, R.J. and J. Gill (2003), 'Managing Instability in Cross-Cultural Alliances', *Long Range Planning*, **36**(3), 543–563.

Chakravarty, B. (1997) 'A New Strategy Framework for Coping with Turbulence', *Sloan Management Review*, Winter, 69–82.

Collins, D.J., P.W. Bane and S.P. Bradley (1997), 'Winners and Losers: Industry Structure in the Converging World of Telecommunications, Computing and Entertainment', in D.B. Yoffie (ed.), *Competing in the Age of Digital Convergence*, Boston, MA: Harvard Business School Press, pp. 159–201.

Dagnino, G.B., F. Le Roy and S. Yami (2007), 'La dynamique des stratégies de coopetition', *Revue Française de Gestion*, **33**(176), 87–98.

D'Aveni, R. (1994), *Hypercompetition*, New York: Free Press.

Davis, S.M. and C. Meyer (1998), *Blur: The Speed of Change in the Connected Economy*, Reading, MA: Addison-Wesley.

Day, G. and P. Shoemaker (2004), 'Peripheral Vision: Sensing and Acting on Weak Signals', *Long Range Planning*, **37**, Special Issue, 117–121.

Depeyre, C. and H. Dumez (2007), 'Le rôle du client dans les stratégies de coopéti-tion', *Revue Française de Gestion*, **33**(176), 99–110.

Doz, Y. (1996), 'The Evolution of Cooperations in Strategic Alliances: Initial Conditions or Learning Processes?', *Strategic Management Journal*, **17**(7), 55–83.

Draulans, J., A.P. de Man and H. Volberda (2003), 'Building Alliance Capability: Management Techniques for Superior Alliance Performance', *Long Range Planning*, **36**(2), 151–166.

Dussauge, P., B. Garrette and W. Mitchell (2000), 'Learning from Competing Partners: Outcomes and Duration of Scale and Link Alliances in Europe, North America and Asia', *Strategic Management Journal*, **21**, 99–126.

Dyer, J.H. and H. Singh (1998), 'The Relational View: Cooperative Strategy and Sources of Inter-Organizational Competitive Advantage', *Academy of Management Review,* **23**(4), 660–679.

Eisenhardt, K. (1989), 'Building Theories from Case Study Research', *Academy of Management Review*, **14**(4), 532–550.

Gambardella, A. and S. Torrisi (1998), 'Does Technological Convergence Imply Convergence in Markets? Evidence from the Electronics Industry', *Research Policy*, **27**, 445–463.

Gavetti, G., R. Henderson and S. Giorgi (2003), *Kodak (A)*, Boston, MA: Harvard Business School Publishing.

Glaser, B.G. and A.L. Strauss (1967), *The Discovery of Grounded Theory*, Chicago, IL: Aldine.

Grant, R.M. (1996), 'Towards a Knowledge Based Theory of the Firm', *Strategic Management Journal*, **17**, 109–122.

Grant, R.M. and C. Baden-Fuller (1995), 'A Knowledge-Based Theory of Inter-Firm Collaboration', *Academy of Management Best Paper Proceedings*, pp.17–21.

Hamel, G. (1991), 'Competition for Competence and Interpartner Learning within International Strategic Alliances', *Strategic Management Journal*, **12**, 83–103.

Hamel, G. (1996), 'Strategy as Revolution', *Harvard Business Review*, July–Aug, 69–82.

Hamel, G. and C.K. Prahalad (1996), 'Competing in the New Economy: Managing out of Bounds', *Strategic Management Journal*, **17**, 237–242.

Hamel, G., Y. Doz and C.K. Prahalad (1989), 'Collaborate With Your Competitors – and Win', *Harvard Business Review*, **67**(1), 133–139.

Heimericks, K.H. and G. Duysters (2007), 'Alliance capabilities as a mediator between experience and alliance performance: an empirical investigation into the alliance capability development process', *Journal of Management Studies*, **44**(1), 25–49.

Henderson, R.M. and K. Clark (1990), 'Architectural Innovation: The Reconfiguration of Existing Product Technologies and the Failure of Established Firms', *Administrative Science Quarterly*, **35**, 9–31.

Hennart, J.F. (2006), 'Alliance Research: Less in More', *Journal of Management Studies*, **43**(7), 1621–1628.

Khanna, T., R. Gulati and N. Nohria (1998), 'The Dynamics of Learning Alliances: Competition, Cooperation and Relative Scope', *Strategic Management Journal*, **19**, 193–210.

Kogut, B. and U. Zander (1992), 'Knowledge of the Firm, Combinative Capabilities and the Replication of Technology', *Organization Science*, **3**, 383–396.

Koza, M.P. and A.Y. Lewin (1998), 'The Coevolution of Strategic Alliances', *Organization Science*, **9**(3), 255–262.

Lane, P.J. and M. Lubatkin (1998), 'Relative Absorptive Capacity and Interorganizational Learning', *Strategic Management Journal*, **17**, 461–477.

Le Roy, F. and S. Yami (2007), 'Les stratégies de coopetition', *Revue Française de Gestion*, **33**(176), 83–86.

Levitt, T. (1960), 'Marketing Myopia', *Harvard Business Review*, **38**(4), 45–56.

Lorenzoni, G. and A. Lipparini (1999), 'The Leveraging of interfirm relationships as a distinctive organizational capability', *Strategic Management Journal*, **20**(4), 317–37.

Moore, J. (1996), *The Death of Competition*, New York: Harper Collins.

Nalebuff, B. and A. Brandenburger (1996), *Coopetition*, New York: Currency.

O'Driscoll, T., D. Reibstein and V. Shankar (2002) 'Mobile E-Business: Disruptive Technology or Untethered Extension of Business as Usual?', Working Paper, Robert H. Smith School of Business, University of Maryland.

Padula, G. and G.B Dagnino (2007), 'Untangling the Rise of Coopetition: The Intrusion of Competition in a Cooperative Game Structure', *International Studies of Management and Organization*, **37**(2), 32–52.

Prahalad, C.K. and R. Bettis (1986), 'The Dominant Logic: A New Linkage between Diversity and Performance', *Strategic Management Journal*, **7**(6), 485–501.

Prahalad, C.K. and G. Hamel (1994), *Competing for the future*, Boston, MA: Harvard University Press.

Prévot, F. (2007), 'Coopétition et management des compétences', *Revue Française de Gestion*, **33**(176), 183–202.
Ratliff, J. (2002), 'NTT DoCoMo and Its I-Mode Success: Origins and Implications', *California Management Review*, **44**(3), 55–71.
Reuer, J. (ed.) (2004), *Strategic Alliances: Theory and Evidence*, Oxford: Oxford University Press.
Sakakibara, M. (1997), 'Heterogeneity of Firm Capabilities and Cooperative Research and Development: An Empirical Examination of Motives', *Strategic Management Journal*, **18**, 143–164.
Sawhey, M., S. Balasubramanian and U. Krishnan (2004), 'Creating growth with services', *Sloan Management Review*, **45**(2), 34–43.
Shankar, V., T. O' Driscoll and D. Reibstein (2003), 'Rational Exuberance: The Wireless Industry Killers', *Strategy and Business*, **31**(Summer), 68–77.
Sleuwaegen, L., K. Schep, G. den Hartog and H. Commandeur (2003), 'Value Creation and the Alliance Experiences of Dutch Companies', *Long Range Planning*, **36**(6), 533–542.
Teece, D.J. (1986), 'Profiting from Technological Innovation: Implication for Integration, Collaboration, Licensing and Public Policy', *Research Policy*, **15**, 185–305.
Teece, D.J., G. Pisano and A. Shuen (1997), 'Dynamic Capabilities and Strategic Management', *Strategic Management Journal*, **18**(7), 509–533.
Van den Bosch, F.A.J., H.W. Volberda and M. de Boer (1999), 'Coevolution of Firm Absorptive Capacity and Knowledge Environment', *Organization Science*, **10**(5), 551–568.
Wind, J. and V.J. Mahajan (2002), *Convergence Marketing: Strategies for Reaching the New Hybrid Consumer*, New York: Prentice Hall.
Wirtz, B. (2001), 'Reconfiguring Value Chains in Converging Media and Communications Markets', *Long Range Planning*, **34**(4), 489–506.
Yin, R. (1994), *Case Study Research: Design and Methods*, London: Sage.
Yoffie, D.B. (ed.) (1997), *Competing in the Age of Digital Convergence*, Boston, MA: Harvard Business School Press.
Zollo, M., J. Reuer and H. Singh (2002), 'Interorganizational Routines and Performance in Strategic Alliances', *Organization Science*, **13**(6), 701–713.

12. Successful strategy for challengers: competition or coopetition with dominant firms?

Frédéric Le Roy and Patrice Guillotreau

INTRODUCTION

> When Sam Walton opened his first Wal-Mart store in 1962, his goal was to sell products at the lowest possible prices. We [Wal-Mart] decided that instead of avoiding our competitors, or waiting for them to come to us, we would meet them head-on . . . Since that time, Wal-Mart Stores, Inc., ('Wal-Mart') has become the world's largest retailer with $93,627,000,000 in net sales in 1996. (Roy Beth Kelley)

As shown by this statement from a Wal-Mart executive, some companies do not hesitate to challenge overtly the leading position of one of their competitors. In this aggressive setting, it is usually hard to retain a long-term leadership position. For instance, Weiss and Pascoe (1983) showed that only 30 per cent of the companies that were market leaders in the United States in 1950 were still in that position 25 years later (Weiss and Pascoe, 1983, quoted in Ferrier et al., 1999). Such companies' rise and fall could probably be explained within the paradigm of the so-called new industrial economics.

A number of related issues are also interestingly addressed within the framework of management science (Pearce, 2006; Hill and Rothaermel, 2003; Smith and Basu, 2002; Smith et al., 2001; Ferrier et al., 1999). How can a company challenge the market leader? How can a leading company maintain or lose its leadership? Adams and Brock (1998) showed that the capacity of leading firms to organize their resistance with respect to challengers essentially relies on the stability of market dominance conditions. Behavioural norms rule the industry, for example, in terms of production capacity building or price levels. These collective norms are set up by the leading company, which retaliates towards any incumbent firm willing to challenge them.

A socio-economic approach (Granovetter, 1985) has been applied to the case of the European tuna industry. The theoretical framework is introduced before showing how, in a European context, social exchanges between the different stakeholders led to coopetitive regulation of economic relations and placed one of the companies (namely Saupiquet) in a leading position. We then show how the entry of new foreign competitors, including Starkist, a US firm belonging to Heinz, challenged Saupiquet's leadership by questioning the coopetitive behavioural norms of the industry and led to the rebuilding of both competitive relationships and market shares to its own benefit.

1. COMPETITIVE AND COLLECTIVE FATE OF RIVAL FIRMS

1.1 A Ticklish Choice between Conformity and Boldness

In order to understand how, in social terms, a supply system is constructed, Abolafia (1998) proposed developing a genuine ethnographic approach to markets. According to this analysis, markets are not created via commercial interaction but rather through the repetition of such interactions. Such a repetition leads to behavioural habits, becoming norms on which the stakeholders can base their decision-making rules. These norms are not in opposition to legal rules laid down by the institutions that regulate markets, but enable the development of actual behaviours.

In the financial markets studied by Abolafia (1998), the rule that is meant to promote efficient markets is not sufficient to define behaviours. Customs, becoming norms, have emerged to foster the rule and make operators comply to achieve social acceptance. Operators who do not comply with these socially constructed norms are rejected as opportunists who may jeopardize market efficiency and thus the welfare of all operators. They are then labelled as 'aggressive' and blamed by their competitors.

From this standpoint, according to Baumard (2000), all companies must begin by accepting their individual fate, that is, their survival and identity, defence of their market position, and protection of their owners' resources and their financial commitments. However, barring a monopoly situation, they are competing with other firms with which they form the unique community that runs the industry's supply sector. Whether their directors like it or not, the individual fate of their companies is bound – to a greater or lesser degree depending on the sector – to the collective fate. A company may then try to alter the collective fate by threatening the community with egotistical behaviour. Conversely, the community may attempt to influence a company's individual fate by exerting pressure in the form of threats or actual reprisals.

Table 12.1   Features of individual and collective norms

Individual behaviour	Collective behaviour
Unembedded	Embedded
Deviance	Conformity
Illegitimacy	Legitimacy
Confrontation	Cooperation
Information secrecy	Information exchange
Privatization of knowledge	Publication of knowledge
Mutual defiance	Mutual confidence
Opportunism	Commitment
Flexibility	Inertia

1.2   Exclusion Risk or Shared Success

All companies must manage their individual and collective fates simultaneously. Pure individual and collective behaviour are thus two ideal-types (Table 12.1). A company subscribes to the collective norm, that is, adopts conformist behaviour, by accepting 'social embeddedness' (Granovetter, 1985) in competitive relationships. The main advantage of such conformity is that it confers legitimacy, which then gives the company access to a number of common tangible and intangible resources (DiMaggio and Powell, 1983). For instance, in most sectors, a very substantial amount of information is exchanged directly between competitors or collected and redistributed by trade associations (Bresser and Harl, 1986; Pennings, 1981). Companies that adopt a behaviour that is deemed legitimate will have access to this information, whereas those that are considered opportunistic may be excluded from information dissemination circuits.

Competitive strategy involves the creation and maintenance of a relationship of mutual distrust with competitors, which may rapidly degenerate into confrontation. For example, as shown by Garda and Marn (1994), any downward pressure on sale prices, however slight and localized, may lead to a paranoid interpretation and thus to a widespread price war. Conversely, adoption of a cooperative strategy reflects an attempt to foster trust relations between rivals (Bresser and Harl, 1986). Frequent exchange of information and publication of knowledge will limit misinterpretation of behaviours and degeneration into confrontation. For instance, Adams and Brock (1998) showed how, in the US tobacco industry, established competitors, through very frequent information exchanges, had kept prices very high for a long time.

Trade-offs between the choice of a competitive or a cooperative strategy are the only explanation for a paradox noted in the US automobile industry. A number of studies have shown that price wars occur in this sector during phases of very strong growth in demand, not during downturns (Bresnahan, 1987), which is out of line with forecasts made by standard economic models. Bresnahan (1987) and Rotemberg and Saloner (1986) interpret this paradox by the fact that during a recession, competitors adopt collectivistic behaviours and exchange information on their plans to avoid overcapacity, which would drive down their profit margins. Conversely, during periods of strong growth, all of these operators – to benefit from the increased demand – adopt opportunistic strategies that generate overcapacity, thus placing downward pressure on sale prices.

1.3 Coopetitive Strategy

The pure 'individualistic behaviour' may be defined as a 'pure competitive strategy' in which a firm tries to develop a competitive advantage to enhance its competitive position, even if it may be detrimental to the competitors' positions (Grimm and Smith, 1997). The 'collective behaviour' may be defined as a 'pure cooperative strategy', through which a firm attempts to develop a competitive advantage with its partners. A third strategy consists of mixing competitive and cooperative strategies. This mixed strategy with direct rivals is named 'coopetitive strategy' by Bengtsson and Kock (1999, 2000).

Such a coopetitive strategy allows firms to enjoy both competitive and cooperative advantages simultaneously. The interest found in competition lies in the induced incentives that are provided (Bengtsson and Kock, 1999, 2000; Lado *et al.*, 1997). The company is constantly forced to develop new productive combinations to remain competitive. The interest of cooperation is found in the access to resources, skills and knowledge which would otherwise stay inaccessible. A firm solely in competition has no chance of accessing such cooperative resources. Similarly, a firm solely in cooperation does not receive any incentive from competition. The combination of both positions simultaneously therefore improves the efficiency of the firm as compared to the exclusive choice of one of the two strategies.

The adoption of coopetition is nonetheless subject to negative effects and costs. In the early 1990s, Hamel (1991) showed that firms in competition do not learn equally from one another. Some learning-by-watching asymmetries may result in a genuine plunder of a firm's know-how by its coopetitors. In the same way, Uzzi (1997), from various case studies, demonstrated that cooperation between competitors can bear several types of risks, such as greater exposure to external shocks and isolation. In that respect, Rindfleisch and Moorman (2003) indicated that allied competitors are likely to lose their customer-oriented behaviour.

The three types of relationships – pure competition, pure cooperation and coopetition – offer alternative choices for a firm. According to Bengtsson and Kock (1999), the adoption of one of these strategies depends both on the need for external resources and on the relative industrial position. The competitive strategy corresponds to the situation where the need for external resources is quite low and where the industry position is strong. The cooperative strategy is the opposite (a strong need for external resources and a weak position). Finally, the coopetitive strategy suits both a strong need for external resources and a strong position within the industry.

Coopetition would thus mean somehow sharing a collective fate with a firm's competitors, usually ruled by the leaders of the industry. In that respect, which strategy could lead a firm to break up the collective rules set up by the leaders and thus reduce existing coopetition?

1.4 Subverting Collective Norms to Secure an Individual Fate

Why would a company choose to behave opportunistically so as to break previous cooperation relationships with the competitors? For Chen and Hambrick (1995), companies that behave opportunistically no longer have a choice, since they are faced with such severe financial distress that they have nothing to lose by questioning the socially accepted norms in their sector. Another explanation is that a company may run the risk of being considered opportunistic or aggressive when it wants to improve its current position. The main effect of cooperative strategies is that they stabilize the relative positions of competitors in a sector. They lead to inertia and deprive companies of some of the latitude they enjoy in their strategic choices (Bresser and Harl, 1986).

For this reason, price wars are usually triggered by outsiders, who have much less to lose than the leading firms, should margins in the sector be driven down across the board (Grimm and Smith, 1997). Conversely, the most conservative firms derive the greatest benefit from stability in the sector, and they are the quickest to organize for retaliation. In the US tobacco industry example, the standard that discouraged discounting below a certain level had been set by the leading firms, which organized joint reprisals against any new entrant or outsider proposing lower prices (Adams and Brock, 1998).

Based on this earlier research, we speculate that any challenge to market leadership is accompanied by a challenge to the current behavioural norms of the industry.[1] Outsiders are willing to impose new social norms that would be beneficial to them, while the leaders would be expected to strive to maintain existing norms. Changes in market position should theoretically depend on the respective stakeholders' ability to impose new norms or maintain existing ones, depending whether the challenge succeeds or the leaders' position is maintained. We thus put forward the following proposals:

> **Proposal 1:** Challengers' success will depend on the extent to which they are able to break collective behavioural norms in the sector.

> **Proposal 2:** Leaders' success in defending their position will depend on the extent to which they can maintain existing collective behavioural norms in the sector.

The more aggressively a firm attempts to challenge the market leadership of dominant firms, the less it will cooperate with the latter. As a result, the challengers will be in a position of reducing or purely avoiding any collective behavioural norm previously imposed by the industry leaders.

Consequently, a corollary result of both proposals, if verified, is that coopetition is less likely to emerge in a challenging context and would rather disappear or be mitigated either if the challenger's strategy is successful, or if the leaders fail to defend the collective norms.

2. STRATEGIES PREVAILING IN THE FRENCH TUNA INDUSTRY BETWEEN 1950 AND 1980: ESTABLISHMENT OF A NORM

It is very clear that a dual rationale has prevailed throughout the history of the French tuna industry. Strategies in the processing sector are quite individualistic – competitive pressure is very strong and results in relocations and the takeover of weaker competitors. Collective strategies predominate in the tuna fishing sector since the feeling of a common fate is stronger than between-company rivalries.

2.1 Relatively Competitive Strategies in Processing Sectors

Since the creation of the tuna packing sector, there has been intense competitive rivalry between processing companies, with each regularly striving to gain an advantage over the rivals. This rivalry has taken the form of competitor take-over and production relocation strategies. We shall demonstrate these trends by tracking the history of Saupiquet and Pêche et Froid, the two main French companies in the 1980s.

Saupiquet was founded in 1881. By 1899, the company was already present abroad (in Portugal) and in the ex-French colonies (Algeria, Morocco), with 11 production units located near the fishing grounds. Throughout the 20th century, it grew by taking over many of its competitors in the canning (or packing) industry. In 1956, to cope with the development of the Atlantic tropical tuna fishery, Saupiquet set up business units in Senegal (Cofrapal) and Côte d'Ivoire (Scodi) through mergers and acquisitions of small competitors, and then competed fiercely with other French-owned firms for raw material until 1962.

Its main competitor, the Pêche et Froid corporation (trawlers and processing plants), had been founded in 1875 by the Delpierre family under the name Pêcheries Delpierre. Its strategy was to diversify both horizontally (tuna canning and freezing) and vertically (fishing, freezing warehouses and processing). The company grew by acquiring warehouses, fishing companies and canneries. Following Saupiquet, Pêche et Froid set up a cannery in Senegal in 1973, and in 1978 opened a second cannery in Côte d'Ivoire (PFCI – Pêche et Froid Côte d'Ivoire). In 1990, Pêche et Froid created a third big cannery in Antsirana, Madagascar (PFOI – Pêche et Froid Océan Indien). After these investments, Pêche et Froid became number two in Europe.

These different paths taken by Saupiquet and Pêche et Froid are fairly typical of the competitive relationships that prevail in the tuna processing sector. Strong rivalry then drove two related trends, that is, relocation and acquisition of competitors, and led to concentration in the sector, which by the 1980s was reduced to four main companies (Saupiquet, Pêche et Froid, Union Cooperative des Pêcheurs de France, and Paul Paulet) and a small competitive fringe. However, this strong rivalry did not preclude a degree of cooperation between canners, essentially because of supply problems.

Therefore the industry had to deal with fishing and shipping companies. In this commercial relationship, packers joined together in trade associations so as to exert more influence collectively on trade conditions. In 1959, for instance, some 100 packers formed a single purchasing structure, called COFICA, to obtain the best prices from shipowners.

This packers' association has a very long history, since it began as of the end of the 19th century with the formation of regional associations. In the early 20th century, a great number of associations and organizations were formed and they had very complex relations among themselves and with fishing and shipping companies, industrial magnets and the government. The most representative contemporary outgrowth of this long history of industrial association is the seafood division of the Fédération des Industries Agroalimentaires de la Conserve (FIAC), whose members are the 17 seafood packers still active in 2008.

2.2 Coopetitive Strategies in Tuna Fishing and Shipping Activities

While tuna processing companies have tended to pursue individualistic strategies, the fishing companies have created joint entities through which cooperation was made possible. One main reason for this is the nature of the activity, which requires some risk sharing because of its exposure to natural conditions and because of highly capital-intensive assets (vessels) for such a small-scale industry. The discovery of new fishing grounds and the negotiation of international fishing agreements (access rights) can only succeed collectively. Finally, the companies' bargaining power vis-à-vis the packers has been enhanced by a shipowners' association.

To solve coordination problems of fishing, shipping and marketing frozen tuna, the various tuna fishing and shipping companies created professional associations. Up to 1992, the Syndicat National des Armateurs de Thoniers Congélateurs (*SNATC*) brought together all shipowners and played the role of social partner (collective agreements). In addition, it looked after other more commercial matters (lobbying of national and European authorities in relation to European trade policy or negotiation of fisheries agreements with third countries having fish-rich waters). In 1992, the commercial function of SNATC was transferred to a producers' organisation, Orthongel, which represents all the shipowners involved in the tropical tuna fishing sector.

Beyond this industrial association, the willingness to act collectively was reflected by the creation of common structures for tuna fishing and shipping activities. Shipowners formed collective entities to manage the fishing vessels jointly and share the associated risks. In 1965, M. Delhemmes created the Compagnie Bretonne de Cargos Frigorifiques (Cobrecaf), which combined tuna fishing, through direct or indirect operation of tuna vessels, with frozen tuna shipping aboard refrigerated ships. Similarly, a few cooperatives merged to create Armement Coopératif Finistérien (ACF) in 1964, and three Concarneau shipowners created a fishing joint company called CMB (Chevannes-Merceron-Ballery).

All of these groups and associations, as well as vertically integrated packers (Saupiquet and Pêche et Froid), marketed their frozen tuna through another collective company, Société de Vente de Thon Congelé (Sovetco). Sovetco was created in 1959 by three Concarneau shipowners, Messrs. Ballery, Delhemmes and Kuhn, as a response to the packers' association Cofica. Its objective was to negotiate jointly the sale of all French-caught tuna. To work as a collective body, it was owned by a holding company (Sovetpar), with shares proportional to the number of vessels selling through Sovetco.

Collective decisions regarding both fishing and shipping were taken by the board of directors of Cobrecaf (mainly shippers and fishing managers). This led to quite an equitable sharing of supply among packers. This company thus operated more like a cooperative, even though it was a limited company. The entire processing industry could use its services on a relatively impartial basis.

This collective trend was even stronger when fishing companies wished to expand their activities beyond their usual geographical areas. The creation of Cobrecaf, ACF and Sovetco thus came at a time when shipowners were developing the tropical tuna fisheries in the Atlantic Ocean in the 1960s. A similar cooperation took place in 1982–83, at the inception of the Indian Ocean tuna fishery.

3.   CHALLENGING THE COOPETITIVE NORM

3.1   Starkist Enters the French Industry

In the 1960s, one of Sovetco's first foreign customers was an American company, Starkist (a multinational firm owned by Heinz), which also became Cobrecaf's first and main international customer (for frozen tuna transport). In 1978, André Delhemmes, the director of Cobrecaf at that time, allowed Starkist to take a 36 per cent share of the company. During the 1980s, Starkist became one of the three main players in the US and worldwide tuna canning industry, ultimately achieving a leading position by the early 1990s. However, due to stagnation of the American market and the arrival of new international competitors, including Thai firms, *Starkist* refocused on the European market. In 1987, *Starkist* acquired the French company *Paul Paulet*.

In 1988, Starkist became even more aggressive and tried to purchase André Delhemmes' shares in Cobrecaf. The managers did not hesitate to take legal action in France to claim the whole capital. This aggressiveness could be explained by Cobrecaf's leading role in the French fleet. Since its creation in 1965, Cobrecaf had rapidly developed its fishing and shipping activities and accounted for 46.8 per cent of the French fishing output by 1991 (Table 12.2).

As the breakdown of Sovetco's capital among shipowners was proportional to the number of vessels selling through this facility unit, in 1988 control of Cobrecaf was tantamount to controlling Sovetco. Starkist's opportunistic behaviour thus prompted collective retaliation by the other economic stakeholders. The reaction was initially quite destructive since Pêche et Froid, Saupiquet and ACF left Sovetco in early 1988. In late 1988, the environment became more constructive as Pêche et Froid and

Table 12.2   Output share of French fishing companies (%)

	Saupiquet	Pêche et Froid	Cobrecaf	CMB	ACF	Other	Total
1977	16.1	11.5	16.9	15.9	16.6	23.0	100.0
1981	14.6	17.4	23.8	15.5	11.5	17.2	100.0
1985	9.8	13.7	37.2	20.8	9.2	9.1	100.0
1988	14.2	12.3	41.0	20.0	10.7	1.8	100.0
1991	20.8	–	46.8	19.7	6.4	6.2	100.0

Source: SNATC

Sopar (another shipowner company) proposed to take equity positions in Cobrecaf.

The French court ruled against *Starkist*. *Sopar* and *Pêche et Froid* then set up a jointly owned company, the *Compagnie Financière de Participation Maritime* (*CFPM*), which bought out the 64 per cent of Cobrecaf shares held by the Delhemmes family and took control of it. Pêche et Froid and ACF rejoined Sovetco, and Pêche et Froid assigned the management of its ships to Cobrecaf. New collective projects could start again, like ordering new vessels in co-ownership. There was no change in this situation until 1993, when a new entrant to the market, Ona, took over Pêche et Froid.

3.2   Ona's Entry and Impact

Ona is a diversified Moroccan group that is particularly active in the agrifood business. It entered the French tuna industry in 1992 when it signed a partnership agreement with Union des Pêcheurs Coopératifs de France (UPCF). At that time, UPCF was the largest French small-scale fishing group. The agreement involved the creation of a new corporation, Pêcheurs de France, jointly held by the two partners.

In 1993, Ona acquired Pêche et Froid through a holding company (Optorg). This acquisition enabled it also to control Cobrecaf through CFPM. The other shareholder in CFPM, the Sopar group directed by M. Le Flanchec, stubbornly opposed this takeover and CFPM quickly became ungovernable. An anonymous complaint was lodged on 16 November 1993, denouncing the acquisition, and the case was swiftly referred to the French antitrust authority. The conflict was so bitter that M. Le Flanchec decided to sell his shares to Starkist, which thus obtained 68 per cent of the capital of Cobrecaf. After a long legal battle, Starkist took control of Cobrecaf, and Ona became a minority shareholder (Guillotreau and Le Roy, 2000).

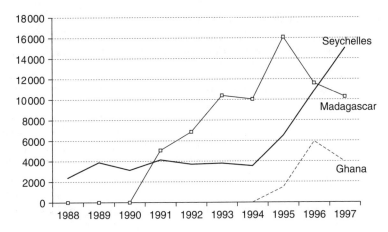

Source: Eurostat-Comext

*Figure 12.1   French vessels' tuna landings (= exports) by destination (in
             tonnes)*

In 1994, Starkist restructured itself by closing several plants in Central
America and France, before investing in new canneries in Ghana and the
Seychelles to supply the European market through a few leading brands.
Ona undertook similar transactions in 1996, closing French plants and
investing in African subsidiaries. All of these operations had an impact on
Sovetco's supply chain. The French exports (that is, landings) of frozen
tuna to the three countries where Starkist and *Ona* had invested in capacity were greatly increased (Figure 12.1), and so were the French imports of
canned tuna from these countries as a consequence.

   These changes had a substantial impact on rivals of ONA and Starkist.
Before the control of Cobrecaf by Starkist, the former acted as a non-
profit centre. Afterwards, when there was a tuna shortage in the Atlantic
Ocean, Starkist put pressure on Sovetco, the selling facility, to supply its
canneries first and by doing this forced its rivals to procure raw materials
from other sources (like the Indian Ocean) through third-party traders,
at much higher prices, which in turn squeezed down packers' margins
(Guillotreau and Le Roy, 2000).

   The behavioural norms in the tuna fisheries and frozen tuna transport
sectors had clearly shifted. These industries were organized collectively
when controlled by fishing and shipping companies (especially to coun-
teract the power of processing firms), but more individualistic strategies
were adopted after control over joint resources was taken by some opportunistic firms. The new entrants proceeded on the basis of an equitable

distribution of supply only where raw material was abundant. As soon as a shortage arose, opportunism led them to secure their own supply despite the concomitant increase in their competitors' costs.

4. DISCUSSION AND IMPLICATIONS

4.1 Challenges to Coopetitive Norms in Shipping and Transport

As shown in Figure 12.2, Starkist and Ona came into the sector by taking control of the packers and the main shipping company. This latter company's carrying and fishing capacity was used to develop a strategy of investment in low labour-cost countries. Saupiquet, the former market leader, then experienced supply shortages, thus limiting its capacity to increase its own production or to sell at the same prices as Ona and, especially, Starkist.

Starkist thus clearly broke up the coopetition norm in the tuna fishing, shipping and transport sectors in order to challenge Saupiquet's leadership position in Europe. By taking control of a major stakeholder (Cobrecaf), Starkist succeeded in imposing American market norms on the French tuna industry, that is, packers' domination over raw material suppliers. By imposing these new norms, Starkist was able to develop its production and sales capacity in Europe. Paul Paulet increased its sales to the extent that its brand became the main challenger of the Saupiquet leading label in France, making it the only large company in the sector that was truly

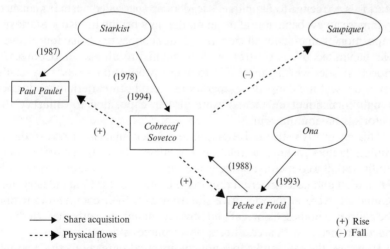

Figure 12.2   COBRECAF's position in the competition dynamics

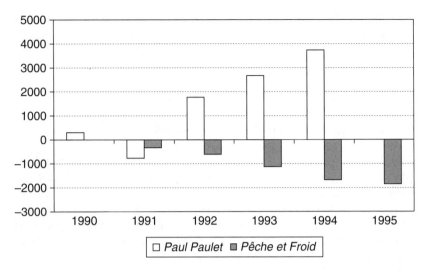

Source: Diane database

Figure 12.3   Paul Paulet's and Pêche et Froid's operating results (€'000)

profitable (Figure 12.3). Nowadays, Paul Paulet belongs to another group (MW Brands) and has become the new market leader in France with a 27 per cent market share in 2007.

Proposal 1 therefore does seem applicable for the case under review. Starkist's challenge to Saupiquet's leadership succeeded when it managed to impose a new behavioural norm on the tuna fishing industry. Starkist's imposition of an individualistic rather than a coopetitive behavioural norm was facilitated by its control over the main French carrier (Cobrecaf). Indeed, parties which gained title to major production assets – especially when the sector's coopetitive operations were both materially and functionally dependent on them – were also in a position to influence the sector's behavioural norms.

This result fits with the Bengtsson and Kock analysis (1999) of determining factors behind a relational strategy. Indeed, the case study confirms that a coopetitive strategy is undertaken when the company leads the market and needs external resources. Leaders of the tuna industry, like Saupiquet, were in a coopetitive situation with their competitors within the collective bodies, Cobrecaf and Sovetco, mainly because the latter provided the former with access to supply resources at lower costs.

However, the case study does not confirm that pure competition strategies are adopted only by leaders who do not need any external resources.

In this industry, the most aggressive and non-cooperative firms are not the leaders, but their challengers (mostly Starkist, but also Ona). A company can therefore be aggressive and poorly cooperative, even starting with a weak market position, as long as its objective is to become the new market leader. In that respect, it will strive to break the coopetitive behavioural norms that benefit the current leader by adopting a predatory strategy to get access to central resources.

Note that the strategy of imposing new norms that are beneficial to outsiders can only work if the latter really have the means to control the central resources or stakeholders of the industry. Ona's failure to take over Cobrecaf in 1993 prevented it from controlling Sovetco and therefore from securing its own supply chain. Ona's subsidiary Pêche et Froid made a loss throughout the 1990s (Figure 12.3) and was then pushed to withdraw its canneries from Senegal in 1997 and its other fish processing plants in France in 1998–99. At that time, trading of Pêche et Froid equities on the stock market had been suspended and Ona had announced its intention to sell the company.

4.2 Weak Reprisals

Starkist's success was facilitated by the fact that French companies found it impossible to jointly organize reprisals against it. The 1988 attempt by Starkist to take control of Cobrecaf led to a collective reaction involving a collective withdrawal from the selling unit Sovetco (Saupiquet, Pêche et Froid and ACF all left). However, the best alternative solution that could be found to achieve control of Cobrecaf was for just two firms, that is Pêche et Froid (shipowner-packer) and Sopar (shipowner), to acquire 64 per cent of Cobrecaf's capital from the Delhemmes family. In other words, in order to oppose Starkist's individualistic behaviour, Pêche et Froid and Sopar took control of Cobrecaf, and thus Sovetco.

Sovetco therefore could no longer be considered a collective entity by the other French shipowners and packers. Mistrust arose, as clearly indicated by the fact that a complaint was lodged, in the late 1980s, by ACF (which had re-joined Sovetco) against Cobrecaf for its refusal to ship ACF fish aboard its refrigerated boats (but the lawsuit was dismissed). This mistrust was also evident in the individualistic strategies adopted by many shipping companies, especially the market leader Saupiquet. Unlike the others, Saupiquet did not come back into Sovetco in 1988, and it even left the union SNATC in 1992.

Saupiquet decided to secure its supplies through an essentially individualistic development of its own fleet. Hence, one of two new Saupiquet seiners launched in the early 1990s was internally funded (and not through co-ownership, a current practice of the industry), while the other was funded by a financial group. Moreover, these seiners were built at the Campbell shipyards in California rather than in France. Saupiquet only established cooperative relationships at the international level, as a sister ship was commissioned from the same shipyards in 1991 for the Italian packer Trinity (which took over Saupiquet in December 1999) and was managed by Saupiquet. In the mid-1990s, Saupiquet developed an ambitious programme independently and ordered two super-seiners at a cost of FF160 million each (€24 million). These two tuna boats had on-board processing capacity to produce high-value tuna loins for the European market.

This programme resulted in a failure and increased Saupiquet's debt substantially (€55 million in 1998, and a net operating loss of €4 million) because of high production costs compared to its rivals,[2] and did not solve the supply problems of its West African or French canneries. Saupiquet's profitability also suffered greatly on account of the difficulties of its subsidiary. As a consequence, in December 1999, Paribas sold its shares in Saupiquet (37 per cent) to the Italian packer Trinity Alimentari Italia.

Clearly, the success of Starkist's challenge was greatly favoured by the French packers' inability to take effective coopetitive reprisals against it. Proposal 2 therefore does seem applicable for the case under review. Starkist succeeded in imposing a new behavioural norm in the tuna industry because the French packers were unable to agree on reprisals that should be implemented. Not only did French firms fail to organize a coopetitive response, but the market leader, Saupiquet, pursued a lonely strategy without any regard for its coopetitors, thus hastening the collapse of the French tuna industry.

This inability to organize retaliation may in turn be explained by the mistrust resulting from a long tradition of rivalry between French packers. These packers – before finding themselves with a common threat – had pursued individualistic strategies that sometimes led to violent confrontations. Paradoxically, in 1988, when Starkist was attempting for the first time to take control of Cobrecaf, Pêche et Froid slashed its canned tuna prices so as to boost its market share instead of adopting a collective strategy in response to the takeover bid, and this move hit *Saupiquet* particularly hard. *Saupiquet* then responded in kind, resulting in financial hardship for all French packers.

This mistrust, produced by long-standing rivalries, explains why the various French packers preferred to sell out to foreign competitors rather than finding domestic solutions. Paul Paulet was thus bought by Starkist, Pêcheur de France and Pêche et Froid were taken over one after the other by ONA, and Saupiquet was acquired by Trinity, concluding nearly two centuries of this French-born industry (Guillotreau and Ferreira Dias

2005). We conclude that the individualistic response by incumbent companies to the individualistic behaviour of an outsider – though understandable in the context of a long history of rivalry – reduced the capacity for coopetitive reprisals and ultimately enhanced the difficulties for these companies.

CONCLUSION

The question of the stability of market leadership and challenges to it has been the subject of some recent papers (Adams and Brock, 1998; Ferrier *et al.*, 1999). The present study builds on these investigations and, through a socioeconomic approach, shows that in the French tuna industry, a distinction may be drawn between the processing sector, characterized by quite competitive behaviours, and the shipping and transport sector, where the behavioural norm has been more coopetitive. This situation lasted until Starkist and Ona broke into the market, succeeding in taking control of a major stakeholder, Cobrecaf, in order – out of self-interest – to impose a more competitive and less cooperative behavioural norm in the French tuna industry.

We have shown that a company that mounts a successful challenge to the market leader's position does so by subverting coopetitive norms in the sector and, conversely, that an industry leader may forfeit its leadership when it loses existing behavioural norms. More generally, we demonstrated that gaining ownership of the shared and symbolic assets of a sector's macroculture is the key factor in the ability to uphold or upset behavioural norms in that sector.

In the light of these findings, a number of other questions should be addressed in future research. How do collective beliefs concerning a company's 'normal' behaviour in a sector arise? How are they perpetuated by the leaders? How does a given company come to be known as 'deviant' or 'aggressive'? How decisive for a company's competitiveness is its reputation in the eyes of its competitors? How far will firms go in attempting to deprive one or more competitors of their legitimacy? How deviant can a company's behaviour be before it is seen as socially illegitimate?

NOTES

1. We use the term 'norm' in the sense given by neo-institutionalists, that is, a habit or social behaviour that is repeated without ever being challenged (DiMaggio and Powell, 1983).
2. There was no comparison between the salaries of workers at its rivals' canneries and

those of French workers aboard the new tuna boats. Moreover, some 80 crew members were needed to run both fishing and processing facilities on board these new vessels, whereas only 25 crew members were needed to run a standard tuna purse-seiner.

REFERENCES

Abolafia, M.Y. (1998), 'Markets as Cultures: An Ethnographic Approach', in M. Callon (ed.), *The Laws of Markets*, Oxford: Blackwell, pp. 68–85.

Adams, W. and J.W. Brock (1998), 'Tobacco: Predation and Persistent Market Power', in D.I. Rosenbaum (ed.), *Market Dominance*, Westport, CT: Prague, pp. 11–38.

Barney, J.B. (1991), 'Firm Resources and Sustained Competitive Advantage', *Journal of Management*, **17**, 249–278.

Baumard, P. (2000), *Analyse stratégique, mouvements, signaux concurrentiels et interdépendance*, Paris: Dunod.

Bengtsson M. and S. Kock (1999), 'Cooperation and Competition in Relationships between Competitors in Business Networks', *Journal of Business and Industrial Marketing,* **14**(3), 178–190.

Bengtsson M. and S. Kock (2000), 'Coopetition in Business Networks – to Cooperate and Compete Simultaneously', *Industrial Marketing Management*, **29**, 411–426.

Bresnahan, T.F. (1987), 'Competition and Collusion in the American Automobile Industry: The 1955 Price War', *Journal of Industrial Economics*, **35**(4), 457–482.

Bresser, R.K. and J.E. Harl (1986), 'Collective Strategy: Vice or Virtue?' *Academy of Management Review*, **11**(2), 408–427.

Chen, M.-J. and D.C. Hambrick (1995), 'Speed, Stealth, and Selective Attack: How Small Firms Differ from Large Firms in Competitive Behavior', *Academy of Management Journal*, **38**(2), 453–482.

DiMaggio, P.J. and W.W. Powell (1983), 'The Iron Cage Revisited: Institutional Isomorphism and Collective Rationality in Organizational Fields', *American Sociological Review*, **48**, 147–160.

Ferrier, W.J., K.G. Smith and C.M. Grimm (1999), 'The Role of Competitive Action in Market Share Erosion and Industry Dethronement: A Study of Industry Leaders and Challengers', *Academy of Management Journal*, **42**(4), 372–388.

Garda, R. and M. Marn (1994), 'Comment échapper à la guerre des prix', *L'Expansion Management Review*, Spring, 6–13.

Granovetter, M. (1985), 'Economic Action and Social Structure: The Problem of Embeddedness', *American Journal of Sociology*, **91**(3), 481–510.

Grimm, C.M. and K.J. Smith (1997), *Strategy as Action*, Cincinnati, Ohio: South-Western College Publishing.

Guillotreau, P. and J. Ferreira Dias (2005), 'Fish Canning Industries of France and Portugal: Life Histories', *Economia Global e Gestão*, **10**(2), September, 61–79.

Guillotreau, P. and F. Le Roy (2000), 'La guerre du thon ou l'élévation des coûts des concurrents par l'intégration verticale', *Annales des Mines, Gérer et Comprendre*, **62**, 53–62.

Hamel, G. (1991), 'Competition for Competence and Inter-Partner Learning within International Strategic Alliances', *Strategic Management Journal*, **12**, 83–104.

Hill, C.W.L. and F.T. Rothaermel (2003), 'The Performance of Incumbent Firms in the Face of Radical Technological Innovation', *Academy of Management Review*, **28**(2), 257–274.

Lado, A.A., N. Boyd and S.C. Hanlon (1997), 'Competition, Cooperation, and the Search for Economic Rents: a Syncretic Model', *Academy of Management Review*, **22**(1), 110–141.

Pearce J.A. (2006), 'How Companies can Preserve Market Dominance after Patents Expire', *Long Range Planning*, **39**, 71–87.

Pennings, J.M. (1981). 'Strategically Interdependent Organizations', in P.C. Nystrom and W.H. Starbuck (eds), *Handbook of Organizational Design*, New York: Oxford University Press, Vol. 1, 433–455.

Rindfleisch A. and C. Moorman (2003), 'Interfirm Cooperation and Customer Orientation', *Journal of Marketing Research*, **40**(4), 421–436.

Rotemberg, J.J. and G. Saloner (1986), 'A Supergame-Theoretic Model of Price Wars during Booms', *The American Economic Review*, **76**(3), 390–407.

Smith, K.G., W.J. Ferrier and C.M. Grimm (2001), 'King of the Hill: Dethroning the Industry Leader', *Academy of Management Executive*, **15**(2), 59–70.

Smith T. and Basu K. (2002), 'A View from the Top: The Impact of Market Share Dominance on Competitive Position', *Journal of Brand Management*, **10**(1), 19–33.

Uzzi, B. (1997), 'Social Structure and Competition in Interfirm Networks: The Paradox of Embeddedness', *Administrative Science Quarterly*, **42**(1), 35–88.

Weiss, L. and G. Pascoe (1983), 'The extent and performance of market dominance', *Annual Meeting of the European Association for Research in Industrial Economics*, August.

Index